GREAT
PERFECTION

Terry F. Kleeman, 1955-

'Great
Perfection

RELIGION AND ETHNICITY

IN A CHINESE

MILLENNIAL

KINGDOM

UNIVERSITY OF HAWAI'I PRESS

HONOLULU

98 99 00 01 02 03   5 4 3 2 1

Library of Congress Cataloging-in-Publication Data
Kleeman, Terry F., 1955–
Great Perfection = [Ta Ch' eng] : religion and ethnicity in a
Chinese millennial kingdom / Terry F. Kleeman.
    p.   cm.
Parallel title in Chinese characters.
Includes bibliographical references and index.
ISBN 0–8248–1800–8 (alk. paper)
1. China—History—Five Hu and the Sixteen kingdoms, 304–439.
2. Taoism—China.   3. Ethnicity—China.   I. Title.
DS748.45.K64   1998
931'.04—dc21   97–25798
                              CIP

Jacket illustration: The image comes from
a Western Zhou zheng-bell found in
Ba Shu qingtongqi (1992).

Designed by Cameron Poulter

Contents

Acknowledgments

This book has been a long time in the making. I was first drawn to the Li family and the Cheng-Han state by comments in the classic article of the late Anna Seidel on Daoist messianism (1969–1970). At the University of British Columbia I wrote an M.A. thesis on the history and historiography of that state under the supervision of E. G. Pulleyblank. I profited at that time from extended discussions with Roberto Ong and from the patient advice and instruction of Chao Yeh Chia-ying, Leon Hurvitz, Dan Overmyer, and Ken-ichi Takashima. Des McMurchy was my computer maven and aided in the inputting.

Leaving Vancouver, I devoted myself to the study of Daoism, first in Japan under Yasui Kōzan, Makio Ryōkai, Kusuyama Haruki, and Fukui Shigemasa, then at Berkeley under Michel Strickmann and Edward Schafer. During a year in Paris, I studied with Kristofer Schipper. These researches encouraged me to take up again the study of Cheng-Han with a clearer idea of the religious and intellectual milieu in which the state was founded. Moreover, new, annotated editions of the *Record of the Land of Huayang* by Ren Naiqiang and Liu Lin made possible a more exacting account of the history of the state at the same time that an explosion of research on Chinese historical ethnography shed much light on the ethnic background of the Lis.

I began serious work on this book while teaching at the University of Pennsylvania, where I profited from the encouragement and advice of Victor Mair, Susan Naquin, and Nathan Sivin. Victor, Alan Berkowitz, and Stephen Bokenkamp all read the manuscript carefully and offered detailed suggestions for its improvement. Others offering valuable comments on some parts of the manuscript include Richard von Glahn, Li Fengmao, and Paul Katz. Any remaining errors are, of course, my own.

During the course of this project I received financial and other support from the American Council of Learned Societies and the

Institute of Literature and Philosophy of the Academia Sinica. Karl Kahler at the University of Pennsylvania and Zhou Yuan at the University of Minnesota were instrumental in securing primary and secondary sources necessary for this study. Finally, the editorial staff of the University of Hawai'i Press and David Goodrich of Birdtrack Press deserve much thanks for their professionalism and competence in putting out a complex and demanding book.

Abbreviations

HHS	*Hou Hanshu* 後漢書. By Fan Ye 范曄 (398–445). Beijing: Zhonghua shuju, 1971.
HHSJJ	*Hou Hanshu jijie* 後漢書集解. By Fan Ye 范曄 (398–445). Ed. by Wang Xianqian 王先謙. Changsha, 1923.
HS	*Hanshu* 漢書. By Ban Gu 班固 (32–92). Beijing, Zhonghua shuju, 1962.
HY	Serial number of work in Daoist canon according to Weng Tu-chien. 1935. *Combined Indices to the Authors and Titles of Books in Two Collections of Taoist Literature.* Harvard-Yenching Institute Sinological Index Series, no. 25. Beijing: Yenching University Press.
HYGZ	*Huayangguo zhi* 華陽國志. By Chang Qu 常璩 (fl. 350). Basic Sinological Series edn. Shanghai: Commercial Press.
JS	*Jinshu* 晉書. By Fang Xuanling 房玄齡 (578–648). Beijing: Zhonghua shuju, 1974.
JSJZ	*Jinshu jiaozhu* 晉書斠注. Ed. by Liu Chenggan 劉承榦 and Wu Shijian 吳仕鑑. Taipei: Yiwen shuju reprint of Beijing, 1928.
LIU	*Huayangguo zhi jiaozhu* 華陽國志校注. By Chang Qu. Ed. by Liu Lin 劉琳. Chengdu: Ba Shu shushe, 1984.
REN	*Huayangguo zhi jiaobu tuzhu* 華陽國志校補圖注. By Chang Qu. Ed. by Ren Naiqiang 任乃強. Shanghai: Guji chubanshe, 1987.
SGZ	*Sanguozhi* 三國志. By Chen Shou 陳壽 (233–297). Beijing: Zhonghua shuju, 1963.
SJ	*Shiji* 史記. By Sima Qian 司馬遷. Beijing: Zhonghua shuju, 1962.
SLGCQ	*Shiliu guo chunqiu* 十六國春秋. By Cui Hong 崔鴻 (?–ca. 525). Quoted in TPYL 123 and elsewhere. Reconstructed in *Shiliu guo chunqiu jibu* 十六國春秋輯補. By Tang Qiu 湯球. Basic Sinological Series edn. Beijing: Commercial Press, 1958.

TPHYJ   *Taiping huanyu ji* 太平寰宇記. By Yue Shi 樂史 (930–
         1007). Taipei: Wenhai chubanshe, 1963.

TPYL   *Taiping yulan* 太平御覽. Ed. by Li Fang et al. Beijing:
         Renmin wenxue chubanshe, 1959.

WS   *Weishu* 魏書. Ed. by Wei Shou 魏收 (506–572).
         Beijing: Zhonghua shuju, 1973.

ZZTJ   *Zizhi tongjian* 資治通鑑. By Sima Guang 司馬光.
         Beijing: Zhonghua shuju, 1956.

Introduction

Fragmentation, not unity, was the rule in ancient China. The early Zhou federation established around 1050 B.C.E. had lost all but symbolic meaning after the fall of the Western Zhou in the early eighth century B.C.E. The Spring and Autumn period (722–481 B.C.E.) was an unending series of battles as larger states swallowed up the smaller while new, powerful enemies were constantly appearing on the horizon. The Warring States (403–221 B.C.E.) was two centuries of near total war as vast, populous states devoted all of their resources to fielding huge armies that annihilated each other in mass battles resulting in hundreds of thousands of casualties. The victor, the state of Qin, maintained power for less than two decades before the empire again disintegrated into competing factions of feudal lords and newly risen peasant leaders. The Former Han empire that emerged from this confusion kept order through most of two centuries, though foreign threats by no means disappeared, but Wang Mang's usurpation in 8 C.E. led to major conflagrations among peasant rebels and local magnates. Latter Han rule was both shorter and more ephemeral. When all of China was convulsed by messianic uprisings in the 180s, warlords became dominant. Although they resolved into three major competing forces, unity was not regained until 280, only to be lost again in minority rebellions and civil war the following decade.

Modern historians, looking back across the centuries of largely peaceful, united imperial rule in China, have tended to see the period treated in this book—the first half of the fourth century C.E.—as an era of exceptional strife and disorder. It was, to be sure, a turbulent period, yet to people of the day it was rather the two or three centuries of stable Han rule that was the exception, a golden age when imperial institutions actually functioned as designed. The Han constituted an ideal that charismatic religious movements tried to recreate again and again. The nascent Daoist religion was but one of these, a movement centered in Western China that offered a Celestial Master to guide the wayward Han emperor back to the Han's cardinal virtues and through impending natural and human disasters to a future utopia of Great Peace. When the Han empire proved unable to make use of their teachings, the Celestial Masters established an independent state that survived in the region around the headwaters of the Han River and Eastern Sichuan for some decades before submitting to the strongest warlord of the day. Although the state perished and its citizens scattered, the movement survived and spread throughout China, becoming the foundation of Daoism, China's indigenous higher religion.

A powerful family from Eastern Sichuan surnamed Li was among the early followers of the Celestial Masters. They were transferred to the far northwest of China along with their entourage of some five hundred families but never lost sight of the Dao and their responsibilities as Daoists. When large-scale warfare followed by famine and epidemic disturbed them in their new home, they led their followers and other refugees, a group eventually numbering more than two hundred thousand individuals, back east, through the site of the old Celestial-Master state and south into the Chengdu plain. They were far from welcome. The entrenched elites of Sichuan sought directly and through their governmental representatives to have them forcibly returned to the devastated Northwest. Having endured the hardships of a mass migration once, they strove mightily to avoid this fate.

The Li family and the other refugees found allies. The Daoist faith was still a vital force in the region, and it recommended them to others in the faith. Long-lived Fan, a Daoist recluse heading a community on a sacred mountain near Chengdu, was one; he supplied the refugees with grain at a strategic point during a famine. Moreover, the Li family name, with its connections to Laozi, was the subject of prophesy and messianic speculation.

Ethnic ties were also important, for the Li family was not Chinese. It belonged to a branch of the Ba people, the indigenous inhabitants of Eastern Sichuan. Many Ba had followed the Lis to the Daoist community in Hanzhong, then out to the Northwest and back again amongst the refugees. Many others had remained in the Sichuan region and now provided support for their returning kinsmen.

Caught between the government and hostile local elites on one side and the death and devastation of a return to the Northwest on the other, the Li family opted for political independence and the chance to realize its utopian dreams. In 302, Li Te inaugurated the state of Perfection, Cheng 成. Te died in battle, but his son, Li Xiong, was able to establish a stable state, making Long-lived Fan his Chancellor and spiritual guide. In spite of constant threats of warfare and invasion, he maintained rule over an extended area and a large population for three decades. There he put into practice Daoist doctrine, simplifying the legal code, regulating the marketplace, living frugally, and refraining from ostentatious display. After Xiong's death in 334, his nephews, sons, and cousins vied for the succession. The next thirteen years saw four rulers take the throne, the longest for five years, and the policies of Li Te and Li Xiong were largely abandoned. Even the name of the state was changed to Han 漢. Meanwhile the Eastern Jin empire was consolidating its power; in 347 it was able to crush the last independent forces and reincorporate the region under Chinese rule. A last attempt to reestablish the utopian state of old under the son of Long-lived Fan was soon crushed.

This book is an exploration of the state of Cheng-Han and its significance for the study of Chinese and world history. It treats first the ethnic identity of the leaders of the state, then their ties to the Daoist faith. Finally, it gives an overview of the development of the state in the context of fourth-century history.

Ethnic identity is a contentious topic even today in China. China is 95 percent ethnic Chinese,[1] and all aspects of culture are dominated by the Chinese tradition. Yet subsumed within the state are many ethnic groups, some granted official recognition and a degree of protection for their native ways, some not. Historically speaking, Chinese ethnic identity has evolved continuously as numerous originally non-Chinese peoples came to identify with Chinese culture,

---

1. Chinese nationalists have sought to assert an overarching Chinese identity that subsumes all the peoples within the political borders of modern China. In this parlance the Chinese are called "Han" after the dynasty that ruled China for four centuries and established the imperial system that held sway for the next two millennia. I eschew this usage for four reasons: First, much of the time I will be talking about ethnic groups before the establishment of the Han dynasty, at which point the term is nonsensical; many of these peoples had become Chinese by the Han. Second, although the Han was the focal point of identity for most northern Chinese in late imperial China, the south, which was non-Chinese during the Han, looked instead to the Tang (618–906) and still call their overseas communities "Streets of the Tang People." Third, this usage disenfranchises the many ethnic Chinese who live outside of modern China's borders yet have maintained Chinese ethnic identity. Fourth, the use of this term is invidious in that it denies to non-Chinese peoples within the People's Republic of China true, independent ethnic identity and has been used as a tool of their oppression.

adopt Chinese names and language, and eventually lose all links with their original ethnic group, but at the same time these sinicizing peoples have enriched the Chinese tradition through the incorporation of their lore, customs, language, religion, and genes into Chinese identity.

The Li family that ruled the state of Cheng-Han was non-Chinese. Its ancestors were Ba, a general term for the indigenous inhabitants of eastern Sichuan and southwestern Hubei. These peoples shared a common founding ancestor called Lord of the Granaries, worshiped a tiger totem, were adept at hunting but skilled in the use of boats, and were cohesive enough to maintain a state or confederation for several centuries. The Lis hailed from a subgroup of the Ba called the Banshun, or Board-shield Man-barbarians, who inhabited the upper to middle reaches of the Jialing and Qu rivers. The Banshun, who were renowned as fierce warriors and repeatedly served the Chinese state as mercenaries, were also known for martial songs and dances, which became a staple of the official repertoire. By the fourth century some of the Banshun were well along the road toward Chinese identity. The Lis are identified as non-Chinese by some of the contemporary inhabitants of Sichuan and by all later histories but seem in other respects indistinguishable from the Chinese with whom they interacted. They had Chinese names, spoke, read, and wrote Chinese, adopted Chinese governmental institutions, and had served in standard governmental positions. The first chapter of this book takes up this question of ethnicity, exploring the origins and development of the Ba people, their relations to the Chinese state, and the nature of their ethnic identity in the long-sinicized world of fourth-century Sichuan.

The Li family members were also converts of long standing to Celestial Master Daoism. Daoism as a religion arose out of the intellectual and religious ferment at the end of the Han dynasty, combining a utopian vision of an egalitarian society with pervasive fears of demonic attack and a strong sense of guilt over lapses in personal conduct. The entry of Buddhism at around this time also provided models for new ritual forms and practices. The movement that arose in Sichuan during the mid-second century C.E. evolved a distinctive social organization that linked followers into communities under religious officiants called Libationers, who maintained rosters of the community, administered communal centers where food was provided to the needy, officiated at rituals of prayer and penance where sins were confessed and illnesses healed, and ordained new members.

The millenarian kingdom that the Celestial Masters prophesied was open to all the faithful, and they gained many adherents among the Banshun and other non-Chinese ethnic groups of the region. When, in the confusion of the last years of the Han, Zhang Lu was able to establish a Daoist state in the Hanzhong region northeast of Sichuan, huge numbers of church members flocked to him. After he surrendered to forces of the central government in 215, these followers were scattered, with many moved to the far Northwest. Among these transferees was a large group of Banshun Man led by Li Hu, the grandfather of the founder of the Cheng state. When Li Te and his family returned to Sichuan, their religious identity was important in gaining support from coreligionists and informed the conduct of their government. The second chapter describes the origins and nature of Celestial Master Daoism, examines the relationship of the Li family to that faith, and considers the influence their faith had on the administration of their state.

The first half of the fourth century was a key period in Chinese history. The ruling family of the Jin dynasty (265–420) had sought to turn back the clock by rejecting the highly centralized, bureaucratic government of the preceding Wei and reinstituting aristocratic feudalism. The result, once the first strong ruler had passed from the scene, was unending plotting and internecine warfare that squandered the resources and energy of the government and allowed large parts of the empire to separate. The first to break off was Sichuan, under the direction of the Li family, but it was soon followed by the Xiongnu state of Liu Yuan in the north, and eventually states of every nationality established kingdoms on Chinese soil in the period known to history as the Five Barbarians and Sixteen Kingdoms. In 316 the Jin capital was overrun and North China was lost to Chinese rule until the seventh century, the first example of a split between a Chinese dynasty in the South and a non-Chinese dynasty in the North, which was to recur in the Southern Song (1127–1280). Although the Jin never reconquered the North, they were able to regroup and bring the Sichuan region back into the Chinese polity in 347. The third chapter places the history of the Cheng state within the context of historical developments across China, demonstrating the role that population movements, religious faith, and political intrigue had on the period.

The translation that follows these three chapters is the foundation upon which these studies were constructed. It presents as complete as possible a record of the state of Cheng through the conflation of all surviving sources for the history of the state, taking as its base the "Illegitimate Annals" record of the state in the *Book of Jin* 晉書, an early Tang compilation. This is supplemented primarily by information from the *Record of the Land of Huayang* 華楊國志, a local history of the Sichuan region by Chang Qu 常璩 that is often said to be China's first regional gazetteer. It is an invaluable source because Chang had been an official of the Cheng state and hence was an eyewitness to many of the events described, with access to original documents from the state. Moreover, the *Record of the Land of Huayang* contains an abridged version of another lost work by Chang, referred to as the *Book of the Lis of Shu* 蜀李書 or the *Book of the Han* 漢之書, which was the ultimate source for all other accounts of the state. All textual material derived from sources other than the *Book of Jin* is set off in italics and its source is indicated immediately following the close of the passage. The *Book of Jin* material has been selected as the base, despite the primacy of the *Record of the Land of Huayang* as a source, because the narrative in the *Book of Jin* is continuous (except for short recapitulations of the previous exploits of each new leader when he assumes control), whereas material in the *Record of the Land of Huayang* is split between two chronologically overlapping chapters, and because the *Book of Jin*, as one of the set of standard dynastic histories, is the best-known and most widely accepted account of the state.

The Cheng empire was remote in time and far from the center of Chinese civilization, but it was neither small nor inconsequential. The state at its greatest extent stretched over eight hundred kilometers east to west and over nine hundred kilometers north to south.[2] In this time of large-scale population movements and limited tax registration, it is difficult to estimate population with any accuracy, but it surely numbered more than a million.[3] Cheng was thus a sizable

2. This is a rough estimate based upon the map in Tan Qixiang 1982–1987, 4:7–8. Historical boundaries are difficult to determine because sources record geographical units in terms of administrative centers rather than the extent of the territory they effectively control. Further, especially in the south, state control extended only to the urban areas, with mountainous regions remaining under the control of indigenous people. Still there can be little doubt that the sphere of influence of the Cheng state was extensive.

3. Chinese population records for this period are difficult to assess. They reflect not the population of the area but the number of households or individuals appearing on the tax rolls. Thus neither clients of great families nor non-Chinese peoples are recorded accurately, and Sichuan was at the time an

state by European standards and ruled for more than four decades, a respectable period in the tumult of the day. For most of that period the Cheng-Han state was an island of peace and prosperity in a perilous, rapidly changing landscape. This is the story of that state and its rulers.

---

area with large numbers of non-Chinese households at various stages of integration into Chinese society. In 140 C.E. the registered population was 4.7 million, but in the census of 280 only some eight hundred thousand are recorded. HYGZ gives partial population figures, presumably for ca. 347, considerably higher than those for 280, but with great variance from place to place. Guanghan commandery, for example, had six times as many households as in 280, whereas Qianwei doubled and Shu commandery is only one-third larger. During the course of Cheng history sizable groups both immigrated and emigrated. The region was certainly underpopulated relative to its Han period population, but could still field several large armies numbering in the tens of thousands simultaneously. See Li Shiping 1987:47, 59–65.

PART I

Ethnicity, Religion, and History

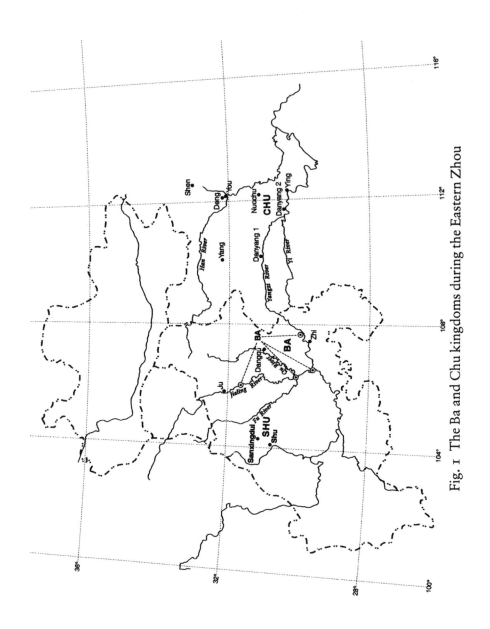

Fig. 1 The Ba and Chu kingdoms during the Eastern Zhou

ONE

Ethnicity and Identity

The Li family, we are told, was of the Ba 巴 ethnicity, belonging to the subgroups known as the Zong 賨 and the Banshun 板楯 or Board-shield Man-barbarians. The exact significance of these designations is a complex question, to be discussed at length below, but it is clear that the ethnic identity of the Lis and their followers was a key factor in determining their reception when entering Sichuan, the establishment and development of their state, their interaction with other peoples of west and southwest China, and their ultimate treatment by Chinese historians. The historical record of the Lis, in turn, is an important source of information concerning the historical development of their ethnic group and the state of other ethnicities of the area in the fourth century C.E. This chapter examines the ethnic identity of the Lis against the diverse ethnological canvas of the Sichuan basin and surrounding areas. It treats both the prehistory of Sichuan and the historical ethnography of all the peoples who interacted with the Lis. We begin with a discussion of the special problems confronting modern scholars seeking to deal with the historical ethnography of ancient China.

IDENTITY AND HISTORICAL ETHNOGRAPHY

There are a number of pitfalls involved in even broaching the subject of ethnicity in premodern China. The first involves the construction of the Chinese ethnic identity. Historical sources identify three successive political entities, the Xia, Shang, and Zhou dynasties, as ruling consecutively over a territory comprising the ancient Chinese heartland (essentially the drainage basin of the Yellow River and its tributaries) and sharing a common culture that was distinctively Chinese. Modern historiography confirms the existence of the Shang and Zhou much as they were recorded, but the Xia remains controversial, with

Chinese scholars readily identifying pre-Shang remains as Xia while non-Chinese scholars have been more skeptical.[1]

Moreover, there are significant cultural breaks between the Shang and the Zhou. The Shang seem to have originated in the east (i.e., lower Yellow River valley and surrounding areas) and are most closely linked to the Neolithic Longshan culture of that region, whereas the Zhou came from the Wei River valley of Shaanxi province (and before that central Shaanxi) and are more directly derived from the Yangshao culture of that area.[2] In fact, early sources characterize the Zhou as being of the Western Barbarians 西戎, and Pulleyblank has argued cogently that they were originally Tibeto-Burmans closely related to the Qiang 羌 and Rong 戎 ethnicities.[3]

In any case, Shang and Zhou do seem to have shared a common language, as evidenced by the oracle bone and bronze inscriptions of the Shang, which were written in a language identifiable both syntactically and lexically as Chinese.[4] A common dialect has been a unifying feature of the Chinese world since at least the sixth century B.C.E., when Confucius advocated the use of a shared "elegant" pronunciation (ya 雅), an ideological if not linguistic ancestor to Mandarin, when intoning canonical texts. Confucius also differentiated Chinese from their neighbors in matters of dress,[5] and about this time we find the terms Xia (same as the dynasty) and Hua 華 ("flowery") used to designate the Chinese states.[6] It is difficult, however, to

1. There has been an international conference on Xia civilization, but Allan has argued in a number of articles (collected in Allan 1991) that much of Xia "history" can be seen as mythological reflexes of Shang history and legend.

2. These archaeological cultures cannot easily be equated with historical groups. The Yangshao culture, for example, extends from the central Yellow River valley all the way into Gansu and Qinghai provinces, where Ren Naiqiang (1984) has linked it to the Qiang ethnic group. Similarly, although Longshan was in some sense ancestral to the Shang, it undoubtedly comprised some members who would later become Yi-barbarians of the East, especially around the lower Huai River area.

3. Pulleyblank 1983:420–422. Cf. *Mencius* 30/4B/1.

4. It is possible, however, that the Zhou adopted the (perhaps related) language of the then dominant culture of the Shang. The present study, filled with members of explicitly non-Chinese ethnic groups who read, write, and speak Chinese fluently, might be seen as support for such a hypothesis.

5. *Analects* 14.17, Lau 1979:126–127.

6. In an entry dated 559 B.C.E. in the *Zuozhuan* (278/Xiang 14/1), a Rong representative says, "We Rongs are different from the Hua in eat, drink, and dress." Hua can be plural, referring to the Chinese states (*Zuozhuan* 258/Xiang 4/fu 1; 431/Zhao 30/4), and is found in collocation with Xia (*Zuozhuan* 313/Xiang 26/fu 6). Cf. Lin Huixiang 1936:45–49.

specify the boundaries of this group, nor can we be sure of the cultural, linguistic, or historical standards employed in defining it.

A second major problem involves the terminology used for non-Chinese peoples. Although Chinese identity may at first have been somewhat nebulously defined, the ancient Chinese seem to have encountered no difficulty in distinguishing those people who were not Chinese. There is a rich vocabulary of names for these non-Chinese people. A common organizational scheme was to array them according to the directions, with Yi 夷 in the east, Rong in the west, Di 狄 in the north, and Man 蠻 in the south. Unfortunately, this neat geographical layout was little more than an ideological construct; Prusek (1971) has shown that Rong and Di, for example, lived in mountainous regions throughout what was nominally Chinese territory and non-Chinese of the far southwest were regularly referred to as Yi.[7] Although Chinese at times allied themselves and intermarried with these non-Chinese peoples, they perceived a great cultural gap separating them from Chinese society. The characters used for the names of non-Chinese ethnic groups often contain elements identifying them with animals or insects and they are said to have "shrikes' tongues."[8]

The imprecision with which terms for non-Chinese peoples were employed is a major source of confusion in analyzing the ethnography of premodern China. The four directionally oriented terms for non-Chinese were often applied on the basis of physical location with no regard to cultural, linguistic, or historical identity.[9] Similarly, there was a tendency, especially evident in the comparatively late material of the fourth century, to take the name of the dominant minority in a region as a general term for non-Chinese, often prefixing some other character to distinguish different ethnic groups. We will see that just such a practice has resulted in a serious misunderstanding of the ethnic filiations of the Li family.[10] Further, we often

7. As, for example, in the "Arrayed Traditions on the Southwest Yi" of the *Shiji* (chapter 116).

8. *Mengzi yinde* 21/3A/4. Cf. *Zuozhuan* 258/Xiang 4/fu 1, "The Rong are birds and beasts."

9. It is difficult to know, for example, whether the various peoples styled "Man" were truly thought to be related or merely shared a geographical location south of Central China.

10. I refer here to the interpretation of the designation Ba Di 巴氐 that assumes from this that the Lis were in fact Di. As Zhang Guanying (1957:70) has pointed out, "The area around Lueyang was originally occupied by Di; since Di were the non-Chinese people that the Chinese were accustomed to

do not know if a given term is derived from a native word in that people's vocabulary or is simply a conventional term applied to them by Chinese neighbors.[11] When the name can be shown to be of indigenous, non-Chinese origin, it often provides persuasive evidence linking that people to a modern ethnic group.

A third problem lies in the thoroughness and reliability of historical sources. Because of the varying fortunes of the Chinese state, it was not able to extend consistent political control into non-Chinese areas. For this reason, accounts of many peoples are episodic and lacking in continuity, detailed for periods when Chinese influence and interest in the region was high, but silent for long stretches when communication was interrupted or the attention of the state was focused elsewhere. There are accounts of the indigenous inhabitants of Yunnan, Guizhou, and the Sichuan periphery in the chapters devoted to the Southwest Barbarians in the *Account of the Historian (Shiji)* and *Book of Han (Hanshu)*, but no description of peoples living closer to the Chinese center in Sichuan or Hubei. The *Book of Latter Han (Hou Hanshu)*, compiled in the fifth century, treats these closer figures, including the Ba people, who are the primary subject of this study; the *Book of Jin (Jinshu)* and *Springs and Autumns of the Sixteen Kingdoms (Shiliuguo chunqiu)* include biographies for those who established their own states during the period of disunion. Some of the closer peoples occur occasionally in belles lettres, but this is rare for those on the periphery.[12]

The reliability of these accounts is also open to question. We know that Sima Qian, author of the *Account of the Historian,* traveled as far as Xichang in southwestern Sichuan, so some of his records of the peoples of the southwest are based on personal observation, but for most works, we must suppose that we are dealing with second- and third-hand accounts deriving from official reports written by government representatives with varying degrees of experience in the region and with various intended purposes. Because it was the policy through most of early imperial history to select for administrators in

---

seeing, the term 'Di' came to be the general term used by the Chinese of the region for non-Chinese." Terms like Ba Yi 巴夷, applied to the indigenous inhabitants of Langzhong, would seem to function similarly.

11. Wang Ming-ke (1992, 1994b) argues that during Shang times the term "Qiang" 羌 was just such an exonym that was applied categorically to all non-Chinese peoples to the west of them.

12. One important source is the "Rhapsody on the Shu Capital" 蜀都賦 by Zuo Si 左思 (ca. 250–305). See Knechtges 1982:341–372.

border regions long-time inhabitants of the region, either Chinese immigrants or highly sinicized locals, we can hope that reports from such men were based upon extensive knowledge of the area, its history, and its ethnic composition, but they also had vested interests in the region that might skew their portrayal of local events or individuals. The *Record of the Land of Huayang (Huayangguo zhi)* of Chang Qu, an important source for the Sichuan and Guizhou area, is a good example of this. Chang was a native of the region and must have written from firsthand experience, but he was also an ethnic Chinese from an elite family with a tradition of Confucian scholarship and this to some degree colors his accounts.

A fourth problem involves the nature of ethnic identity and the ongoing process of sinicization that continually expanded the bounds of Chinese ethnicity. An important characteristic of ethnic groups of this region was their living in close proximity to and in constant contact with other groups. Although one ethnic group might clearly dominate a given region, there were often other groups living in the area, some related, some of totally different strains. In Chinese such groups are normally described as "living intermixed" (*zaju* 雜居).[13] Although individual cases may differ, for most of these peoples we can assume regular interaction with members of other ethnic groups and the complex of cultural borrowing, accommodation, and assimilation that such sustained contacts engender.

The influence of Chinese culture must be singled out of this ethnic congeries. As the dominant prestige culture of East Asia, its impact was greater and more widespread than that of any other ethnic group. To be sure, the Chinese also adopted local habits, and some of these may have made their way back to the center. Nor can the role of native peoples of the southwest as transmitters of Indic culture and material civilization be dismissed.[14] Still, we must acknowledge that a knowledge of Chinese and of Chinese forms of government was essential for advancing one's wealth or status. This gave a great impetus

13. At least in some locales this must have meant a situation such as obtains now in parts of northern Thailand, where a Lisu village may have a Lahu village as its nearest neighbor on one side, a Chinese settlement on the other, and a Karen village just down the road. In 1981 I encountered just such a grouping and met on the road many Akha who must have lived nearby. A Chinese trader married to a Lisu woman ran the only store in the area, in the Lisu village.

14. The role of the "second silk road" through the southwest has been the object of much recent interest in Sichuan, but demonstrated examples of cultural diffusion through this route are still largely lacking.

to sinicization, the conscious adoption of Chinese dress, speech, culture, and worldview. We will see that most of the non-Chinese we encounter in accounts of the Cheng-Han state are highly sinicized; they are not only trained in Chinese language but possess the extensive knowledge of Chinese history and literature necessary to run a Chinese-style bureaucratic state. Absent other evidence, we cannot assume that, because they belong to a given ethnic group, they maintain the cultural traits of that group as recorded in our earliest sources. But we should also be prepared to find a great deal of internal variation, with non-Chinese from urban or densely settled rural areas speaking, acting, and dressing essentially the same as their Chinese neighbors and more remote elements of a people maintaining traditional social organization and culture.

Finally, recent anthropological scholarship on the nature of ethnic identity and its relationship to historical memory raises very basic questions about the significance of both exonymic appellations used by other ethnic groups and autonymic terms based on the group's name for itself. In brief, this scholarship holds that historical memory itself is a shifting and adaptive entity that is being continually reshaped to fit the needs and circumstances of the moment.[15] Since the accounts in Chinese historical sources are more or less accurate transcriptions of the historical memory of the peoples involved, both Chinese and non-Chinese, we must understand that the historical situation and the events leading up to it, as they are presented in these accounts, are themselves narratives created for specific purposes rather than objective representations of historical reality. For example, the account of Taibo 太伯, son of the Zhou King Taiwang, fleeing to the far southeast, adopting the local customs, and establishing the state of Wu, has long been accepted as historical fact and has shaped our understanding of the archaeological record of that region. More recently, Wang Ming-ke has argued that this tale is in fact a narrative created by the Zhou and Wu peoples at a much later date to establish and strengthen relations between the two peoples; it provided a type of fictive kinship that was instrumental in bringing the inhabitants of the southeast into the Chinese ethnic group.[16]

15. See Wang Ming-ke 1994a and 1994b. A good presentation of the theoretical arguments concerning ethnic identity and collective memory is found in the essays collected in Keyes 1981.

16. See Wang Ming-ke n.d. Wang points out that tombs containing Zhou-style bronzes are treated as the product of a different culture from living sites in the same area, which show no sign of Zhou influence.

Thus in evaluating such accounts, we must always keep in mind what function they might have played during the period of their creation and currency.

With the preceding caveats, let us now look at the ethnic composition of the areas under discussion. We will first treat the primary occupants of the Sichuan basin, the Ba and Shu, beginning with prehistory and our first historical records.

PREHISTORY

The last two decades have seen a dramatic shift in our understanding of Chinese prehistory. Prompted by a series of startling archaeological discoveries, a highly sinocentric model of prehistory seeing the traditional homeland of the Chinese people in the Yellow River drainage basin and the North China plain as the dominant culture and the source of all cultural innovation has given way to a new understanding of the East Asian Neolithic as composed of a number of equally advanced, competing cultures spread throughout the region. Sichuan has shared in this reevaluation of prehistory.

Sichuan was inhabited in Paleolithic times, but so far remains are insufficient to give us a clear picture of the culture(s) involved and their dating.[17] Similarly, the early Neolithic in Sichuan remains shrouded in mystery. For the late Neolithic period, however, we are fortunate to have the finds around modern Guanghan, specifically, the site known as Sanxingdui 三星堆. There a cultural sequence in four stages spanning fourteen hundred years, from roughly 2500 B.C.E. to 875 B.C.E., has revealed a flourishing culture that developed independently yet actively interacted with both the Central Plain cultures and those of the Middle and Lower Yangzi.[18]

It is the latest stratum of this site that holds the most interest for us. It corresponds to the period from the end of the Shang dynasty through the first half of the Western Zhou (roughly eleventh through ninth centuries B.C.E.) and is best known for two hoards of sacrificed objects discovered in 1986.[19] These reveal a highly developed

---

17. The following discussion is based primarily upon Sage 1992, the first major treatment of early Sichuan in a Western language. See also Meng et al. 1989:14–18.

18. In this I follow Meng et al. 1989:16 rather than Sage, who distinguishes only three major stages.

19. The sacrificial purposes of these objects is indicated by the broken and burned condition of many of the objects. See Sage 1992:25 and the articles in *Wenwu* 1987.10.

civilization with an independent bronze industry capable of casting pieces of great size and intricate design, an advanced jade-working industry, as well as experience in materials as diverse as gold, bone, and ivory. The richness of the find indicates a highly stratified society with an ample agricultural surplus and a governmental apparatus sophisticated enough to extract it for use by a king or other ruling group. Particularly striking is a life-size crowned bronze figure, large bronze masks (one 134 centimeters wide and 70 centimeters from chin to brow), and numerous bronze heads, all in a distinctive style sporting non-Chinese dress and ornamentation. Gold and gold-leaf masks as well as a gold-encased scepter that may have functioned as a symbol of authority also stand out. There is evidence of Sanxingdui-type goods as far away as Yichang, Hubei, to the east, Hanzhong to the northeast, and Yaan to the south, but we cannot assume that the state at this time actually extended so far. A set of sandstone rings of various sizes, some as heavy as sixty-three kilograms, have been identified as balance weights, suggesting extensive trading relations, as do bronze and ceramic vessels of central China typology.[20]

No true continuation of the Sanxingdui culture has as yet been found, but there is an increasing amount of archaeological evidence for the succeeding centuries, and much of it seems derivative of Sanxingdui. A large ritual mound in Chengdu may have had its origins in the late stages of the Sanxingdui site; its size suggests a well-developed state organization, but we have yet to find the assemblages of luxury goods indicative of an aristocratic ruling class.

One intriguing continuity with later sites is a bowl or ladle with a handle in the shape of a hook-billed bird, which is found beginning in the second layer of Sanxingdui. This bird, which has been identified as a cormorant, is among the most common of a small number of designs found on weapons and vessels from Spring and Autumn and Warring States sites throughout the Sichuan region. Examples of these vessels have been found as far away as the Yichang region of Hubei. Various scholars have sought to link this bird to the name Yufu 魚鳧, a mythical ruler of Shu, and through this name to a number of similarly named sites over a wide area centering on the Yangzi gorges.[21]

---

20. Meng et al. 1989:17.

21. These sites include: Yufu 漁復 west of Changsha (*Yi Zhoushu jixun jiaoshi* 7/196); Yufu 魚腹 city near Mianyang, Hubei (TPHYJ 144:11a); Yufu Ford 魚符津 near Nanxi, Sichuan (cited as Yu 魚 Ford in TPHYJ 79:5a); the Yufu 魚腹, formerly Yuyi 魚邑, that is now Fengjie, Sichuan (HS 8A/1603);

The discoveries at Sanxingdui are recent and surprising. The assessment of this culture and its relation to other early centers is ongoing, as is the process of archaeological discovery in Sichuan. We can confidently assert that Sichuan was home to an advanced, independent culture at an early date, but the relationship of this civilization to the later historical inhabitants of the region remains a topic of contention and speculation. We turn now to these successor states.

SHU

Historical sources for the Sichuan area divide it into two major regions, Shu 蜀 in the west along the Min River and extending across the Chengdu plain and Ba 巴 in the east. Since Shu was traditionally centered on the Chengdu area, it seems the logical historical correlate of the Sanxingdui culture and its successors. As we shall see, the historical record of Shu is far from clear.

Our earliest historical source for ancient China is the terse divinatory statements recorded on turtle plastrons and bovine scapula that have come to be called "oracle bone inscriptions" (jiaguwen 甲骨文).[22] Among these inscriptions is found a character variously written 𤔌, 𤔌, 𤔌 that has by some been identified with Shu.[23] The graph would appear to be an animal, with a large eye (often standing by principle of synecdoche for the head) atop a sinuous curling body. The eye/head is sometimes topped by antennae or feelers, and the body in some cases is depicted with a number of hairs, or perhaps legs, projecting from both sides of the length of the body. Chen Mengjia interpreted the graph as xuan 旬.[24] The character xun 旬, meaning the cyclical ten-day week, has a curving body that matches the graph in question, with a simple cross at the head; the "eye" 目 element that replaces "sun" 日 in the middle of the later graph is then interpreted as a semantic radical. There is a site in Shanxi province known to have been an early Zhou fief by this name (usually written xun 郇), and it is assumed that this is the place referred to in the oracle bone inscriptions as well.[25] This interpretation requires

Yufu Ford 魚涪津 near Pengshan, Sichuan (HHS 18:681); and others. See Meng et al. 1989:17.

22. For a general overview of oracle bones, their discovery early this century, and the process of their interpretation, see Keightley 1979.

23. Relevant inscriptions are collected in Shima 1971:106.3-4.

24. Chen Mengjia 1956:273. This identification is accepted by Zhong Bosheng 1972:61 and Jao 1959:189.

25. For references to this place on Western Zhou bronzes, see Shaughnessy 1991:6, 79.

that the original oracle bone graph be interpreted as a radical-phonetic compound, with the eye element functioning as radical or signific and the body of the beast being phonetic, but the graph found on the oracle bones is almost certainly a pictograph.

Among the inscriptions found on a horde of oracle bones unearthed at Zhouyuan, the predynastic Zhou capital, there are two occurrences of a character that has been identified as Shu. Written 蜀, these characters are nearly identical to an "ancient orthography" form recorded in *Shuowen*, which defines Shu as "a silkworm within a musk mallow" (*kuizhong can* 葵中蠶) and specifies that the insect *chong* 虫 is the signific, the eye represents the insect's head, and the rest of the character its body.[26] It would seem, then, that the signific *chong* was added to the character after it had lost its obviously pictographic character. Thus the Zhouyuan oracle bone character and, through it, the earlier graphic form, can be confidently identified as *shu*.

This does not, however, permit us to assume that the Shu mentioned in the oracle bones is in fact the Shu of the Chengdu plain or even a state ancestral to that Shu and located farther north, perhaps in the upper Han River valley. There was a Shu in Shandong (west of modern Taian) that was the site of an interstate meeting in 589 B.C.E., and Shu Mountains in Shandong, Jiangsu, and Zhejiang provinces.[27] The occurrence of the state in the Zhouyuan oracle bones, however, suggests that it was in the general vicinity of the Zhou, to the west of the Shang rather than far to the east.

Examining the inscriptions themselves, we find that Shu was at least at times an ally of the Shang, reflected in Shang divinations about Shu's harvest[28] that are thought to indicate a commonality of interest, in the absence of any record of hostile military action against Shu, and in the fact that Shu is never referred to as a *fang* 方, a term reserved for often-hostile states like Gui 鬼 in the north and Yi 夷 to the east. The Shang king once visited Shu and made divinations there.[29] The extensive divinations preceding the trip suggest that it

26. *Shuowen jiezi zhu* 13A/35b. The Qing commentary of Duan Yucai notes that the Tang philologist Lu Deming's glosses to the *Erya* quotes *Shuowen* with mulberry (*sang* 桑) in place of musk mallow, but in spite of the frequent association of silkworms with mulberry trees, this seems an insufficient reason to emend the *Shuowen*. For the musk mallow, see Stuart 1911:256.

27. Zang 1936:1059.4–1060.1; *Chunqiu jingzhuan yinde* 226/Cheng 2/9–10.

28. Dong Zuobin, 5280, 6422; Guo Ruoyu et al. 1955:248.

29. Chalfont and Britton 1935:993; 981. The Zhouyuan inscriptions have

was hazardous. Mention of the state of Fou 缶 in these inscriptions indicates that the trip was generally westerly, since Fou was subject to attacks from the Qiang. The record of divinations made during the trip has been analyzed by Shima Kunio (1958:378–379), who on this basis argues that the trip took thirty to sixty days; he places the state of Shu south of the great bend of the Yellow River, in western Henan.[30] It is not inconceivable that the sphere of influence of a Chengdu-area Shu might extend far to the north,[31] but it is usually assumed that when a Shang king is said to have visited a place, he visited the capital.

An early historical source provides additional evidence. The "Oath at Shepherd's Field" ("Mushi" 牧誓) chapter of the *Book of Documents* purports to record an address by King Wu of Zhou to his assembled troops preceding the attack on the Shang. It mentions eight non-Chinese tribes or states, including Shu, who are said to have joined with the Zhou in their attack on the Shang.[32] The "Oath at Shepherd's Field" has been dated to the Warring States period but may record traditions of an earlier era.[33] A chapter of the *Lost Zhou Documents* (*Yi Zhou shu* 逸周書), on the other hand, describes an expedition against Shu by a subordinate of King Wu shortly after the conquest.[34] Both sources agree that a state called Shu was in contact with Zhou during the eleventh century B.C.E.

Archaeology provides an intriguing confirmation of such contact. Shu bronze halberd blades show clear influence from Central Plains models in the late Shang–early Zhou period but then develop

---

Zhou divining about attacking Shu. See Xu Xitai 1979:189 and Shaughnessy 1980–81:73n22.

30. The relevant inscriptions are *Kufang* 681 and 683. The thirty-day date is based upon rather speculative reconstructions of missing texts. The sixty-day date also makes assumptions about the order and frequency of divination as well as the speed of travel and overall geographical extent of the Shang state that are open to challenge.

31. Sage 1992:225n41.

32. *Shangshu zhengyi* 11/15a. The eight states are Yong 庸, Shu, Qiang, Mao 髳, Wei 微, Lu 盧, Peng 彭, and Pu 濮. All have been plausibly located in the Wei River valley area, southern Henan, northern Hubei, or northern Sichuan. See Ikeda 1976:237–238.

33. Ikeda 1976:234–235 has an excellent review of the various arguments for dating this text to the Warring States, which center on matters of vocabulary, syntax, and official titles. See also Qu Wanli 1969:71 and the comments of Edward Shaughnessy in Loewe 1993:379.

34. Shaughnessy 1980–81:58; *Yi Zhou shu jixun jiaoshi* 4/96. Shaughnessy argues that this chapter is an authentic early Zhou text providing a comparatively reliable account of the conquest.

independently, with no apparent further influence, as Central Plains styles were evolving into new forms. The famous "willow-leaf" sword blades characteristic of Spring and Autumn and Warring States Sichuanese tombs are also based on Shang models with little evidence of influence from later Zhou innovations.[35] This archaeological situation is confirmed by the absence of Shu from almost all Zhou literature up until Qin began to plot its conquest at the end of the fourth century.[36]

For most of the Zhou dynasty we have no reliable historical records concerning Shu. The *Annals of the Kings of Shu* (*Shuwang benji* 蜀王本紀), traditionally attributed to Yang Xiong 揚雄 (53 B.C.E.–18 C.E.), survives only in quotations.[37] The *Record of the Land of Huayang (Huayangguo zhi),* by Chang Qu, is the earliest surviving history of the Sichuan region. Chang made extensive use of the *Annals of the Kings of Shu,* and surviving quotations from the *Annals* suggest that it presented a similar picture of Sichuan's early history. In these sources we find that preconquest history is pure myth, consisting of wonder-working kings and their feats.[38] The first was said to be Cancong 蠶叢, or "Silkworm-bush," who was later worshiped as the founder of silkworm cultivation, a major Sichuanese industry. He was followed by Boguan 柏灌, or "Cypress-irrigator";[39] little is known of this figure, but he may be related to the lumber industry. Next came Yufu 魚鳧, or "Cormorant." All three are said to have transformed into transcendants and flown away. They were followed by King Duyu 杜宇, or "Cuckoo," who descended from the heavens, married a woman who emerged from a well, taught the people agriculture, and transformed upon his death into the bird that was his namesake. He was followed by Bieling 鱉靈, or "Turtle Spirit," who is said to have floated up the Yangzi from Chu as a corpse, then

---

35. Sage 1992:38–39.

36. Exceptions are the *Yi Zhou shu* passage discussed above and a passage from the *Zhushu jinian* (Wang Guowei 1917:2/14b) that records the presentation of jades by a representative of Shu in 864 B.C.E. Dates follow Shaughnessy 1991.

37. These have twice been collected, by Hong Yixuan 洪頤烜 (1763–?) and Wang Renjun 王仁俊 (1866–1913). Their reconstructions are to be found in *Jingdian jilin* 經典集林 and in the *Yuhan shanfang jiyishu bubian* 玉函山房輯佚書補編.

38. The following material is taken from HYGZ 3/117–118 and from the *Shuwang benji,* quoted in TPYL 888/2b–3b.

39. *Shuwang benji* gives Bohuo 柏濩 ("cypress drippings"?). The two characters are graphically quite similar and easily confused. See TPYL 888/2b.

revived in Shu, where he became Prime Minister to Duyu and was cuckolded by him while off performing wondrous terraforming feats aimed at controlling the flood waters. When Duyu abdicated out of shame, Bieling came to the throne as Kaiming 開明, or "Enlightened."[40] He married a sex-changing fairy and was aided by the Five Stalwarts (*wuding* 五丁), heroic siblings who moved monoliths, built roads through impenetrable mountains, and were killed by a giant snake. All of this material is presented by Chang Qu as history but with relatively few euhemerizing embellishments.[41]

In spite of the obviously fantastic elements in these accounts, they are accepted by nearly all Chinese historians of Sichuan, and even by some Western scholars, as true accounts of early history, with each mythic ruler representing a dynasty of unspecified length.[42] Such myths are of course products of history and can perhaps be understood as representing different stages of cultural development, but they do not record historical events per se, and great care must be used in reconstructing history on such a basis. In the case of the myths of central China, for example, we know, largely from the work of the "doubting antiquity" (*yigu* 疑古) movement of the 1930s, that myths concerning the (purportedly) earliest figures were actually the last to be created, as successive authors sought increasingly loftier (that is, more ancient) pedigrees for the mythical embodiments of their ideals.[43]

40. *Kaiming* is the term used to describe Danzhu 丹朱, the rightful heir to the sage Emperor Yao who was rejected by his father as "obstinate and vicious." An ironic interpretation of this name fits well with his portrayal as a hedonistic adventurer who brought his state to ruin. See *Shiji* 1/20.

41. Emperor Kaiming is described as having "lived for nine generations" (*jiushi you Kaimingdi* 九世有開明帝), which could be interpreted as a succession of nine reigns, but he is said to have a son. He seems, in any case, more anthropomorphic than any of his predecessors, who reign then pass away without forebears or issue. Again, there is mention of his ancestral temples, but in fact these are temples to the Thearchs of the Five Directions, color-coded divinities of a Chinese cult that may have originated in the state of Qin (see Kleeman 1994b) and are five in number rather than eight.

42. Chinese representatives of this trend are too numerous to list exhaustively. Some good examples are Tong Enzheng 1979; Meng Wentong 1981:42; Deng 1983:135ff. The primary Western exponent is Steven Sage 1992. Compare the treatment of Duyu in Birrell 1993:197–198, where the tale is said to be "a singular expression of classical mythic motifs."

43. These seminal discussions, which seem to have been forgotten by some modern Chinese scholars, are collected in Gu Jiegang's seven-volume *Gushi bian* 古史辯 (1926–1941).

We are on firmer ground when we reach the end of the fourth century B.C.E.[44] It was at this time that the state of Qin, centered in modern Shaanxi province, began the expansion that would eventually lead to its conquest of all of China through a decisive move toward the south. Qin was at the forefront of a wave of administrative and tactical innovation that was sweeping through the Zhou states. It actively promoted the cultivation of new land and administered this new territory directly through a system of commanderies and counties, then sought to gradually expand this system to other parts of the state. Through application of universal legal codes, household registration, and a system of mutual responsibility, Qin reduced the power of subinfeudated local nobility and increased governmental control of the populace. It also standardized weights, measures, and axle widths and established a monopoly over iron production, both to promote commerce and to facilitate taxation. Beginning with the reign of Huiwen in 337 B.C.E., and especially after he assumed the royal title of King in 324, Qin began to focus on Sichuan as a possible area of expansion as well as a route through which Qin could directly attack its greatest rival, the state of Chu.[45]

In 316 B.C.E. Qin moved into Sichuan, at first allying with Ba in the conquest of Shu and the death of its king, then turning on Ba and its northern neighbor Ju 苴. Soon Qin controlled all of Sichuan and the Hanzhong region as far east as Yong 庸 (near modern Zhushan, Hubei).[46] The son of the former King of Shu was enfeoffed as Marquis, but a Qin official was appointed his Prime Minister and a Warden (shou 守) was also appointed to govern in Qin's name.[47] This

44. The following discussion is entirely based upon accounts from sources external to Sichuan. Local Sichuanese history remains suffused with myth, recording an encounter between the rulers of Shu and Qin in which Shu's gifts transform into soil and the construction of a road, presumably the famed scaffold road (zhandao 棧道), from Shu to Qin by the Five Stalwarts in order to fetch five gold-defecating oxen. Sage (1992:112) characterizes these events as being "in a literary grey area set somewhere between history and legend."

45. The "Discourse Faulting Qin" (Guo Qin lun 過秦論) of Jia Yi 賈誼 (201–169 B.C.E.) implies that Qin's annexation of Hanzhong and conquest of Ba and Shu were entrusted to King Huiwen by his predecessor, Duke Xiao. See Shiji 6/279.

46. Shiji 5/207; Sage 1992:115.

47. Following Shiji 70/2284, which states that the King of Sichuan's rank was reduced to that of a Marquis, and Sage 1992:256n13. HYGZ 3/29, however, clearly states that the Kaiming line was extinguished and that the new Marquis was the son of the Qin king. Ren 128n6 presents evidence that a son of this line fled to the far south, where he was killed by the King of Yue.

condominium government lasted only three decades, experiencing three revolts, before Qin assumed final direct control over the region.

Following its conquest of the region, Qin immediately embarked upon an ambitious program to convert Ba, Shu, and Hanzhong into military strongholds and economic resources. The capital of Chengdu and two other cities were walled, and from the pits excavated for building materials giant fish-growing ponds were created. Agricultural land was divided into regular, equal-sized plots and redistributed (perhaps primarily to Qin immigrants). In the third century, a major irrigation system was created by the Qin Warden Li Bing 李冰. Large numbers of people were marched into Shu in orderly groups and resettled. These transferred populations included criminals and war captives from other parts of China as well as voluntary migrants and encompassed merchants and aristocrats as well as peasants.[48]

The preservation of a Shu Marquis during the early years of Qin occupation suggests that the traditional Shu nobility was not immediately displaced, and graves clearly reflect differences between natives and colonists. Still, from this time forward we hear no more in historical sources of the native population of Shu. Assimilation to a new Qin-Chinese identity must have proceeded rapidly among most of the settled populace, while more resistant or remote groups were reclassified as "barbarian" minorities.

BA

The eastern portion of the traditional Sichuan region is known as Ba 巴. The area usually indicated by this term is the Yangzi valley from Fengjie up to Yibin, the middle and lower reaches of the Jialing River 嘉陵江 that feed into it, and the tributaries of the Jialing, the Fu River 涪江, and the Qu River 渠江 (the upper reaches of which are known as the Ba River 巴河). The term Ba is also used to refer to an ethnic group, the Ba people, and to a state that was conquered by Qin in 316 B.C.E. As we shall see, the relationships between the geographical region, the people, and the state are by no means simple.

The evidence for this entity called Ba differs from that for Shu in both date and type. The upper Yangzi was home to an early Neolithic

48. An example of the use of Shu as a place of banishment is found in the "Fengzhenshi" 封診式 document excavated from a Qin tomb in Hubei province. In a sample verdict meant to act as a precedent for future rulings, a father asks that an unfilial son have his feet cut off and be banished to a border county of Shu. See Shuihudi Qinmu zhujian zhengli xiaozu 1990: "Fengzhenshi shiwen zhushi," 155.

Fig. 2 Ba Chunyu 錞于 Bronze Drum (Western Han).
Chinese Museum of History collection.

culture, the Daxi 大溪 culture, which has been documented for a period from roughly 5500 B.C.E. to 2750 B.C.E.[49] Daxi sites show evidence of contact with the Qujialing culture of the Middle Yangzi and had some influence on sites in the Jialing River basin.

Yang Quanxi 楊權喜 has identified a series of second millennium B.C.E. sites along the Yangzi in Western Hubei as "early Ba culture," and Zhang Xiong would extend this horizon to sites in Eastern Sichuan.[50] The inhabitants seem to have subsisted primarily on hunting and fishing, and their primary cultural artifact is a handmade, sandy gray pottery.

Ba does not occur in the oracle bone inscriptions of the Shang, indicating either that there was no such state at that time or that it was so distant as to be out of touch with Shang.[51] Ba is not mentioned in the "Oath at Shepherd's Field" among the states that aided the Zhou in their conquest of the Shang, but later there was such a tradition.[52] There is a fairly early tradition that the ruler of the Ba state had the surname of the Zhou royal house, Ji 姬.[53] Given the wide

49. Sage 1992:47–50.

50. Zhang Xiong 1993:34. Zhang cites an article by Yang in *Hubeisheng kaogu xuehui lunwenji* 湖北省考古學會論文集, vol. 2, which I have been unable to consult.

51. Some Chinese authors do indeed find reference to it in the character 𠂤, which bears a superficial resemblance to the modern character Ba. The character in question designates a distant state *(fang)* that is in an adversarial relationship to Shang. Although the interpretation of this graph is problematic, Ba is not a likely possibility. Chen Mengjia (1956:284) interpreted this graph as *yin* 印 and placed the state of Yin in southern Shanxi. Li Xiaoding (1965:entry 2783) follows Guo Moruo in identifying the character as a variant form of *yi* 夷, hence referring to the well-known state in the southeast. Cf. Shima 1958:390–391. All agree that the oracle bone character in question depicts a human figure, and such an analysis is never made for Ba.

52. HYGZ 1/3–4. Chang Qu records that the first Han emperor, Liu Bang, in ordering the adoption of the Ba songs into the state repertory, said, "These are the songs to which King Wu (of Zhou) attacked Zhou (last king of the Shang)." Such a comment does not occur in earlier accounts of this music discussed below but may reflect an authentic tradition concerning Liu Bang's understanding of ancient history. By Chang's time, in any case, Ba's role in the expedition was a well-accepted fact. Ren 1/5n6 points out that the reference to the Zhou conquest saying that King Wu's troops "sang before (the battle) and danced after it" derives from the Latter Han *Baihu tong*, where there is no mention of Ba peoples. See *Baihu tong* 13/6/3. By Chang's time the Ba songs and dances had been part of state ceremony for more than five hundred years, and it is not surprising that legends developed concerning their even greater antiquity. See also Dong Qixiang 1987.

53. *Zuozhuan* 382/Zhao 13/fu 1. This account concerning the events of 529

distribution of this surname and its presence among non-Chinese peoples, it is uncertain what significance this has.[54] There is also a record from later Spring and Autumn or early Warring States that Ba had been part of Zhou territory after the conquest.[55]

The best early evidence concerning the Ba people derives from the *Zuozhuan*, a historical work compiled in the fourth century B.C.E. that preserves documents from a variety of sources concerning the history of the Spring and Autumn period.[56] Ba makes an early appearance in this document, in an event that occurred in 703 B.C.E.:[57]

> The Baron of Ba dispatched Han Fu 韓服 to make an announcement to Chu 楚, asking permission to establish friendly relations with Deng 鄧. The Baron of Chu dispatched Dao Shuo 道朔 to lead the Ba visitor to offer presents to Deng. The You 鄾 people on the southern border of Deng attacked them and stole their woven goods, killing Dao Shuo and the ambassador from Ba. The Baron of Chu dispatched Wei Zhang 蓬章 to offer a reproach to Deng. The men of Deng would not accept it. Summer. Chu dispatched Dou Lian 鬭廉 leading troops together with Ba troops to besiege You. Yang Sheng 養甥 and Nan Sheng 聃甥[58] of

---

records that King Gong of Chu (r. 590–560) had as consort a woman of Ba with that surname. The source of the tale must be a Chu history, since it uses Chu titles, and in that it narrates a key event that determines the Chu succession, it was sure to be recorded and well remembered some thirty years later. The consort from Ba is an incidental figure to the story, and even if key events were changed to favor one or the other aspirants of 529, her name is unlikely to have been altered.

54. Ba is not among the twenty-five Ji-surnamed states listed at *Zuozhuan* 124/Xi 24/2 under the year 636 B.C.E.

55. *Zuozhuan* 370/Zhao 9/fu 1, where we read, "When King Wu conquered Shang . . . Ba, Pu 濮, Chu, and Deng 鄧 were our southern lands." This occurs in the context of a territorial dispute with the state of Jin, hence we can expect the speaker to maximize Zhou claims. The list forms a curious group, including an old state of the Man 蠻 surname and Marquis rank, Deng, with two distant states of Baron rank that never participated in Zhou ritual, Ba and Chu, plus the Pu, who seem to have had no state structure or fixed abode and were likely still at a tribal level of organization. It is interesting testimony as to the degree to which these southern states had been integrated into the Zhou worldview in 536 B.C.E., but poor evidence for events five hundred years earlier.

56. On the dating of the *Zuozhuan*, see Karlgren 1926; Kamata 1963. On the nature of the individual accounts in the *Zuozhuan* and their possible sources, see Egan 1977; Johnson 1981; Wang 1977.

57. *Zuozhuan* 35/Zhao 9/fu 1; Yang Bojun 1981:125; *Chunqiu Zuozhuan zhengyi* 7/5a–b.

58. I follow Du Yu's phonetic gloss in reading this surname, which is other-

Deng led a force to the rescue of You. Three times they drove off the Ba troops and You did not fall.[59] Dou Lian arrayed his force transversely (*heng* 衡) across the center of the Ba forces. When battle was joined, they turned their backs and fled. When the men of Deng pursued them, they turned their backs on the Ba force and were attacked from both sides. The Deng force suffered a great defeat. The men of You scattered into the night.

Deng was a state with close ties to Chu on the Han River north of modern Xiangfan, Hubei. You was slightly to its south. Since the Ba and Chu forces pass by You on their way to Deng, they must be approaching from the south. This gives an important indication of the location of the Chu and Ba capitals at this time, a point of some dispute, though it does not permit us to choose between two traditional sites for the Chu capital of Danyang 丹陽 at this time, in modern Zhijiang county or slightly further up the Yangzi near Zigui.[60] Ba is a state accorded equal status with Chu by the author of the account (a northerner subscribing to the Zhou feudal system). It is not impossible that the Ba conceived of themselves as in some sense within the Chu sphere of influence, but the term "visitor" applied to Ba's representative in at least one case refers to the emissary of an enemy state.[61] Ba must ask permission to establish relations with Deng because it must transit Chu territory to get there. Placing Ba on the upper Yangzi, either at the closer site of Yufu (modern Fengjie) or the traditional Ba at modern Chongqing, would accord well with this series of events. Ba is sophisticated enough to engage in the intricacies of interstate diplomacy and powerful enough to dispatch an army into the central Yangzi and far up the Han River.

wise pronounced Dan. It is possible that Nan Sheng is to be linked to the place Nuochu 邧處 discussed below. The phonetic in Nan (on the right) is a graphic variant of the phonetic in Nuo (on the left). Sheng means "nephew," specifically, the son of a sister, and it may be that here it indicates the relationship of these two men to the Deng ruler rather than their personal names.

59. The change of subjects in this sentence is confusing. Du Yu understands that it is Deng which, having thrice repelled the Ba, is undefeated. Yang Bojun, on the other hand, paraphrases, "[Deng] three times charged the Ba force, but could not defeat them." The object of the Ba and Chu attack, however, was the city of You. When the Ba army could not defeat its Deng defenders, Ba and Chu plotted to draw the Deng army into their midst.

60. Here I reject the tentative conclusions of Blakeley 1988. There is no credible evidence that puts Chu anywhere but in the Yangzi valley at this time. I am preparing a detailed refutation of Blakeley's argument.

61. *Zuozhuan* 242/Cheng 16/7; Yang Bojun 1981:887. Cf Yang Bojun and Xu Ti 1985:453.

Since Ba was the aggrieved party, it takes the lead in the campaign against You and its protector, Deng, but the description of the battle suggests that the Chu forces are similar in size and power. It is not the entry of Chu forces into the fray that turns the tide but the combination of Ba and Chu forces strategically applied.

Whatever the exact relations of Chu and Ba at the time of the incident of 703, a quarter-century later Ba forces were again allies of the Chu, contributing troops to one of their expansionist campaigns. The second incident concerning the Ba occurs in 676–675:[62]

> King Wu of Chu 楚武王 (r. 740–690) conquered Quan 權.[63] He dispatched Dou Min 鬬緡 to administer it. When Dou revolted from there, Chu besieged and killed him, then transferred [the population of] Quan to Nuochu 那處[64] and dispatched Yan Ao 閻敖 to administer it. When King Wen 文王 (r. 689–677) succeeded to the throne, he, together with men from Ba, launched an attack on Shen 申.[65] He frightened their troops.[66] The men of Ba revolted against Chu and attacked Nuochu, capturing it.

62. This account ends abruptly in the eighteenth year then continues into the nineteenth year. See *Zuozhuan* 64/Zhuang 18/fu 3–65/Zhuang 19/fu 1; *Chunqiu Zuozhuan zhengyi* 9/16a, 17a; Yang Bojun 1981:208–210.

63. Du Yu identifies this Quan with the walled city of Quan southeast of Dangyang.

64. Du Yu identifies Nuochu with Nuokou 那口, a walled city southeast of Bian 編 (west of Jingmen, Hubei). Tan Qixiang 1982–1987:1, 28 places both the original and relocated Quan southeast of Jingmen with the new Quan (i.e., Nuochu) perhaps twelve kilometers further southeast.

65. Shen is modern Nanyang, Henan. This campaign against Shen took place in 684. See *Chunqiu Zuozhuan zhengyi* 8/12b. There is no mention at that time of the participation of Ba troops. On the way to Shen, the Chu ruler stops in Deng, where he is acclaimed as paternal nephew of the ruler of that state. Three officers of Deng, including the Ran Deng of the previous encounter, urge the Marquis of Deng to kill the Baron of Chu, but he refuses. The following year, after conquering Shen, Chu obliterates Deng. These events no doubt are related to the enmity aroused by the events of 703, some twenty years earlier.

66. Du Yu and subsequent commentators understand by this passage that the Chu in some way frightened or startled the Ba army. *Guanzi* 2:22–1 extols the strategic value of displays of military might in order to intimidate an opponent. Rickett (1985:394) translates: "Now whenever calculating [expense incurred by] the use of armed forces, three [mobilizations] to warn [the enemy] equal one expedition." The commentary to this passage reads: "*Jing* means to glorify your awesome might and display your martial prowess (*yaowei shiwu* 耀威示武), which can startle (*jing*) your enemy and cause them to fear." Yang Bojun records the opinion of Tao Hongqing 陶鴻慶 that it was Yan Ao who, through his mistreatment and insults, forced the Ba to revolt.

Consequently they attacked the gates of Chu. Yan Ao fled, swimming down the Yong River. The Baron of Chu killed him. His clan arose in rebellion. The men of Ba took advantage of this to attack Chu. . . . [Nineteenth year] The Baron of Chu sought to repel them and suffered a great defeat at Jin 津.[67]

This account is in several places ambiguous, and the narrative sequence is not completely clear. The events described must have taken place over at least a twelve-year period. Further, whereas the opening elements derive from a Chu source that claims the title of King for the Chu ruler, the end of the tale refers to him as Baron, indicating conflation with an account of non-Chu origin. The break between the two sources probably follows the line, "Consequently they attacked the gates of Chu." We are never told the result of this attack, but soon there is a Ba force bearing down on the Chu capital. The events described are consistent with a location of Ba on the upper Yangzi, with Chu, which by this time had moved its capital to Ying 郢, in the area around Jiangling.[68] Having assembled in Chu, Chu and Ba troops set out for Shen in the north. Either on the way there or on the way back there is a falling out. Most probably this occurred on the return. Perhaps Chu's destruction of Deng, a state to which it was allied by marriage, was at the insistence of Ba and a dispute then arose over the spoils. In any case, the Ba turned on their Chu allies and seized the city of Quan, thus affording them a path back to the Yangzi without traversing the Chu stronghold at Jiangling. Some years must have passed between Ba's seizure of Quan/Nuochu and the Ba expedition of 676. Perhaps Chu had by then eradicated the Ba force there and it was in retaliation for this action that troops again descended from Ba. Perhaps they had managed to survive and the Ba force was meant to reinforce this salient into Chu territory. In any case, the direction of attack is clearly from the west along the Yangzi.

Ba enters history again in 611, at the time of a great famine and a general uprising of southern tribal peoples:[69]

67. Du Yu, after identifying Jin as a place in Chu territory, notes that according to one source there is a Jin township in Jiangling county. Takezoe 1911:3/52 identifies it with a Jin township three *li* west of Zhijiang county, upstream from Jiangling, and this is followed by Tan Qixiang 1982–1987:vol. 1. Yang Bojun suggests Jiangjin Outpost 江津戍, twenty *li* south of Jiangling.

68. On the location of Ying at this time, see Cheng Faren 1967:54–55.

69. *Zuozhuan* 172/Wen 16/6; *Chunqiu Zuozhuan zhengyi* 20/2b–4b; Yang Bojun 1981:617–620.

Chu was experiencing a great famine. The Rong attacked its southwest, reaching Mount Fu 阜山; Chu set up a camp at Dalin 大林.[70] They also attacked from the southeast, reaching Yangqiu 陽丘 and thereby invading Zizhi 訾枝.[71] The men of Yong led the many Man in rebellion against Chu. The men of Jun 麇,[72] leading the Hundred Pu, gathered in Xuan 選 and were about to attack Chu.[73] Thereupon they closed the northern gates to Shen and Xi.[74] The men of Chu planned to move to Bangao.[75] Wei Jia 蔿賈 said, "No. Anywhere we can go, the bandits can also go. It would be better to attack Yong. Jun and the Hundred Pu think we are enfamished and cannot form an army. That is why they attack us. If we field an army, they will certainly be terrified and will return to their homes. The Hundred Pu live in scattered communities. Each will flee to his town. Who will have the spare time to plot against others?" They proceeded to field an army, and in fifteen days the Hundred Pu had ceased operations. From Lu 盧 on, they opened the granaries and shared the food. They made a stage at Jushi 句澨 and dispatched Yi Li

70. Mount Fu is 150 *li* south of Fangxian 房縣, Hubei. Cheng Faren (1967:169) suggests that Mount Fu may refer to a large mountainous area between Fangxian, Jingshan 景山, and Badong that is called Shennong's Table (*Shennongjia* 神農架). Yang cites the imperial collation of 1669 (*Qinding Chunqiu zhuanshuo zuanhui* 欽定春秋傳說纂彙) in identifying the Great Forest *(Dalin)* with the Long Forest (*Changlin* 長林) northwest of Jingmen, Hubei. Cheng Faren notes a quotation from the *Jianglingji* 江陵記 of Wu Duanxiu 伍端休 that a forest sixty-five *li* northwest of Jiangling is the Dalin of the present tale. Cheng prefers this location because it accords better with an attack coming from the west.

71. Cheng Faren, noting that both places must be to the southeast of Chu, suggests that Yangqiu must be around modern Yueyang, Hunan, and identifies Zizhi with modern Zhijiang 枝江. This was also the opinion of Shen Qinhan 沈欽韓 (1775–1831), adopted by Yang Bojun.

72. Cheng Faren (1967:166) cites two opinions putting Jun in the north, near Yunxian 郧縣, Hubei, and notes another opinion placing it near Baihe, just over the border in Shaanxi, which is the location adopted by Tan Qixiang 1982–1987:vol. 1. But Cheng also quotes TPYL placing Jun sixty *li* southeast of Dangyang, then argues that the Juncheng east of Yueyang must be where the people of Jun were moved after their state was exterminated.

73. The 1669 *Huizuan* places Xuan on the southern border of Zhijiang county.

74. Shen and Xi were on the northern borders of the Chu realm. As Du Yu remarks, this comment indicates Chu's fear of a further invasion from the Central Plains states.

75. Du Yu says simply that it is a strategic location in Chu.

戡黎 of Lu to invade Yong.[76] When he reached the walled city of Fang in Yong, men of Yong routed him, capturing his son Yang Chuang 揚窗. After three nights he escaped and reported, "The Yong troops are numerous. The many Man have gathered there. It would be better to return to the main force, raise the royal troops, and advance only after uniting the forces." Shishu said, "No. For the moment we should continue engaging them in battle in order to make them overconfident. When they are overconfident and we are angry, then they can be defeated. This is the way our former lord Fenmao 蚡冒 conquered Xingxi 陘隰."[77] They met again in battle seven times, and each time Chu was defeated. The men of Pi 裨, You 鯈, and Yu 魚 alone routed them.[78] The men of Yong said, "Chu is not worth fighting." Consequently they did not make adequate preparations. The Baron of Chu, riding in post carts, met the army at Linpin.[79] He divided his army into two groups. Ziyue 子越 led one through Shixi 石溪, and Zibei 子貝 led the other through Ren 仞 in order to attack Yong. Men of Qin and men of Ba followed the Chu army, and the many Man followed the Baron of Chu in concluding a covenant, then they exterminated Yong.

Here again some of the places mentioned cannot be located with any confidence; still, the overall shape of the campaign seems fairly clear. The Rong, who invade from the southeast and southwest, are

76. Lu was fifty *li* east of modern Nanzhang county. Du Yu says only that Jushi was on the western border of Chu. *Huizuan* gives a location west of modern Junxian, Hubei. See Cheng Faren 1967:168–170.

77. The location of Xingxi is also a problem. The name indicates a marshy area below a steep rock face. Cheng Faren 1967:170 proposes a place between Yidu and Yicheng, near Tigertooth Mountain 虎牙山. Huizuan suggests someplace east of Jingmen Mountain.

78. Yu was a state based at modern Fengjie, Sichuan. The other two sites cannot be located. Cheng Faren suggests that they are Man cities between Fengjie and Zhushan. He further argues that Du Yu is incorrect in identifying these three places as Yong cities and that they are instead members of "many Man" then allied with Yong. Cheng Faren 1967:170.

79. *Huizuan* puts Linpin on the borders of Junxian. Cheng Faren, on the basis of a personal investigation of the terrain, suggests that Linpin was at Caodian 草店, thirty-five *li* south of Junxian. From there two roads diverge, then converge on Zhushan. He identifies a road that passes by the foot of Wudang Mountain and through Fangxian as the course described below as passing through Shixi 石溪 and one that follows along the Du River 堵水 as that said to pass through Ren. See Cheng Faren 1967:171.

never identified and may even have represented mutually unrelated ethnic groups. At the same time there is a major uprising of tribal peoples to the west and northwest, led by older and more established states. Chu is able to put down this uprising only by enlisting the aid of the states of Qin and Ba as well as some of the tribal peoples. The description of these events is so uncertain that it is difficult to draw conclusions as to whether Ba at this point joined the Chu army through the Yangzi gorges and fought with it toward the north or came down the Han River valley with Qin troops. If the latter, it would mean that Ba was already extending its power north.[80]

As noted above, King Gong of Chu (r. 590–560) had a favored consort who was Ba, presumably a daughter of the Ba ruler. This testifies to continuing close ties with Chu, but a century later, relations had again deteriorated. In 477 a Ba force invaded Chu and besieged the city of You.[81] No reason is given for the attack on You. With its key location on the Han, it would be an important site for a force moving up the Han to the upper Han valley or toward Shen (modern Nanyang) in the northeast but also for a force moving down the Han toward the Chu capital, now at Yan 鄢.[82] The invasion ended in failure, but whatever the route taken, this marked a deep penetration into territory that had been Chu's for two centuries.

In 377 Shu invaded Chu and captured Zifang 兹方 (modern Songzi, south of the Yangzi), apparently crossing overland to the headwaters of the Qingjiang 清江 and down that valley. Ba troops may have participated in this campaign.[83] If not, Shu was able to transit Ba territory with impunity.

---

80. This may be supported by an incident in 632, when Ba is said to have presented tribute to Qin. The claim occurs in the midst of a conversation with Shang Yang extolling the accomplishments of the minister Baili Xi 百里奚. Tong's dating of the incident to 632 is open to debate, but Baili was only in power "six or seven years," so it cannot be far off. The *Shiji* account is at earliest mid-fourth century B.C.E. and perhaps considerably later. See *Shiji* 68/2234; Tong 1979:23.

81. *Zuozhuan* 496/Ai 18/fu 2. The point of this tale seems to be the irrelevance of prognostication, but to be believable and persuasive, it must have been constructed around true historical events. Sage (1992:63) inexplicably dates this event to 475.

82. Near modern Yicheng. Chu had moved its capital to Yan in 504, where it came to be called Northern Ying. Cheng Faren 1967:56–57 places this new capital on the west side of the Han, whereas You was on the east, making the siege of You less obvious an objective if the ultimate goal was this new Ying at Yan. See *Zuozhuan* 448/Ding 6/fu 1.

83. Tong 1979:25. Tong cites as evidence TPHYJ quoting the Tang dynasty

Chu posed a constant threat to Ba throughout this period. In 361, at the time of the accession of Duke Xiao of Qin, we are told that Chu possessed both the Hanzhong region to Ba's north and the originally Ba territory of Qianzhong 黔中 south of the Yangzi in southeast Sichuan, northwest Hunan, and northeast Guizhou.[84] The Ba capital was moved repeatedly. Chang Qu tells us that, "During the time of the Baron of Ba, although the capital was at Jiangzhou (modern Chongqing), sometimes the administrative center was in Dianjiang (Hechuan), sometimes in Pingdu (Fengdu); later it was in Langzhong. Most of the tombs of their former kings are in Zhi (Fuling)."[85] This identification of Fuling as an ancient center of the Ba preceding its capital at Chongqing accords well with what we have seen of Ba's early contacts with Chu.

One interesting example of Chu participation in Ba affairs, and its continuing desire for Ba territory, is the case of Manzi 蔓子, a general of Ba faced with rebellion sometime in the mid-Warring States period.[86] Manzi requested an army from Chu in order to quell the rebellion, promising in return to transfer control of three walled cities to Chu. Once the Chu army had served its purpose, an emissary from Chu appeared demanding the promised cities. Manzi instead cut off his own head, saying, "By borrowing the spiritual might of Chu, we were able to forestall disaster. I did in truth promise cities to the King of Chu. Take my head to repay him. You cannot have

---

Jingnanji 荊南記 of Su Cheng 蕭誠, which explains the place-name Bafu 巴復 as referring to the return home of defeated Ba soldiers from the campaign, but it seems much more likely that *fu* here refers to the tax exemption given the Ba people who once inhabited this region.

84. *Shiji* 5/202. This would seem to be the better understanding of the phrase *nan you Ba Qianzhong* 南有巴黔中, which has also been interpreted to mean that Chu at this time possessed both Qianzhong and Ba. Cf. Sage 1992:241n73.

85. HYGZ 1/8.6. Sage understands this as a slow retreat up the Yangzi then up the Jialing River under the pressure of Chu. Ren (1984:28n4) understands the direction of movement similarly but suggests that it was in response to Ba's expansion toward the north. We have no evidence of Chu intrusion into Sichuan, but its fourth-century activities in the western Hunan-Guizhou area may have caused some trepidation among the Ba rulers. Still, evidence for the motivation behind these transfers of the Ba administrative center is inconclusive.

86. HYGZ 1/2–3. This event is attributed to "the end of the Zhou dynasty" but must have antedated the Qin invasion of 316 B.C.E. Tong Enzheng (1979:26) argues that this was a slave rebellion against Ba's "reactionary slave system," but it seems more likely that some competing faction had gained control of the Ba army.

the cities." Manzi received an honorable burial appropriate to a minister of state from both Chu, for his head, and Ba, for his body. This would suggest that at the time of the event Ba remained a distinct political entity, possessing numerous walled cities and a historical identity and traditions sufficient to command the unswerving loyalty of an elite warrior class.

The Qin conquest of Sichuan was prompted by a dispute among the powers of Sichuan. The younger brother of the King of Shu (or perhaps the cadet line?) was enfeoffed at Ju 苴 (modern Jiameng), an area on the border of Ba territory.[87] Ju established close relations with Ba, thus siding against Shu in the chronic warfare between Ba and Shu.[88] When Shu launched a campaign against Ju in 316, the ruler of Ju fled to Ba, and Ba requested aid from Qin. After Ba, with the aid of Qin, had exterminated Shu, Qin turned on its allies and conquered Ba. This version of events differs considerably from that presented by Qin, which concentrates on Qin's actions and gives Ba no role in the conquest of Shu other than to provide a pretext for invasion.

We have little direct evidence for Ba culture and society at this time other than the results of archaeological excavation. The economy seems to have centered on hunting and fishing, supplemented by simple agriculture, practiced largely in river valleys.[89] There is no evidence of irrigation works or of large-scale architectural construction, probably because there was no cohesive central power to direct such projects. Society seems to have consisted primarily of local clans, largely independent but owing some sort of ultimate loyalty to higher authorities referred to in Chinese sources as "king" or "marquis." Warfare was an important element of life, reflected in the widespread use of Ba mercenaries, the martial songs and dances discussed below, and the prominent place of weapons among Ba grave goods.

87. HYGZ 1/2.3 affirms that Ba territory stretched north to Hanzhong; Langzhong, some sixty-five kilometers south of Jiameng, was one of its later capitals. Ju's unbrotherly behavior toward its sibling state and the conflicts occasioned thereby remained a portion of Sichuanese lore and resurface in the *Book of Transformations of Wenchang,* a revealed twelfth-century scripture from northern Sichuan. See Kleeman 1994a:194–195.

88. HYGZ says that Ba and Chu "fought for generations" 世戰爭, which would seeem to contradict Tong Enzheng's claim that Shu was now ruled by a Ba ruling house.

89. The following synopsis of Warring States Ba culture is based primarily upon Huang Xiaodong and Zeng Fanmu 1993.

Ba had an advanced bronze industry that specialized in distinctive willow-leaf-shaped swords and halberds, as well as musical instruments, vessels, and tools. Ba bronzes are softer than contemporary Central Plains products and the weapons do not take as sharp an edge, indicating a technologically less developed industry, but they have won praise for their elegance and simplicity. Ba bronze vessels show relatively little influence from Central China and for the most part are distinct from Shu examples, which exhibit much greater Central Plains influence.[90] Still, Warring States archaeological sites often reflect a melding of east and west as well as influences from outside the region. Thus we find Ba-style halberds and even one example of the famous Ba *chunyu* 錞于 bronze drums in Shu areas.[91]

Beginning in 1954, boat burials have been discovered in the Sichuan region. Best documented are the two initial discoveries, one near Chongqing and the other on the upper reaches of the Jialing River, near modern Zhaohua.[92] At both sites, in burials dating between the fourth and second centuries B.C.E., actual boats placed in shaft graves gradually gave way to coffins placed within boats, then just coffins. There is a similar progression at these sites from grave assemblages consisting solely of Ba-Shu relics to assemblages closely resembling those of the Central Plains. More recently, boat burials have also been found in the Chengdu region, and some are as early as or earlier than the earliest discovered boat burials in Eastern Sichuan. These tombs contain a variety of implements and vessels, reflecting trade or influence from Ba and Chu.[93]

Unique among all early non-Chinese cultures of East Asia, Sichuan developed two scripts. The first is a pictographic script with a limited repertoire of symbols. Prominent among them is the tiger and a compound symbol of a crooked arm with open hand and a flower bud (see Fig. 3). This script, closely associated with Ba, has been found primarily on bronze weapons and drums, leading to speculation that an important function of this script was to impart magical efficacy to articles on which it was inscribed.[94] The second is more diverse and seems to be more functional; the small number of symbols

90. Huang Xiaodong and Zeng Fanmu 1993:56.
91. Sage 1992:66–67. Whereas Shu halberds maintained the triangular shape inherited from early Zhou models, Ba developed a scythe-like curved blade similar to later Central Plains models.
92. Sichuansheng bowuguan 1960.
93. Described in Sage 1992:67–70. Sage does not refer to the earlier finds.
94. Huang Xiaodong and Zeng Fanmu 1993:56.

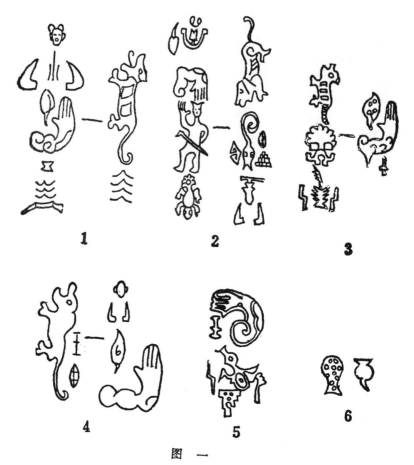

图 一

1.剑，巴县冬笋坝M12　2.矛，峨符　3.矛（成百）　4.剑，（采自《西南文物展览》专刊）5.矛，新飞　6.斧，绵竹M1

Fig. 3 Examples of the Ba script. Reprinted from Xu Zhongshu, ed., *Ba Shu Kaogu lunwen ji* (Beijing, 1987), p. 90.

has led some to speculate that it is phonetic in character. Neither has been deciphered, but their use on seals confirms their status as writing. There is as yet no evidence of a literature written in either script.[95]

We hear little of the former rulers of the state of Ba following the Qin conquest. The Qin are said to have treated the Ba clan as leaders of the non-Chinese peoples and repeatedly provided them with wives.[96] In the early third century C.E. there is a record of a King of the Ba Barbarians 巴夷王, but he seems to be the leader of a much smaller subgroup.[97] For the most part we find records of individual members of Ba tribes and occasionally of the leaders of these tribes, often designated kings, but there is no evidence of large-scale organization that would encompass all of the region formerly identified with Ba.

Prominent among early records of the region are accounts of signal acts by Ba tribesmen that win for their people special treatment from their foreign rulers, especially with regard to taxation. The earliest of these tales involves the Qin state before its unification of China:[98]

> During the time of King Zhaoxiang of Qin 秦昭襄王 (r. 306–251), a white tiger was wreaking havoc. From Qin[99] through Shu, Ba, and Han, it was a danger. The King of Qin accordingly offered to anyone in his state who could kill the tiger a hefty reward, an appanage of ten thousand households, and a corresponding amount of gold and silk. Thereupon the barbarians Liao Zhong 廖仲 and Yao He 藥何 of Quren and the tiger-shooter Qin Jing 秦精[100] made a crossbow from white bamboo

95. Li Xueqin 1985:215–216. Sage 1992:58–59 mentions a third type represented so far on only one vessel. On the relationship of these two scripts, see Sun Hua 1987, Li Fuhua and Wang Jiayou 1987, and Qian Yuzhi 1993.

96. HHS 86/2841.

97. *Wenxuan* 44/13b. The King was subsequently made Grand Warden of Badong; he must have been highly sinicized to fulfill the duties of this office.

98. HYGZ 1/3.6–10. A similar passage is found in HHS 86/2842; major differences are noted in the annotation below. HHS 86/2841 records a tax exemption granted the followers of the Ba ruler by this same Qin king with no justification for the exemption and different payment figures: the ruler is to pay 2,116 cash annually and 1,800 cash once every three years whereas commoners pay eighty-two feet of cloth and an amount of chicken feathers.

99. Ren 15n2 argues on the basis of the following reference to "four commanderies" that this Qin is a mistake for Qian(zhong) 黔中.

100. Here I follow the interpretation of Ren Naiqiang 15n2. HHS (86/2842) lists only one hunter, a nameless "barbarian from Langzhong." Ren assumes that this barbarian was Qin Jing and that *shehu* 射虎 was a sort of epithet. This

and shot the tiger from atop a high tower. They struck him in the head, the arrow penetrating three nodes deep. The white tiger always had a pack of tigers following him. In his anger he mauled all of them to death then, with a great roar, died. The Qin king praised them: "The white tiger traversed four commanderies and killed one thousand two hundred people. Now in one day the problem is eliminated. No achievement could be greater than this!" The king wanted to observe the terms of his promise, but he despised them for being barbarians. So he had inscribed in stone the essentials of a covenant: the barbarians would pay no land tax for one *qing* of land, up to ten wives would be exempted [from tax]; those who injure others would receive a reduced sentence; those who kill others could redeem the death through payment of *tan* 賧 cash. The covenant said, "If Qin transgresses against the barbarians, it will pay with a pair of yellow dragons.[101] If the barbarians transgress against Qin, they will pay a barrel of pure wine."[102] The barbarians were comfortable with this arrangement.

This is a teleological myth intended to justify a *modus vivendi* between the bureaucratic Qin state, with its complex system of universal population registration and mutual responsibility, and tribal peoples who possessed neither the economic power to pay standard taxes nor the social organization necessary for a bureaucratically administered community. A number of non-Chinese peoples had similar myths to explain their relationship to the Chinese. The Man of the Hunan region and the later Yao told of a dog who fetched the head of an enemy general then, denied the proper reward because of his nonhuman identity, fled to the south with his promised princess where his descendants became the Man or Yao.[103] The broken

---

is perhaps the best sense we can make of the existing text, but I suspect that in fact some characters have dropped out of the text. If so, it was before the Song. Funaki 1974:42n5 suggests that *shehu* may be excrescent. The Tang commentary to HHS 86/2842n1 quotes HYGZ reading simply, "The Ba barbarians Liao Zhong et al. shot and killed it," but this quotation may paraphrase the original text rather than accurately reproduce it.

101. Ren 15n3, following Deng Shaoqin, argues that *long* 龍, "dragon," stands for *long* 瓏, meaning a circular jade with a dragon carved on it.

102. A "barrel," literally, a "bell" (*zhong* 鍾), is variously reported as six *hu* 斛 four *dou* 斗 (approx. 128 liters), eight *hu* (160 liters), and ten *hu* (200 liters). Values are for the Han dynasty. Dubs 1938–1955:I, 279.

103. Eberhard 1982:81, translating HHS 116. For other examples, see the stories of the Miao in Eberhard 1982:125–127.

promise motif common to these stories represents resistance on the part of the subjugated non-Chinese to the Chinese historical narrative of their defeat. The Zong myth rationalizes acquiescence in Chinese rule as a willing act of friendship rather than a humiliating surrender but expresses discontent with the resulting relationship by claiming that the Zong are in fact deserving of better treatment.

Whether this tale is based on some historical tiger slayer or created from whole cloth to legitimize an existing *modus vivendi* between Qin and Ba, its value as a narrative of real historical events is at best slight. But precisely because it was created or adopted to justify real practice, its value in determining the historical situation during the time the myth was current is great. Thus we can be sure that there were marauding tigers in the Eastern Sichuan region and probably the occasional ferocious white tiger. Similarly, we can assume that the indigenous people of this region had a reputation as hunters and sometimes killed even tigers with crossbows. That the Qin ruler reneged on his initial promise because of the hunters' ethnic identity reflects a real or perceived disdain on the part of the Qin Chinese for their subject minorities, and since this story must have circulated among the natives as well to be effective, it probably reflects a resentment on their part at this treatment. Finally, the accommodations promised the non-Chinese with regard to taxation and penal law must also have reflected a historical situation at some time, though we cannot be sure when that was or if these provisions were still in effect at the time the tale was initially recorded, much less at the time of our source, the fourth-century C.E. *Record of the Land of Huayang*.

A similar deal was struck with the Han but this time in recompense for a much greater contribution to the state.[104]

> After the rise of the Han they followed Gaozu (Liu Bang) in putting down rebellions, thereby attaining achievements. Gaozu therefore exempted them, making them responsible solely for shooting white tigers.[105] Each household would yearly

104. HYGZ 1/ 3.10–11.

105. The Liao collation, followed by Ren, suggests that the "white" here is excrescent. Ren 15–16n4 explains that the white tiger was an unusual occurrence during the reign of King Zhaoxiang and that if the "white" is not excrescent, then it must refer to the White Tiger barbarians. Here Ren establishes a false dichotomy between tribes worshiping the white tiger and those who kill them. As for the Banshun's responsibility to kill tigers, white or otherwise, this is a ceremonial role meant to explain their excusal from corvée duties and does not depend on the prevalence of tigers. "White" occurs in every surviving edition and should not be excised.

pay *zong* 賨 cash, forty per person. For this reason men of the day called them the White Tiger Exempted Barbarians. One source calls them the Board Shield Man-barbarians (Banshun Man 板楯蠻). They are the ones we call the Hard-headed Tiger Cubs (*Jiangtou huzi* 弜頭虎子).

Ying Shao, writing around 200 C.E., gives a different version of this event:[106]

> In Ba there are Zong people who are valiant and brave. When Gaozu was King of Han, Fan Mu 范目 of Langzhong persuaded him to recruit Zong people to quell 定 the Three Qins. He enfeoffed Mu as Marquis of Langzhong Cifu District 閬中慈凫鄉侯. He also granted a tax remission to the seven clans of Zong people whom Mu had sent, the Lu 盧, Pu 朴, Ta 沓, E 鄂, Du 度, Xi 夕, and Xi 襲: they need not contribute taxes 租賦.

The *Book of the Latter Han,* composed a century later than the *Record of the Land of Huayang,* records that the clans of the seven shield-leaders, Luo 羅, Pu, Du 督, E, Du, Xi, and Gong 龔, were wholly exempted from land taxes while other clans had to pay the token forty *zong* cash. The *Record of the Land of Huayang* states that Fan Mu, having rejected a marquisate in Chang'an and the one in Langzhong mentioned above, was finally made Marquis of Dumian 渡沔.[107] Fan Mu then goes on to exempt seven clans from taxes, the Luo, Pu, Zan 昝, E, Du, Xi, and Gong.[108] Absent other corroboration, differences in the names of clans are difficult to resolve, but Chang Qu's list seems preferable.[109] Ying Shao's account, indicating that only seven clans fought for Liu Bang, seems less credible than accounts (such as *Hou Hanshu*) naming them only as battle leaders. Chang Qu's version leaves open the question of on what authority Fan Mu was able to absolve these clans of their responsibilities. The *Book of Jin* account translated below attributes

106. This passage is from a lost portion of the *Fengsu tongyi* but is preserved in the commentary to *Wenxuan* 4/18a.

107. HYGZ originally had Dumian County, but there is no county by this name. Cf. Ren 14.

108. HYGZ 1/3.14.

109. Lu and Luo may be different renderings of the same native name, but Ta/Du and Xi/Gong would seem to be graphic errors. HYGZ has a number of Gongs from the Langzhong area, but no Xis, hence Gong must be correct here. There are both Lus and Luos, however. Neither Ta nor Du occurs as a surname, but Zan occurs among the refugees; both Li Xiang[a] and Li Zhi married women of the Zan family. See Taniguchi 1973:82.

the imposition of the Zong tax to the Qin and follows Ying Shao in referring to their task as "quelling the Three Qin" but says only that Liu Bang exempted them from taxes, with no mention of specific clans and no distinction between leaders and followers.

Luo Kaiyu (1991) has made a detailed analysis of all the surnames mentioned in these accounts. Luo argues that each leader (*qushuai* 渠率) represents a "tribal alliance" of groups sharing the same surname and hence a putative common ancestor. He then proceeds to trace each of the eleven surnames mentioned, finding their antecedents in states that existed in areas from northwestern Sichuan to Hubei, including some that purportedly participated in the Zhou conquest, or if no likely candidates exist, to cite later examples of individuals with that surname in Sichuanese regions.[110] If Luo is correct, then Ba in the early Han was an extremely cosmopolitan place and the Zong were an unusually diverse ethnic group, the result of the merger of several distinct, unrelated tribal alliances. There is, however, as yet no compelling evidence demonstrating the identity of any of the surname groups mentioned by Luo to those in the Ba lists.[111] Moreover, Luo does not try to reconcile clear graphic variants in the surname lists (e.g., Du, Zan, and Ta or Xi and Gong) but rather treats all as members of the Ba people.

We can assume from this evidence that the Ba did not constitute a coherent, monolithic group, but rather was composed of a number of subgroups.[112] This is evident also from historical and epigraphical

110. For the Du surname, for example, Luo (1991:137) can find no individual earlier than the Ming.

111. Luo assumes that all references to a given surname indicate branches of one tribal alliance, but by late Warring States China encompassed tens of millions of people, and we know that the same surname sometimes occurred among different ethnic groups, as in the case of the royal Ji surname's occurring among the Qiang and the Ba.

112. The "Record of Ba" chapter in the *Record of the Land of Huayang* lists the following varieties of Man-barbarians within the Ba region: Pu 濮, Zong 賨, Ju 苴, Gong 共, Nu 奴, Rang 獽, Yi 夷, and Dan 蜑. It is unclear whether these terms refer to distinct ethnic groups, subgroupings within a larger Ba ethnicity, remnants of former political entities, or clan associations. We have discussed the Zong, and the Dan, who are said to have lived on water, will occur in the following section. The Pu are an ancient and far-flung group, appearing in the seventh century B.C.E. and recorded over a vast area stretching from Henan though Hubei, Hunan, Eastern Sichuan, and Guizhou. Because of the many variations within the group and the lack of political cohesion, they are often referred to as the "Hundred Pu." It is uncertain if the term actually refers to a single ethnic group or is a more general term for non-Chinese like Man. You Zhong (1979:15) argues that they are the ancestors of the later Mon-Khmer peoples of Southwest China. Ju was a state in north central Sichuan, with

records of subinfeudated statelets scattered across Sichuan.[113] The exact relationship of these smaller states or tribes to the larger entities of Ba and Shu is difficult to assess and, in any case, probably varied considerably through time as the power of the larger states waxed and waned. That the different surnames were treated as a group by their dominant neighbors (the Qin kingdom and the Qin and Han empires) does imply a certain degree of cultural similarity and perhaps a self-cognizant common ethnic identity.

Ba men were prized as mercenaries throughout their history. We have seen that Chu used them in its eastern campaigns. One version of Sima Cuo's speech advocating a Qin invasion of Sichuan points out the value of the "valorous troops of Ba" in attacking Chu.[114] After their important role in Liu Bang's victory over Xiang Yu, they continued to serve the Han. During the Latter Han, they were instrumental in repelling repeated Qiang invasions.[115] Men from a particularly backward and bellicose region of Ba, near Fuling 涪陵,

---

cultural ties to Ba but ruled by a cadet branch of the Shu royal house. Gong is probably to be identified with the homophonous Gong 龔, one of the seven surnames of the Banshun Man. Ren cites a number of prominent men from the lower reaches of the Jialing River who were surnamed Gong 龔 during the Han. Nu literally means "slave," and there has been some speculation that this group was often the victim of slavers. Ren suggests that Nu may be an alternate writing for Lu 澧, a group that occurs in the Warring States era "Oath at Shepherd's Field" chapter of the *Book of Documents* (see note 32 above). Ren notes that there was a walled city of Lu in the Dangqu area. Another possibility, not mentioned in any previous scholarship known to me, is that Nu is an alternate writing of *nu* 弩 or "crossbow." Whatever the ultimate origin of the crossbow (India has also been proposed), it occurs early in the Southwest, the Ba were famed for its use, and words with pronunciations similar to *nu (*na)* are found in many languages of the region (Norman and Mei 1976:292–293). Rang (also written Lang 狼) were located in the southeastern portion of Ba and were famous for cliff burials. Ren uses this name to associate them with the early state of Yelang 夜郎in Guizhou. Yi is a general term for non-Chinese, originally of the East, but already applied to the Southwest by Sima Qian. In HYGZ it often occurs in collocation with other terms for ethnic groups and it is possible that here it should be read as Rang-Yi or even Yi-Dan. See Ren 9–10n12.

113. Meng Wentong 1981:27–35 uses a miscellany of historical and literary sources spanning over a millennium (including the surname lists discussed above) to enumerate dozens of these statelets. Meng's methodology is open to severe criticism, but there are still quite a few feudal lords whose existence at this time can be considered adequately demonstrated, and we can assume that only a portion of the total complement of minor nobility has been preserved.

114. HYGZ 3/29.7.

115. HHS 76/2843, 87/2889.

were recruited for a Han elite force called the Red Armor Army.[116] Zhuge Liang 諸葛亮, master strategist of the Shu-Han state, also trained three thousand of them to fire volleys of crossbow bolts, then stationed them at the strategic crossroads of Hanzhong.[117] The centrality of warfare to their culture is reflected in the fact that some Ba place-names refer to different types of shields (e.g., the Lis' native Dangqu, or "curved shield"), as does the name of the Banshun or Board-shield Man.

The Ba people were also famous for their musical abilities. They gave to the Chinese a distinctive dance style and music that proved popular among the Chinese and other peoples for centuries. It was Liu Bang who brought them to national prominence:[118]

When Emperor Gaozu of Han was preparing to subdue the Three Qins region (southern Shaanxi) from his base in Shu and Han(zhong) provinces, Fan Mu 范目[119] of Langzhong brought Zong men to follow him and they formed his vanguard. After the Qin area had been subdued, Gaozu enfeoffed Mu as the Marquis of Langzhong and remitted [the taxes and corvée of] the seven clans. Their customs included a delight in dancing. Gaozu enjoyed their fierce, keen spirit and frequently went to see their dances. Later he had his musicians learn them. The Yu River flows through Langzhong and the dances are named for their residence; hence they are called the Ba Yu dances. Among the dance-songs 舞曲 are: "The Yu Song of the Lance" 矛渝本歌曲, "The Yu Song of the Crossbow" 弩渝本歌曲,[120] "The Song of the Peaceful Pavilion" 安臺本歌曲, and "The Song of the Parting Words" 行辭本歌曲, four pieces in all. Because their language was ancient, no one could parse them. At the beginning of the Wei dynasty, the Libationer for Military Planning Wang Can 軍謀祭酒王粲 was ordered to remake their lyrics. Can would ask Li Guan 李管 and Zhong Yu 种玉, the leaders of the Ba Yu, the meaning of the songs, then have them

116. "Red armor" here would seem to mean bare-breasted. There is a mountain near Fuling called Red Shoulder (*chijia* 赤岬／胛) where the red rocks on its slopes are said to resemble a man with bare shoulders. It seems likely that the Han troop was made up of men from around Red Shoulder Mountain. See Ren 37–38n6.

117. HYGZ 1/11.7–8 *sub* Fuling commandery; Sage 1992:169.

118. *Jinshu* 12/693–694; see also *Fengsu tongyi tongjian* 491, *Tongdian* 145/759b.

119. Here I follow the reading in HYGZ 1/3. JS originally had Fan Yin 范因.

120. Omitting *an* 安 in accordance with JS 12/695n12.

try to sing [the new lyrics], listen to them, and compare them to the melody. He changed the song titles to "The Yu New Blessings Song of the Lance" 矛渝新福歌曲, "The Yu New Blessings Song of the Crossbow" 弩渝新福歌曲, "The Yu New Blessings Song of the Peaceful Pavilion" 安臺渝新福歌曲, and "The Yu New Blessings Song of the Parting Words" 行辭新福歌曲. In "The Parting Words" he extolled the virtue of the Wei. In the third year of Huangchu (222) the name of the Ba Yu dances was changed to the Zhaowu 昭武 ("Illuminating the Martial") dances.[121]

These large-scale performances involving the brandishing of various weapons occurred to the accompaniment of drums and songs in Ba language. Toward the end of the Former Han there were thirty-six drummers and twenty-four singers performing these pieces at court, and they were also performed in the wealthy households of the capital.[122] Wang Can's rewriting of the song lyrics, preserved in the *Book of Song (Songshu* 宋書), maintains the martial air of the original, but the lyrics have been modified to celebrate the founding of the Wei dynasty.[123] The dances remained popular through the Tang and spread as far as Central Asia.[124]

121. The account goes on to mention that in the early Jin dynasty the dances were renamed Xuanwu 宣武, "Disseminating the Martial" (no doubt because of a taboo on the name of Sima Zhao 司馬昭), and paired with "Disseminating the Civil" dances. In 275 their performance was discontinued, but they were revived around the middle of the fourth century and continued in use until the Sui. During the mid-Tang, the lyrics to these dances (presumably Wang Can's rewritten version) were among the few to have survived the disruptions at the founding of the dynasty. See *Tongdian* 146/761a; Dong Qixiang 1987:174.

122. HS 22/1073. *Yantielun jianzhu* 9/69. Cf. Sage 1992:169–170. Dong Qixiang (1987:172–173) argues that the drums were probably of the bronze variety employed at the time by the Dian culture of Yunnan and later with the Lao people of Guizhou. Dong's identification of the Lao with the Ba, based on a single remark attributed to Guo Pu, who was not native to the region, is not persuasive. Similarly, Dong's use of illustrations on Dian drums of ceremonial dances, while suggestive of what such a martial dance might have looked like, cannot be taken as direct evidence of Ba practice.

123. *Songshu* 20/571–572. Cursory inspection of these songs indicates that line lengths were irregular as were the number of lines per song.

124. Ren 1/16n7. Dong Qixiang 1987:175–177 suggests several later dance and song traditions of the south that may be successors to the Ba Yu dances, including the feathered dancers portrayed on southwestern bronze drums, shield dances recorded in South China during the Ming, seasonal dances involving weapons current among the Tujia minority groups, and folk dances of Eastern Sichuan during the Tang.

THE LORD OF THE GRANARIES

The myth of the Lord of the Granaries translated below is also of great importance in understanding the significance of names like Ba, Zong, and Banshun Man. Briefly, this myth relates the origin of five surname groups, the achievement of supremacy by the representative of one of these groups through a series of magical contests, a migration under his leadership, a test of his leadership by a divine/demonic temptress, and the eventual establishment of a fixed dwelling place. Upon his death, this founder transforms into a white tiger. It is a founder myth, meant to explain the dominance of one clan over the others, but it can tell us much more about the Ba and their history.

There is a considerable degree of agreement among scholars concerning the place-names mentioned in the tale. The two caves from which the four surname groups emerge are said to be on a mountain called, in the *Book of Latter Han (Hou Hanshu)* and *Book of Jin (Jinshu)* texts, Wuluozhonglishan 武羅鍾離山. The *Generational Origins (Shiben),* quoted in the commentary to the *Book of Latter Han* account, says instead that they emerged from Wudan 巫誕, and the Qing commentator Hui Dong 惠棟 (1697–1758) quotes the same work as reading Wudanluozhongshan 巫蜑落鍾山.[125] No single mountain by any of these names exists, but the Wu Mountains 巫山 extend north-south across the Yangzi between Fengjie and Badong, and a people called the Dan 蜑 is noted by Chang Qu among the ethnic groups inhabiting Ba. *Luo* 落 and *luo* 羅 are both used to write a non-Chinese suffix meaning "village."[126] This suggests that the name refers to a Dan village in the Wu area, on Zhongshan, or Bell Mountain.[127] Although no specific Bell Mountain is recorded in the area, it is a common name based upon the physical appearance of the mountain.

The myth is, again, teleological, meant to sanction and legitimize

125. HHS 86/2840n2. The source of Hui Dong's quotation is unclear since the *Shiben* was long lost by his day, and none of the reconstructions in *Shiben bazhong* give this reading.

126. Von Glahn 1987:32 says specifically a fortified hilltop village. Von Glahn documents these terms for the Song, but they were in use already in the Jin, as in the place-name Muluo 木落 in the translation below, p. 177.

127. The Zhongli Mt. of HHS and JS would seem to be the result of confusion with a mountain near Fengyang, Anhui, that was the site of a Spring and Autumn period state. Wuluo was also the name of a Spring and Autumn period state recorded in *Shiben*. Apparently Fan Ye or some earlier editor of the *Shiben* he drew upon in fashioning this tale had tried to "correct" this incomprehensible name by drawing upon the closest parallels in other parts of the *Shiben*. See Zang 1936:1304.1; *Shiben bazhong,* Lei Xueqi reconstruction, 51–52; Chen Qirong reconstruction, p. 12.

the claims of the Ba clan to dominance over a number of other groups in the Sichuan area. The other four clans represent constituent elements of Ba society, either major families within the general populace or subinfeudated leaders of minor states with the Ba confederation. That the leadership of this group was, at least purportedly, determined by magical combat involving the performance of miracles implies that the winner had a religious role as well as a political one. This fits well with our understanding of the sacerdotal role of leadership in ancient China and is confirmed by the explicit statement that the contest was to determine who would become "god" (shen).

The title of the Lord of Granaries implies a people already practicing agriculture at the time of the myth's creation, for whom custodianship of the tribal grain storehouses was a vital and respected function.[128] The magical contests, however, reveal a different aspect of Ba life. The first contest involves throwing large double-edged swords with enough force to penetrate stone. Clearly, the chief to be selected would be a military figure who could lead his followers into battle. The competition to create an earthen boat reveals the riverine side of the culture, one demonstrated in the boat burials discussed above. Despite their tiger lore, with its alpine associations, the Ba were people familiar with water and accustomed to moving about on rivers. This must have given them considerable mobility, a mobility evidenced by the contacts with Chu downstream and by the eventual expansion of the culture far up the Jialing River and its tributaries.[129]

The encounter with the salt spirit is also informative. Salt is, of course, vital to all human life, and the meeting can be interpreted as a simple quest for this necessity. But salt is also an extremely valuable commodity, and the salt wells of the Eastern Sichuan region were one of the most important sources for it in all China. Ren Naiqiang has argued that the Ba state was founded upon a service industry transporting and merchandising salt up and down the Yangzi River basin.[130] Ren's evidence is rather speculative, but salt must have been an important resource for the Ba people from an early time.

A more conventional reading of this incident would stress the need

128. Zhang Guanying (1957:70) suggests a different interpretation for this name. Pointing out that among the Tujia, putative descendants of the Ba, "tiger" is called li 力, he speculates that lin might also be a non-Chinese word meaning "tiger," hence linjun would mean something like "tiger lord."

129. Zhang Xiong (1993:35) argues on the basis of usage of the term Bazhong 巴中 in the Hou Hanshu account that the territory controlled by the Ba clan of this myth extended to the Jialing River area of East Central Sichuan.

130. Ren 1986:219–290. Ren sees competition for these salt wells as an

of any people moving into a new and unfamiliar region to secure themselves by subjugating or co-opting any existing gods. The concern with dispelling clouds and letting in sunshine reflects an agricultural interest in sunshine for the crops; the cloudy skies that predominate in the region are immortalized in the local maxim that "Sichuanese dogs bark at the sun."

The direction of the migration down the Qingjiang and into Hubei has been linked to the reported movement of peoples into the Five Streams 五溪 of central Hubei and northern Hunan province after the Chu capture of the Ba capital at Zhi 枳 (modern Fuling). This speculation is founded in part upon an identification of the Tujia peoples of Hubei as remnants of the Ba, but the links between these two peoples, though intriguing, are made across a gap of many centuries, and we cannot be sure when, if ever, Ba became Tujia. Further, the evidence for such a migration of the Ba into the Five Streams region is late and unreliable (a Tang work recording ancient legend).[131] Dating the Lord of the Granaries tale to a time after the fall of the Ba state would not accord with the function of the legend in justifying Ba rule. It seems preferable to assume that the legend ultimately derives from, or records a historical memory of, a time when the Ba people were still centered in the Qingjiang Valley and the Yichang area, after which they moved west up the Yangzi into Sichuan. This would indicate a very early date for the genesis of the tale, perhaps Western Zhou or earlier.

Finally, the linkage of the Lord of the Granaries to a white tiger fits perfectly with tiger emblems found on Ba weapons and musical instruments, with records of Ba tribal groups called "tiger boys" or "white tiger [tax-]exempted barbarians" 白虎復夷, and with legends of special government dispensation won through tiger hunting. Comparative anthropology, beginning with Durkheim, does not support the claims of some Chinese scholars that because the Ba worshiped the tiger as totem, they could not have killed them. On the contrary, the right to kill a totemic animal is often restricted to the group claiming that animal as totem.[132]

---

important factor in disputes between Qin and Chu after the Qin conquest of Sichuan (p. 264).

131. See *Tongdian* 183/975b; the same passage records an alternate tradition that the inhabitants of this region are descendants of the Panhu Man-barbarians.

132. If totemism is even the proper term for the relationships seen here. Lévi-Strauss 1964 argues that the term should be narrowly construed to apply only to Australian aboriginal groups and those groups that follow this model exceedingly closely.

BA IDENTITY

The historical evidence presented above gives us many insights into the historical development of the Ba state and the ethnic groups that inhabited it. We are left, however, with a number of questions concerning how these peoples understood their own identity across the vast expanse of Ba territory and the thousand plus years of Ba history.

The insights of modern anthropological research on minority peoples and ethnic identities can throw much light on this question. A key distinction involves paradigmatic differences expressed as cultural markers by the people themselves and syntagmatic differences arising from the groups' interactions with other ethnic groups.[133] Stevan Harrell has presented a detailed analysis of identity and ethnicity in three Yi 彝 (Lolo) communities in southwestern Sichuan, discovering three different types of Yi identity founded upon different social and cultural conditions and different relations with Han peoples.[134] All three of these communities can be seen to reflect a portion of the Ba experience through this geographical and temporal range.

The first group, the Nuosu, or Black Yi, of Yanbian county live in relative isolation (primarily in territory above 1,800 meters elevation) and maintain a variety of distinctive cultural markers in terms of language, housing, dress, social organization, and religion. Although most Nuosu can converse in Chinese, they use their native language exclusively within their own community. A limited traditional script is monopolized by religious professionals who used it in ritual and to maintain genealogies of the community. Han names are possessed only by those individuals who have received some formal education in Chinese schools. Nuosu maintained until "liberation" (1949) a traditional, endogamous caste structure of aristocrats, commoners, and slaves and a bilateral cross-cousin marriage system. Han outsiders, lacking caste status and clan affiliation, still do not intermarry with Nuosu and traditionally could only be accommodated within Nuosu society as slaves. Harrell stresses the congruence of understanding between the Nuosu and Chinese as to the Nuosu identity.

The Lipuo of Pingdi occupy a highland community where Lipuo and Han have long lived together. The Lipuo speak exclusively Lipuo

133. Keyes 1976.
134. Harrell 1990.

at home but are almost all bilingual in Chinese, use Chinese for certain major rituals, and employ written Chinese to communicate, even with other Lipuo. Harrell notes that the Lipuo's literacy in Chinese is of long standing, perhaps dating back to the beginning of the Qing dynasty (1644). The sizable Han minority (38 percent) is overwhelmingly bilingual in Lipuo. The two groups are economically and politically integrated, but before 1949 wealth seems to have been concentrated in Lipuo hands. The two groups intermarry extensively, with children tending to adopt the ethnic identity of the father. All of this has resulted in a "remarkable identity of culture, politics, and social structure."[135] Ethnic markers center on minor elements of ritual.

The Shuitian of Zhuangshang live in a community where Shuitian dominate (90 percent) but in a lowland region that is almost exclusively Han. Although the Shuitian once spoke a Yi language, they now speak exclusively Chinese but have a very low level of literacy in Chinese. They are otherwise identical to the Han people around them in dress, housing, religion, and social organization, though in general their standard of living is considerably below that of the local Chinese majority. Intermarriage for the Shuitian is a one-way affair: daughters marry out, but sons cannot attract Han brides. Their identity is based on ancestry and upon their disadvantaged status. Although they maintain that they are not Han, they are also adamant in rejecting identification with the less-sinicized "wild" Nuosu. Having rejected Yi as a "stigmatized identity," they seek to be recognized as a distinct ethnic group, the Shuitian, but have been unable to win official recognition of this position.

These three divergent patterns of interaction between Chinese and non-Chinese provide an excellent model for conceptualizing the ethnic world of Ba over the six centuries between its conquest by Qin and the reemergence of a Ba ethnic state, Cheng-Han. Despite formidable cultural and economic pressures to become Chinese, Ba peoples were able to preserve a distinct ethnic identity. Ba is a geographically vast and topographically diverse region that was settled by Chinese peoples and sinicized over an extended period of time and at widely varying rates. We might expect that all three patterns of interaction were adopted at different times and places within the area.

The Nuosu pattern no doubt typifies most of Ba at the beginning of Chinese immigration and more remote portions of Ba throughout

135. Harrell 1990:533.

the period. Like the Nuosu, the Ba were a fierce warrior people famed for their hunting exploits. Those Ba inhabiting highland areas or inaccessible river valleys, as well as those who moved to these areas to escape the Han influx, would have preserved their native traditions of housing, social structure, and religion largely intact. Without the universal Han education provided by the postliberation Chinese government, earlier Nuosu no doubt seldom spoke Chinese. The Yi did, however, develop and use their own script, just as did the Ba. In the Yi case, the script was used by a limited group of religious professionals, the *bimuo,* who kept primarily historical and genealogical records; the Ba script may have functioned similarly.[136]

Communities similar to that of the Shuitian may well have formed in lowland areas with heavy Han settlement. At some point before the Tang the last vestiges of Ba identity disappeared; a Shuitian-type identity, fully assimilated to Han language, culture, and society, must have preceded final merger of the Ba into Chinese identity in many communities. Note, however, that the Shuitian are economically and socially disadvantaged; if and when they integrate into Chinese society, it will probably be as an underclass.

The Lipuo model is most helpful in understanding Han-Ba interactions during this period. There significant Han immigration has led to a balanced assimilation of both Han and Yi to the other's culture. Like the Lipuo's Libie, Ba language would have survived in tandem with Chinese in these communities, though Chinese writing must have soon replaced the more limited Ba script. That such bilingual communities thrived in ancient China can be confirmed by a medieval account that most of the Di (discussed below) spoke Chinese from their intermingled residences.[137] In such a mixed community, Chinese religion, with its impressive ceremonies and intricate cosmology, would have had an advantage over native beliefs, especially after use of the Han script stripped traditional religious professionals of their historiographic function and introduced a system of thought founded on Chinese cosmological principles. The Lipuo adoption of Chinese gods and festivals is paralleled by the Ba acceptance of early Daoism.

136. The Yi logographic script was in use by 1485. Literary remains in this script include philosophy, belles lettres, art, astronomy, medicine, agriculture, and religion, in addition to the genealogical records mentioned above. A number of these texts have been reprinted. See Chen Yongling 1987:1252; Harrell 1990:527.

137. SGZ 30/858n1; Huang Lie 1965:101.

The Lipuo model is important in economic terms, as well. It is only in the Lipuo community that Yi master the Chinese system, becoming rich and influential while maintaining their identity. In Nuosu communities the old ways are too strong; unable to adapt to the intensified agriculture and trade of the Chinese community, they are pushed into increasingly more remote regions. The Shuitian are overwhelmed by their Chinese neighbors, stripped of all vestiges of ethnic identity, and reduced to a permanently subjugated people. It is only among the Lipuo that Yi succeed in Chinese terms, monopolizing the roles of landowner and rich peasant within their community. Ba natives were similarly successful in Chinese Eastern Sichuan. Many of the "great surnames" recorded in the fourth century by Chang Qu were also major clans within the Ba mentioned in the tax exemptions discussed above. Further, the Li family itself is an example of a clan that became fully conversant and well-educated in Chinese, attained the status of local leader with many retainers, and adopted Chinese religion, while still maintaining their distinctive identity as Zong.

We also see in the Lipuo a key to questions concerning the relationship of non-Chinese peoples to Chinese immigrants at a much earlier stage of their history. Harrell notes that Chinese have been contributing populace to the Lipuo for centuries. Chinese legends also record individuals, the most famous being Taibo, the son of Zhou Taiwang, who moved into non-Chinese areas and adopted minority dress, customs, language, and identity. We must get away from the model that sees Chinese culture as an inexorable force converting the non-Chinese. In a variety of situations it was advantageous to be something other than Chinese, and ethnic Chinese converted. Only through this realization can we understand the continuity of Ba identity through a millennium of contact with Chinese civilization.

To sum up, then, we find that the Ba people, whatever their ultimate origins, were occupying the Yangzi River area west of the gorges from at least the eighth century B.C.E. They seem to have diversified internally over time, with some elements absorbing Chu, Central Plains, and Sanxingdui culture and developing an indigenous higher culture, including advanced bronze-casting and ceramic industries as well as two distinctive scripts, while other groups remained at a comparatively primitive level of organization, hiring themselves out as mercenaries and subsisting primarily on a hunting-gathering economy, perhaps supplemented by some trading. The Ba people were united by religious beliefs focusing on tiger worship, by a common spoken language, and by cultural features such as communally performed songs and dances. Following the Qin conquest and colonization of Sichuan, the Ba people came into a complex relationship with Chinese culture and with its representatives, Chinese migrants. Some portion of the Ba people, centering on the cities and increasing over time, identified with Chinese culture and eventually lost all Ba identity. By the fifth or sixth century this process must have overtaken all but the most remote regions of Eastern Sichuan. Some Ba in extremely remote settings maintained their native culture much longer and may survive today in the person of the Tujia. A significant portion of the Ba, however, became fully conversant in Chinese culture while maintaining their Ba identity and distinctive features of Ba culture, such as religion. The Lis were part of this group, as were many of their followers. We will see in the following section that a new Chinese religion was to form a rallying point for these people at the same time that it may have hastened their ultimate sinicization.

QIANG AND DI

The Qiang 羌 and Di 氐 peoples are ancient neighbors of the Chinese. Speakers of Tibeto-Burman languages, they are closely related to the modern Tibetans. Both these peoples played important roles in the history of the Cheng-Han state and hence merit fairly detailed consideration. Both the Ba and Shu peoples have been identified as related to the Qiang and Di.

The Qiang are among the oldest and most intimately related neighbors of the Chinese. Their name indicates an association with sheep/goats, and an early Chinese dictionary says they are "of the race of the goat" (*yangzhong* 羊種), perhaps indicating a totemic as well as occupational identification.[138] The Qiang occur frequently in the oracle bone inscriptions, which date to the latter half of the Shang dynasty (ca. 1250–1050 B.C.E.).[139] They seem to have been primarily in an adversarial relationship to the Shang state, though at one point a Qiang leader received the title of Protector (*bo* 伯), which indicated a regional leader viewed as a bulwark of the state against the incursions of other groups.[140] Qiang occur commonly in the inscriptions

138. *Shuowen jiezi zhu* 4A/36a. Lewis 1990:198n125 discusses this association of the Qiang with goats.

139. Inscriptions referring to the Qiang fill nearly five pages in Shima Kunio's index (1971:14d–19b).

140. This title by Warring States times became integrated into a graded system of peerage as "earl" but at this time was much closer to its Spring and

as sacrificial victims.[141] Since these victims were war captives, this is another indication of the bellicose relations that prevailed between the Shang and the Qiang. The Qiang state was also militarily powerful; one inscription records a Shang force of thirteen thousand assembled for an expedition against them.[142] Qiang seems to have functioned at this time as a fairly broad designation, including a number of subgroups, some of whom served the Shang.[143] Some scholars have in fact argued that Qiang is similar to other directional terms for ethnic minorities in that it was applied to all non-Chinese peoples living to the west of Chinese civilization.[144] Pulleyblank suggests that Rong may have been a general term for Tibeto-Burmans living all across Central China and that the Qiang were in fact, as Xu Shen (ca. 58–147 C.E.) claimed, a type of Western Rong.[145]

The Zhou had a special relationship to the Qiang. They were also said to be originally a western, non-Chinese people and regularly intermarried with a house surnamed Jiang 姜. This surname Jiang is

---

Autumn usage as Hegemon, the preeminent member of the feudal lords responsible for preserving the Zhou royal house. King Wen of Zhou held the title Protector of the West (*xibo* 西伯) from the Shang. See *Shiji* 4/116.

141. Ran, Li, and Zhou (1985:22–25) calculated that the sacrifices of at least 7,750 Qiang are recorded in the oracle bone inscriptions, comprising at least half the total number of individuals sacrificed. It would seem that they had some special religious significance. Keightley (1979:180) notes that the phrase "take Qiang" occurs only in inscriptions from periods III and IV.

142. See Chalfant and Britton 1935:310. Huang Lie (1965:105) calls them "the most powerful enemy" of the Shang.

143. Huang Lie 1965:105.

144. Yang Ming (1991:20–21) cites two facts in support of this position: first, that the Qiang did not occupy a clearly defined area or region and, second, that since Qiang slaves performed agricultural, pastoral, and hunting duties, they did not share a common economic structure. Both these statements are equally true of the contemporaneous Chinese population, yet it is commonly considered a single ethnic group. Wang Ming-ke (1992:103) focuses on more formal but equally inconclusive elements, arguing that the term Qiang is an exonym rather than an autonym because its graphic representation sometimes depicts a bound Qiang tribesman, because of the broad distribution of the peoples referred to by this word, and because the term Qiang "almost disappeared" for five hundred years following the conquest. The graphic representation of a word does not indicate its semantic content (Chinese characters, like all writing, are arbitrary signs, and Wang gives no etymological evidence that the graph writes a Chinese *word*). Further, the supposed distribution of the Qiang at this time was no broader than that of the Yue during later periods or of a group like the Miao today.

145. Pulleyblank 1983:418–419. *Shuowen jiezi zhu* 4A/35b glosses "Qiang are Western Rong."

cognate with Qiang, sharing a similar graphic and phonetic structure, and the legendary ancestress of the Zhou, Jiang Yuan 姜嫄, sports a name that would seem to mean "ancestress of the Jiang." Further, both Jiang and the surname of the Zhou ruling house, Ji 姬, are found among the Qiang. Pulleyblank, pointing out the close phonetic relationship between Jiang and Ji and their practice of intermarriage, suggests that they may represent two exogamic moieties at the heart of both the Qiang and the Zhou people.[146]

The Qiang had several distinctive cultural characteristics. The first and to the Chinese most startling was cremation. The *Mozi* records that in the land of the Yiqu 儀渠, a Qiang tribe, "When a parent dies they collect firewood and burn him. When the smoke rises they call this 'ascending into the distance' (*dengxia* 登遐) and say that only after one has done this does he become a filial son."[147] Xunzi, writing around the middle of the third century B.C.E., says that Qiang and Di (see below) captives "do not fear being bound, but fear not being cremated."[148] This custom is still practiced among the Qiang, especially among less-sinicized villages in remote areas.[149] Hairstyle provides another distinctive feature; whereas the Chinese wore their hair up and covered by a cap and other minorities tied their hair into distinctive shapes, the Qiang let theirs hang loose (*pifa* 披髮). This was explained by a tale of the legendary chieftain Wuyi Yuanjian 無弋爰劍, who after escaping from Chinese servitude met a Qiang woman with a cut-off nose who wore her hair hanging down to cover her ugliness.[150] During his escape Wuyi Yuanjian is said to have taken refuge in a cave, and when his pursuers tried to burn him alive, he was protected by a tiger spirit.

Although we can be certain that the Qiang inhabited a region generally to the northwest of the ancient Chinese, it is difficult to be

146. Pulleyblank 1983:420.

147. *Mozi* 39/25/79–80; *Mozi jiangu* 6/31. Although Mozi lived in the late fifth century B.C.E., the book *Mozi* is certainly later, and this passage occurs in the third and latest version of the chapter on "Regulating Burials." Still we can assume that the passage is from the third century B.C.E., perhaps even the late fourth century. On the dating of the *Mozi* see Loewe 1993:336–341. The chapter on the Qiang in HHS (87/ 2872) places Yiqu north of the Jing 涇 River in Gansu.

148. *Xunzi* 98/27/63.

149. Graham 1958:41.

150. HHS 87/2875. Wuyi Yuanjian is said to have been a war captive under the reign of King Li of Qin 秦厲公 (r. 608–604 B.C.E.). Cutting off the nose (*yi* 劓) was one of the five corporal punishments practiced in antiquity and condemned as excessive in the "Lüxing" chapter of the *Book of Documents*. See Karlgren 1950:74.

more specific. On the basis of evidence of burial practices and hair-styles, Neolithic sites in Gansu, Qinghai, and Xinjiang provinces that have been classified as Gansu Yangshao have been linked to the Qiang.[151] Oracle bone inscriptions seem to indicate that their primary geographical area of activity extended into southern Shanxi and northwest Henan.[152] There is a puzzling dearth of references to the Qiang during the mid-Zhou, but if we assume that references to the Rong often actually refer to Qiang, this is not a serious problem. Coming into the imperial period, we find that the Qiang are very widely distributed, with tribes in modern Xinjiang, Qinghai, Gansu, Tibet, and western and southwestern Sichuan. The *Book of Latter Han* explains that the southern component of this group is the result of Qiang migrating south in the face of the expanding power of the state of Qin.[153] It further chronicles the division of Wuyi Yuanjian's descendants into one hundred fifty groups, nine of which settled north of Hanzhong and fifty-two of which dispersed or merged with other groups; it is estimated that during the reign of Emperor Shun (126–144) the remaining eighty-nine groups could field around two hundred thousand soldiers.[154] Today Qiang are concentrated around the upper reaches of the Min River, especially in the Aba Tibetan Autonomous Province, and number slightly fewer than ninety thousand.[155]

151. He Yaohua 1988:52–53; Ran et al. 1985:8–16. He cites the Siwa 寺窪 site in Lintao, Gansu, and the Xiangbaobao 香保保 cemetery in the Tajik Auton-omous County, Xinjiang, as examples of cremation. Ran et al. also adduce as Qiang burials coffinless burials in a squatting position, which have been found at the Kayue 卡約 site near Huangzhong, Qinghai. This type burial was still in use until recent times along the upper reaches of the Min River. He Yaohua argues that a number of Yangshao sites in the area, such as Mayaiyao, Qijia, and Xindian, should also be considered Qiang; Ren et al. are more cautious but still venture that they are "related" (9n1). He does confess to some uneasiness at attributing these agriculturally oriented sites to a nomadic people but argues that this was the result of internal variation with the Qiang, with Qiang living in areas less suited to settled agriculture maintaining a nomadic lifestyle: Ran et al. find ample evidence of a pastoral economy in the large number of animal bones found in burials and in historical records of the worship of sheep deities.

152. Ran, Li and Zhou 1985:18. It should be noted, however, that recon-structions of Shang geography (Shima 1958) assume a quite modest size for the Shang state, resulting in the placement of Shu in east-central Shaanxi, near the Great Bend of the Yellow River. If there is any truth to the identification of the Sanxingdui culture near Guanghan as Shu, these plottings are all wildly inac-curate.

153. HHS 87/2875–2876.

154. HHS 87/2898.

155. Sichuansheng minzu yanjiusuo 1982:36.

The Qiang had their greatest influence on the Li family while they were still in the north. Li Te's father, Mu, elder brother Xiang, and younger brother Liu all held military appointments with Eastern Qiang in their titles, indicating that supervision of the Qiang was a significant portion of their official duties, and Liu was rewarded for his role in suppressing a Qiang rebellion. Most important, it was this protracted rebellion by Qiang and Di peoples during the last decade of the third century that led to famine, a breakdown of the social order, and eventually the displacement of a huge number of refugees, the Lis among them, who traveled south into Sichuan and Hanzhong in search of food and security.[156] We should not automatically assume the existence of ethnic tension between the Qiang and the refugees; there were Qiang among the refugees. But the Qiang threat did not cease with the refugees' entry into Sichuan. Li Qi revived the office of Colonel of the Eastern Qiang when he came to the throne in 334, and Li Shou also appointed an ally to this office in 338.

THE DI

The Di have a much more prominent role in the history of the Cheng-Han state. Lueyang, the Lis' adopted homeland in the northwest, was populated largely by Di and was home to all of the prominent Di clans that gained political power during the fourth century, the Yang 楊, the Fu 苻, and the Lü 呂.[157] Many Di participated in the revolt of the Di strongman Qi Wannian in Shaanxi that led to the Lis' flight.[158] Di were also members of this refugee band that entered Shu together. The Di leaders Fu Cheng and Wei Bo and their followers were among the four thousand cavalry who responded to Li Xiang's summons in support of Zhao Xin. When Zhao Xin turned on the Lis and circulated wanted posters, and Li, in order to gain the support of the other refugees, changed the wording of the posters to include other leaders of the group, the Di were again mentioned. Clearly they were an important and militarily powerful element within this group. After Te's death, when the refugees were besieged within their camp, a group of Di and Qiang led by Fu and Wei rebelled from

156. HYGZ 8/106.11–12 specifies the Qiang of Malan Mountain 馬蘭山 (sixty *li* northwest of Baishui) and the Di of the Guanzhong region (essentially the Wei River valley).

157. On the Yang clan, see Taniguchi 1976 and Yang Ming 1991; on the Fus, see Rogers 1968; for the Lüs, see Mather 1959.

158. On Qi Wannian's rebellion, see Yang Ming 1991:59–62.

within, and it was only through the valiant efforts of Li Xiong's mother that complete defeat was averted.

There was also an important Di force competing with the Cheng state for power in the northwest. This group was led by the Di King Yang Maosou and, later, his son Yang Nandi. The Yangs had originally hailed from Lueyang but had established themselves at Chouchi 仇池 in Wudu 武都 at the end of the Han. During the time of the Qi Wannian rebellion, many of the inhabitants of the Shaanxi-Gansu region took refuge with them. The Yangs played all sides against each other, simultaneously offering tribute to all the major powers in the region and accepting offices from them. In 313, when Jin was under heavy attack from the Xiongnu, Yang Maosou aided Cheng forces in the capture of Hanzhong, then proclaimed allegiance to Cheng. Shortly thereafter, his son Yang Nandi, having been defeated by the Xiongnu Liu Yao, fled to Jiameng, in Cheng territory, and submitted hostages in token of his fealty.[159] In 220, a major expedition was launched against Nandi, who had returned to Wudu; in this campaign, Cheng suffered a major defeat and lost several important members of the government. Another campaign ten years later gained at least the temporary submission of Yang Nandi.[160] Thus over the course of three decades the Yangs of Wudu interacted repeatedly with the Lis in Sichuan, now allying with them against common enemies, now opposing them when the vital interests of their two states were in conflict. Although relations were not always cordial, no other state was so closely tied to Cheng for such a long period.

Although the Di are thought to have been related to the Qiang, by the fourth century many if not most of the Di had abandoned the nomadic pastoral economy of their forebears and adopted a settled, agricultural lifestyle. Moreover, they seem to have been quite successful at agriculture. When Xiahou Yuan 夏侯淵 attacked the Di and Qiang of Wudu in 216, he confiscated more than one hundred thousand pecks (hu 斛) of grain.[161] Similarly, the Di King Yang Nandi claimed that it was only through food supplied by the Di that the

---

159. The dating of this incident is somewhat unclear. According to the *Jinshu*, it was after 313 and before 318, the next dated entry. ZZTJ would seem to place it in 323, but this does not agree with the next incident dealing with Yang, in 220. See note 71 of the biography of Li Xiong below. These few years, when north China was lost to non-Chinese, represent a major lacuna in the historical record.

160. ZZTJ 94/2927.

161. SGZ 9/272.

army and civilians governed by the Jin Governor of Liang Province
Zhang Guang survived in a time of famine, indicating that Di living
near Hanzhong were producing a substantial agricultural surplus at
a time when food supplies all across West China were in short supply.

The Di had not, however, completely forsaken their fierce, barbarian heritage. The adopted son of Yang Nandi, when sent on a
trading mission to Hanzhong, purchased as a slave a young man of
good family, an act prohibited by Chinese law. This contravention
of the Chinese social order, through which a mean barbarian sought
to enslave a Chinese of the ruling class, so enraged Zhang Guang
that he executed the man.[162] This no doubt reflects an imperfect
understanding of Chinese society. Nandi was puzzled by this response
because he regarded his son's action as a minor offense that should
have been redeemable through a fine. The death of even an adopted
son, however, was a matter of great import to the Di. After finally
capturing the capital of Liangzhou, Nandi had the body of the now-
dead Guang exhumed and burned.

Bands of armed Di seem to have roamed across vast portions of
southern China, fighting and plundering. In 310 we find a large
force of them in the Middle Yangzi region, taking the important
commandery of Yidu in southern Hubei, then moving upstream to
Badong, where they drove off the provincial governor, ransacked
the town, and drove off the entire population. When Zhang Guang
reoccupied Hanzhong, there were Di already in the area, and in 313
they overthrew his successor, taking Hanzhong. The apex of Di power,
however, was to come in the second half of the fourth century, when
the Di leader Fu Cheng established a large state in the northwest
and at one point threatened to conquer south China.[163]

162. We can get some idea of the contempt Chinese of the day held for the
Di from the tale of Tian Song 田崧, the Governor of Yi Province under the
Xiongnu Liu Yao. Tian so preferred the Xiongnu Yao over Yang Nandi that he
died rather than kneel before Nandi, whom he called "Di dog" and "bandit."
Tian proclaimed that he would rather be a ghost of his nation than a vassal of
Nandi, then seized a sword and tried to kill him. See JS 103/2697.11–14.

163. On Fu Cheng, his family, his rise and fall, see Rogers 1968.

TWO

Religion

Daoism is China's indigenous higher religion. Originating in Sichuan in the latter half of the second century C.E., Daoism sets itself apart from all other forms of Chinese religious expression. Its priesthood possesses a full complement of ceremonial regalia and is trained in the performance of elaborate rituals, both public and private, as well as techniques of self-cultivation, meditation, and divination. Although parts of Daoist doctrine can be seen as outgrowths of earlier mantic, cosmological, theological, and ritual systems, Daoist eschatology and the Daoist pantheon were distinctive new creations that marked a sharp break with the profane past and the beginning of a new dispensation for mankind.

The history of the Cheng-Han state is closely interwoven with this new faith. The Li family ancestors had been among the first followers of the church and were citizens of the original Daoist theocracy, the Hanzhong community of Zhang Lu at the end of the second century. Their descendants maintained ties to the Daoist church and continued to look to Daoist religious leaders for guidance and leadership. Governmental policy was influenced by Daoist beliefs in a number of ways, specifically in the promotion of egalitarianism, in charity works, and in attitudes toward corporal punishment. Moreover, support from fellow Daoists and the Daoist community played a key role in the establishment and development of the Cheng-Han state. This chapter will explore the nature of early Daoism and the role it played in the history of Cheng-Han.

HAN RELIGION

The Han dynasty was a turning point in Chinese religious history. The contentious debates of the Warring States philosophical world finally began affecting religious life during this time. The creation of new imperial institutions and the relative stability of four centuries of Han rule led to the coalescence of new schools of thought and permitted new theories of man and the divine to diffuse through various social milieux. It is during the Han that we first see the rise of popular religious movements in China. The extension of Han power into Central Asia and the resulting trade with India, Rome, and the West brought new influences into China. Communities of foreign merchants in the major cities of North China included educated exponents of different worldviews who challenged the Chinese to reassess long-held assumptions. Buddhism, in particular, offered new ontological and eschatological models. From this fertile soil arose Daoism. To understand the background of this phenomenon, let us first examine the archaic religion of the Shang and Zhou dynasties.

Most early evidence for religion in China refers exclusively to state worship. The oracle bone inscriptions of the Shang reveal a world without clear distinctions between the living and the dead.[1] Royal ancestors remained kings in the other world, occupying the same position in a hierarchically arrayed agnatic lineage that they had while alive. The ancestors sent blessings and misfortune to their descendants in response to sacrificial offerings (or lack thereof) of livestock, liquor, and sometimes human beings. The ancestors also acted as divine intercessors with the high god or gods, Di 帝.[2] The pantheon of the time encompassed a variety of nature deities, including gods of the Yellow River and the sacred peak(s). The Shang king had a special role as the sole authorized intermediary between man and the gods. The performance of ritual and the production of goods used in ritual (bronze ritual vessels, meat, vegetable, and liquid offerings, etc.) were primary occupations of the state.

Zhou practice on the whole followed that of Shang, except that Zhou royal ancestors replaced those of the Shang, and a figure called Tian 天, usually translated Heaven, was superimposed upon the pantheon.[3] The rituals of state continued to hold great symbolic significance even after the Zhou kings had lost effective political control of the empire. Feudal lords maintained sacrifices to the gods of the major geographical features within their domains. Altars to the gods of the soil and grain (*sheji* 社稷) were established at every level of feudal organization; continuous seasonal sacrifices at these altars

1. On Shang religion, see Akatsuka 1977, Chen Mengjia 1936, K. C. Chang 1983, and Keightley 1978.
2. On the number of Di in the Shang, see Eno 1990b.
3. Treatments of Zhou religion include Bilsky 1975, Dubs 1958, Granet 1922, and Maspero 1927.

were synonymous with the existence of the state. The world of the dead was conceived of as rather like that of the living, with social classes, a bureaucratic elite, and a legal system, all in a subterranean location called the Yellow Springs, where the dead depended upon male descendants for sacrificial provender. Since this was not a popular destination, attention focused instead on prolonging physical existence, with schools of macrobiotics, alchemy, sexual regimens, and yoga developing in the Warring States period along with a widespread belief in transcendent, often feathered, beings with extended lifetimes.

The Han was a period of intense religious ferment through all segments of society, but the situation at court is best documented. Emperor Wu (r. 140–87 B.C.E.), often credited with establishing Confucianism as the state religion, took a personal interest in imperial ritual. In addition to performing five times the solemn Feng and Shan sacrifices to Mount Tai that confirmed his mandate to rule and making numerous ritual processions to visit and sacrifice at sacred sites, he gathered about him a large number of occultists who promised him long life through various regimens and summoned gods and ghosts. Another royal patron was Liu An, King of Huainan, who sponsored a compilation of esoteric lore that combined Daoist philosophy with the cosmological speculations of the Eclectics (*zajia* 雜家).[4]

The diversity of Han religious expression is reflected in the prognostications and apocrypha (*chenwei* 讖緯) of this era. The prognostications, in particular, were used politically by the usurper Wang Mang 王莽, by the Sichuanese separatist Gongsun Shu 公孫述, and by Liu Xiu 劉秀, the future Emperor Guangwu of the Eastern Han (r. 25–57), in their contestations for power. The apocrypha, conceived as esoteric commentaries on the Confucian classics and often attributed to Confucius, have been shown to presage in their terminology and ideas the rise of Daoism later in the dynasty.[5]

Another important product of the Han was the *Scripture of Great*

4. The compilation and textual history of this book, the *Huainanzi* 淮南子, is described in Roth 1992 and Loewe 1993:189–195. Roth (1991) has argued that the *Huainanzi* is an authentic representative of Huang-Lao Daoism in that it combines cosmological, psychological, and political aspects of the Daoist worldview.

5. On the prognostications and apocrypha, see Dull 1966, Yasui 1979, and the essays collected in Yasui 1984. The texts of the apocrypha are now mostly lost, but surviving fragments have been collected in the multivolume series *Isho shūsei* 緯書集成, edited by Yasui and Nakamura (1971–).

Peace. The earliest record of this work, under the title *Scripture of Great Peace Securing the Beginning of the Calendar of the Heavenly Offices* (Tianguanli baoyuan taiping jing 天官曆包元太平經), was presented to the throne during the reign of Emperor Cheng (32–7 B.C.E.) by a man from the state of Qi (modern Shandong).[6] During the reign of Emperor Shun (126–145 C.E.) we read of a *Book of Great Peace with Green Border* (Taiping qingling shu 太平青領書) that again originated with a master on the eastern littoral, this one named Yu Ji 于吉 (or Gan Ji 干吉).[7] The goal of this work is said to have been a flourishing state and numerous descendants. The relationship of this text to the received *Scripture of Great Peace* has been the subject of much debate, as has the relationship of either text to the Yellow Turban and Celestial Master movements discussed below.[8] We can, however, be confident that works promoting a new era of peace and equality were circulating in some parts of China through most of the Eastern Han.

Interest in religious topics was not limited to the court. In 3 B.C.E. there was a major movement of ecstatic worshipers of the Queen Mother of the West across a large portion of northeastern China. Thousands of believers took to the roads in singing and dancing processions that culminated in the capital, where it seems that an epiphany of the goddess was expected.[9] Less than two decades later, most of north China was disrupted by the revolt of the Red Eyebrows. We know comparatively little about this movement, but worship seems to have focused on Liu Zhang 劉璋, who was instrumental in foiling the attempted usurpation by Empress Lü in the early second century B.C.E.; a prime goal of the rebels was the restoration of the Han after the usurpation of Wang Mang. They traveled in communities of families rather than military bands, showed unusual deference to women, and were advised by spirit mediums.[10]

6. HS 75/3192. The proper interpretation of this title is uncertain. The Heavenly Offices of the title probably refers to the stars and planets in their role as celestial officials. The text advocated a renewal of the Han mandate through a change of reign titles. The disseminator of this text, a certain Gan Zhongke 甘忠可, died in prison, but during the following reign the text found new advocates in the government in reponse to whom the emperor did emend the official calendar.

7. HHS 30B:1080–1081, 1084.

8. Kaltenmark 1979; Beck 1980; Kandel 1979; Kusuyama 1983.

9. See Cahill 1993:21–23 and Dubs 1942.

10. For historical accounts of the Red Eyebrows, see Bielenstein 1959:83, 94–96.

The next two centuries saw a steadily increasing number of popular, religiously inspired insurgencies. Speculation about the reappearance of a divinized Laozi reached a peak around the middle of the second century. In 147 and 154 men surnamed Li 李, the reputed surname of Laozi, rose in rebellion, the second of these in Sichuan, and declared themselves Emperor.[11] Men of other surnames arose in 148, 165, and 166.[12] Emperor Huan (r. 147–168) was a devotee of Laozi. Immediately upon his ascension to the throne, he had a temple erected at Laozi's supposed birthplace. Eunuchs were dispatched to worship there in 165 and 166, and an imperial sacrifice was performed in the palace in 166.[13] It is also in a record from 166 that we first hear of the theory that the Buddha was a transformation of Laozi after he had left China to go among the barbarians.[14] An "Inscription on Laozi" from 153 tells more about his religious identity, describing him as a divine figure who was born from primordial essences and dwells among the stars.[15] Most instructive is a scripture preserved in Dunhuang and translated by Anna Seidel, called the *Scripture of the Transformations of Laozi* (*Laozi bianhua jing* 老子 變化經).[16] This traces Laozi through a series of avatars in this world, feigning death only to be reborn in a new age with a different, though related, name, often as a famous counselor of sage rulers of the past. Seidel attributes this scripture to an otherwise unknown sect operating in Sichuan toward the end of the second century. She believes that the Celestial Masters saw themselves as the successors to Laozi in his role as advisor to rulers.

There was a major outbreak of religiously inspired rebellion in 184, a year with special significance as the beginning of a new sexagesimal cycle. In Eastern China a man named Zhang Jiao 張角 (or Zhang Jue), preaching the Way of Great Peace 太平道, had gathered great numbers of converts across a wide swath of the lower Yellow River valley and the Huai River basin. Jiao worshiped the Great One 太一, who had been placed atop the state pantheon in 130 B.C.E. Jiao gained followers primarily through faith healing; patients would kowtow, confess the sins that had led to their illness, and

11. HHS 7/291, 300.
12. HHS 7/293, 316.
13. Seidel 1969:36–37; HHS 7/313, 316, 317. The second sacrifice at Laozi's birthplace is recorded under the eleventh month of 165. It is unclear where Seidel gets 166.
14. HHS 30B/1082; Seidel 1969:49.
15. Seidel 1969:37–50, 121–128.
16. Stein manuscript 2295 (British Library, London); Seidel 1969:92–120.

drink water imbued with magic. Ma Xiang 馬相, proclaiming himself
a Yellow Turban, led a revolt in Sichuan in 184, and by some accounts
Zhang Xiu 張脩 also led such a group.[17] These rebellions were put
down only with much bloodshed; the local and national military forces
formed to suppress them were beyond the control of the central government and eventually carved up the empire among themselves.

THE CELESTIAL MASTERS

The founding of Daoism is attributed to a shadowy figure known as
Zhang Ling or Zhang Daoling 張 (道) 陵. He is said to have been
born in Pei 沛 (near modern Suxian, Anhui, though Zhang's specific
birthplace is usually placed in Jiangsu) but migrated to Sichuan, where
he began to teach disciples. Our earliest account is from the *Record
of the Three Kingdoms* of Chen Shou 陳壽 (233–297) in a biography
of Ling's grandson, Lu:[18]

> Zhang Lu 張魯, cognomen Gongqi 公祺, was a man of Feng 豐
> in the kingdom of Pei. His grandfather Ling sojourned in Shu,
> where he studied the Dao on Mount Swancall 鵠名山. He fabri-
> cated Daoist writings to delude the masses. Those who accepted
> the Dao from him would supply five pecks of rice. For this
> reason they were known at the time as "rice bandits." When
> Ling died, his son Heng 衡 took over his Dao, and when Heng
> died, Lu continued it.

A fuller account, in the *Biographies of Divine Transcendents* (*Shenxian zhuan*) of Ge Hong, tells us more about his background and
motivations:[19]

> Zhang Daoling was a man of Pei. He was originally a student
> in the Imperial Academy and was broadly conversant in the
> Five Classics. As he grew older, he sighed, "This is of no benefit
> to my lifespan." Consequently he studied the Dao of longevity.

17. HYGZ 5/70.8; Ren 2/73n1.
18. SGZ 8/263.
19. *Taiping guangji* 8, entry 3. Questions have been raised about the authenticity of the *Shenxian zhuan,* but it seems on the whole a reliable attribution.
Moreover, most of the content of this account accords with other information
concerning the early cult. A portion of the tale, concerning Ling's interest in
alchemy and his transmission of alchemical lore to a certain Zhao Sheng, does
not tally with other sources and may derive from a later source, perhaps a
hagiography of Zhao Sheng. Given Ge Hong's interest in alchemy, it is not
surprising that such material was included, but it should not be regarded as
reliable information concerning the early Celestial Master cult.

He obtained the Nine Cauldron Elixir Formula of the Yellow Thearch and wanted to compound it but exhausted his wealth on the drugs needed for it. Ling's family had heretofore been poor. He wanted to make a living by farming the fields and raising livestock, but he was not good at it and consequently gave up the idea. He heard that most of the people of Shu were pure and sincere and open to moral instruction, and that, moreover, there were many famous mountains there. So, accompanied by his disciples, he entered Shu and lived on Swancall Mountain, where he composed twenty-four fascicles of Daoist documents.

We do not know what Daoist documents are referred to here; if they ever existed, they probably do not survive today. In the biography, they are treated as distinct from the major revelation of 142, which is usually considered the founding of the Daoist faith. That encounter with the divine is recorded in the following terms:[20]

Suddenly a Heavenly Man (*tianren* 天人) descended, accompanied by a thousand chariots and ten thousand horsemen, in a golden carriage with a feathered canopy. Riding dragons and astride tigers, they were too numerous to count. At times the man referred to himself as the Scribe Below the Pillar 柱下史, sometimes others would call him the Lad from the Eastern Sea 東海童子. He bestowed upon Ling Newly Emerged Correct and Unitary Dao of Covenanted Awe (*Xinchu zhengyi mengwei zhi dao* 新出正一盟威之道). Having received this, Ling was able to heal illness.

The Scribe Below the Pillar is a title reputedly once held by Laozi as court historian to the Zhou kings.[21] The Lad of the Eastern Sea is the god of the east, also known as Goumang, the Earl-Father of the East, and the Blue Lad; together with the Queen Mother of the West, he forms a pair often depicted in Han art.[22] In later cult documents, the revealing deity is clearly identified as Laozi in his divine form, the Supreme Lord Lao (*Taishang Laojun* 太上老君). The "Covenanted Awe," or perhaps "Covenant with Awe-inspiring Powers," refers to a new way of dealing with sin through confession and pledges not to repeat the evil act, discussed below.

20. *Taiping guangji* 8, entry 3.
21. *Shiji* 63/2140n5.
22. See Riegel 1989–90; Cahill 1993, esp. pp. 27–28.

The revelation to Zhang Daoling marked the beginning of a new religion but also the inauguration of a new religiously organized community. Ge Hong's biography goes on to describe certain key features of this community and its organization:[23]

> Thereupon commoners flocked to serve him as their teacher. His disciples came to number several tens of thousands of households. He therefore established Libationers to divide up and take charge of the households, just like government officials. He also established a code (*tiaozhi* 條制) by which his various disciples would on appropriate occasions contribute rice, silk, vessels, paper, brushes, firewood, and a variety of other goods. They would lead the people in repairing roads, and those who did not participate in the repairs he would cause to fall ill. If there were bridges or roads that should be built within the county, the commoners would cut weeds and clear out latrines; there was nothing they would not do, all at his initiative.

The term used for local leaders of the new religion, Libationer (*jijiu* 祭酒), derives ultimately from the local level, much as the Red Eyebrows had named their leaders after the village elders known as the Thrice Venerable (*sanlao* 三老).[24] The term seems to have had its origin in an informal designation accorded the senior member of a village community, who officiated at the sacrificial ceremony that preceded every banquet. It came, to be sure, to be applied to the official realm, becoming an honorific title used in referring to distinguished elder ministers and a part of the title of educational officials, especially the Chancellor of the Imperial University. But it continued to have a wider usage, referring to low-level officials and distinguished members of the local community.[25] Although the term literally refers to one who sacrifices alcoholic spirits, it does not seem that this was part of the Libationer's function in the Celestial Master church.

The early history of the Celestial Master movement is sketchy, and it is difficult to know what portion of the movement can be reliably attributed to Zhang Ling or Zhang Heng, but there is good evidence that the religious office of Libationer was in existence before the time of Zhang Lu. An inscription dated 173 records the initiation of six

---

23. *Taiping guangji* 8, entry 3.

24. On this title, see Hucker 1985:entry 542; Ōfuchi 1991:149–151.

25. Ōfuchi cites the example of Ban Chao 班超 (32–102 C.E.), who while still a young man in a minor office was referred to as "Libationer" by a physiognomist. See HHS 37/1571; Ōfuchi 1991:150.

men to the rank of Libationer and the conferral upon them of twelve scrolls of secret scriptures (*weijing* 微經).[26] The initiating deity is a certain Hu Jiu-X, Demon Soldier of the Celestial Elder 天老鬼兵胡九□.[27] The Libationers, having received the scriptures, vow to "disseminate the Way and Law of the Celestial Masters without limit."[28]

An administrative framework was set up for the church consisting of twenty-four *zhi* 治, or administrative centers, commonly translated as "parishes." Only three of these parishes were within the territory of Zhang Lu's Hanzhong state. It is unclear how long the other parishes continued and to what degree they maintained administrative or religious ties to the Zhangs. Below these parishes were numerous "lodges of righteousness" (*yishe* 義舍). Historical sources compare these lodges to the lowest level of the Han administration, *ting* 停, or "hostels."[29] This type of hostel, headed by a local Chief (*zhang* 長) who was not a formal member of the central bureaucracy, administered a neighborhood but also functioned as inns for traveling officials and sometimes served meals or offered lodging to non-official travelers. The Daoist parish, controlled by a Parish-Heading Great Libationer (*zhitou dajijiu* 治頭大祭酒), had a similar range of functions. The most famous of these was its role as a distribution point for food for the needy. Rice and meat were hung in the lodges

26. *Lixu* 3/8a–b; Sawa 1994:134n11.

27. The second character in this title is irregular and has also been interpreted as *zu* 卒, *qu* 去, and *biao* 表.

28. Interpretations of this inscription beginning with that of Hong Gua 洪适 (1117–1184) have been skewed by a misinterpretation of this god's title. Equating Demon Soldier (*guibing* 鬼兵) with the Demon Troop (*guizu* 鬼卒) mentioned in historical accounts of the Celestial Masters as the initial rank of new members (a title, it must be noted, that is not found in any Celestial Master source), it has been assumed that the Hu Jiu or Hu Jiu-X (there is a lacuna of two characters' length following *jiu*) was a new member. It has never been explained, though, why it would take six Libationers to initiate one Demon Trooper, nor why it is the Libationers who promise to promulgate the cult's teachings. In fact, the term Demon Soldier is not unknown. When Guiji was under attack from the rebel Sun En 孫恩 at the beginning of the fifth century, Wang Ningzhi 王凝之, a particularly devout member of the Celestial Master church, invoked Demon Soldier Xu of the Great Dao 大道許鬼兵 to protect him. See JS 80/2103. Ren Naiqiang (442n4) also goes astray in assuming that Hu is a newly deceased member of the church. He argues that the twelve *juan* of scriptures was the *Laozi,* but that text would not fill twelve *juan,* and all Libationers must have already possessed it; nor does Ren explain why Libationers should receive scriptures for performing what was basically, in his view, a funeral service.

29. On the relationship of these lodges to Han hostels, see Ōfuchi 1991:163–166.

and were free for the taking, but those who took more than they needed would be punished by the spirits.[30]

Sin, in the sense of behavior offensive to the Dao, was a major concern of the Celestial Master Daoists. The concept grew out of more specific taboos, such as that on digging into the earth, that led the men of Han, when burying their dead or digging wells, to perform rituals and make offerings to Sovereign Earth (*Houtu* 后土) in order to "dispel [the curse of] the earth" (*jietu* 解土).[31] Another aspect of divine punishment was vengeance wreaked upon the living by dead individuals for offenses done to them while alive. The fifth-century B.C.E. philosopher Mozi had constructed an entire system of divine justice on the concept of just such spectral retribution for misdeeds.

In the Daoist heavens, gods as divine bureaucrats enforced laws and regulations, punishing those who violated them, but they also operated a judicial system through which the dead might lodge complaints against the living and seek divine punishment in recompense.[32] In this way, an originally highly particularist system based on the personal animosities and vengeances of the gods and the dead was transformed into an effective enforcement power for a wide-reaching moral code that protected both the interests of the divine administration and the individual interests of all those wronged while alive.

Sin was eliminated by acknowledgment of the transgression, a vow not to commit the offense again, and various acts of penance. There were special Quiet Rooms (*jingshi* 靜室) where the faithful could meditate upon their transgressions. They then wrote in their own hand three confessions, acknowledging their sins. They directed these documents to the Three Offices (*sanguan* 三官): the document to the Heavenly Office was placed on a mountain peak; that to the Earthly Office was buried in the ground; that to the Water Office was cast into water.[33] That these documents must be written in the supplicant's own hand would seem to imply quite a high rate of literacy, but Ōfuchi may be right in suggesting that an educated priest would write out an appropriate document that the petitioner could then copy.[34]

Sin was not clearly differentiated from criminal behavior. Both

30. SGZ 8/263.
31. See Seidel 1987.
32. On these sepulchral plaints, see Maruyama 1986.
33. These documents are described in the account from the *Dianlue* quoted in SGZ 8/264 and HHS 75/2436.
34. Ōfuchi 1991:152.

prompted what was for the day an amazingly lenient response: "Those who transgressed against the law were first granted three pardons; only after this were punishments applied."[35] Even when punishments were applied, they often involved only what would today be called public service: "Those who had committed a minor transgression (*xiaoguo* 小過) were to repair a one-hundred-pace stretch of road." No doubt other public works were also assigned (e.g., the bridge repair mentioned in the *Biographies of Divine Transcendents* above), but repairing a road *(dao)* had special significance because it was symbolically equated with cultivating the Dao.[36] The Code of Great Perfection, a Celestial Master document preserved only in a scripture of the Six Dynasties period, details more stringent punishments for repeat offenders, including the contribution of three thousand sheafs of reeds to be used in thatching the Celestial Master's residence and the supply of two thousand *ge* 合 of roof tiles.[37]

At least some of the prohibitions of the Celestial Masters had their origins in earlier, more mainstream codes of conduct. One such rule was a general prohibition on killing and slaughter during the spring and summer.[38] This taboo, rooted in a conception that spring and summer are times of fertility and growth that would be stunted by violent actions contrary to these cosmic currents, is derived from the "Monthly Ordinances" (*Yueling* 月令), a code of seasonal behavior so important that it was included in variant forms in three major works, the *Springs and Autumns of Master Lü (Lüshi chunqiu)*, the *Huainanzi*, and the *Record of Rites*.

Another distinctive feature of the Celestial Masters was a prohibition on the consumption of alcohol. Alcoholic beverages had long been popular in China and played an important role in the cycle of banquets through which social ties were established and affirmed. The

35. HHS 75/2436; HYGZ 2/17.3.

36. Ōfuchi 1991:157, on the basis of recently excavated Latter Han documents, points out that the repair of roads was normally a local responsibility and that a special tax was extracted for this purpose. The significance of the Daoist regulations would seem to be that the repairs were performed personally and willingly by the faithful.

37. *Chisongzi zhangli* (HY 615) 2/19a, cited in Ōfuchi 1991:156. The lowest level of punishment in this code involves sweeping the roads for a period of twenty days. A *ge* was roughly twenty cubic centimeters in the Han. It seems curious to measure roof tiles by volume, but perhaps it is the unformed clay that is measured. The character can also refer to a pair of objects, but there seems no good reason to count tiles in pairs and two thousand pair of tiles would be an exceedingly large amount. See Dubs 1942, 1:279.

38. HHS 75/2436, quoting the *Dianlue*.

ritual codes prescribe a seasonal "Community Drinking" (*xiangyin* 鄉飲) in which the members of local society would come together and, seated in order appropriate to their age and standing in the community, engage in a series of formalized toasts.[39] Similar feasts were held at the time of major sacrifices to the altars of grain and soil and to any local deities with a significant following. Because of the Celestial Master prohibition on sacrifice, a communal feast called a "kitchen" (*chu* 廚) was substituted.[40]

The early church also held periodic gatherings of the community on the dates of the Three Primes (*sanyuan* 三元), on the seventh day of the first, seventh, and tenth months. In addition to a communal feast, these days were occasion for a stock-taking of the community. Every member of the local parish was recorded in a roster (*ji* 籍) maintained by the local Libationer. On the Three Primes, members of the parish reported deaths, births, and movements of peoples so that these registers could be adjusted accordingly.[41]

A complex system of graded registers (*lu* 籙) also served to unify and order the community.[42] In a sense, each member of the Celestial Master community was a priest. Each possessed a register that specified his or her identity, parish, and rank. Rank was graded according to the number of otherworldly generals and troops one had at one's disposal to do one's bidding and protect one from nefarious influence and according to the number of divine scriptures that had been conferred upon the individual. Children were first initiated at the age of seven *sui* (usually six years old) and received at successive periodic ceremonies registers for one, three, and finally ten generals. At the age of capping (usually nineteen years), they received the full initial complement of seventy-five generals, recorded in a document which

39. The social import of this rite is discussed in the "Significance of the Community Wine Drinking" chapter of the *Record of Rites*. See *Liji zhengyi* 61/12a–23a; Legge 1885, 2:435–445.

40. Daoist scriptures describe the number of guests to be entertained at kitchens given for various reasons, such as the birth of a son or daughter, marriage, or when seeking to cure illness or avoid misfortune, but also mention kitchens to be held every month or at the three Daoist yearly meetings (*sanhui* 三會). Whereas the former were primarily for laymen to feast priests, the latter were sponsored by the church and open to large numbers of members. Since this evidence all comes from the Six Dynasties period, we cannot be certain how these kitchens were conducted in the early church. See Ōfuchi 1991:396–400.

41. These periodic meetings are described in *Lu xiansheng daomen kelue* (HY 1119): 2a–b.

42. The best description of this system to date is Schipper 1985. See also Benn 1991, which describes in some detail the system of the mid-Tang.

they wore belted at the waist. Marriage brought the union of two sets for a total of one hundred fifty spirit generals, perhaps accompanied by the infamous sexual ritual known as the Joining of Pneumas (*heqi* 合氣). A Libationer officiated at each ordination and, later in the Six Dynasties period if not now, a set of precepts imposing progressively stricter codes of conduct was also transmitted. A plethora of higher ranks, some quite specialized, awaited the adept, but advancement was no longer simply by age but rather by religious accomplishment.

We can get some idea of how these ranks might have functioned in early Celestial Master communities by looking at Yao 傜 minority communities in southwest China and northern Thailand.[43] The Yao are converts to Daoism of long standing. Although their initial conversion seems to have taken place in the Song under the influence of Tianxin thunder rites, the basic structure of their community and most of their rituals still reflect Celestial Master usage.[44] In Yao society one's position within the community is determined by one's religious rank.[45] Children are ordained beginning at age five and pass through a series of progressively higher ordinations during their lifetimes. Although social status ultimately derives from Daoist rank, wealth is an important consideration because well-to-do Yao can better afford the elaborate ceremonies with multiple priest-officiants through which one gains higher ordination, more spirit soldiers, and higher rank. All fully ordained males can perform simple rites, but in order to officiate at the more complex rituals, they must apprentice to an acknowledged master, copy and study his scriptures, and assist him in ritual performances. The result is a tight-knit society where the village headman and village chief priest have nearly equal influence.

The Celestial Masters were further unified by a strong millenarian belief. I have mentioned that such beliefs were common at this time, perhaps due to the widespread disorder and societal breakdown. The Celestial Masters believed that they were among the chosen "seed people" (*zhongmin* 種民) who would survive the coming conflagration and repopulate the world.[46] In an early cult scripture the

43. The following discussion is based upon Strickmann 1982b and Skar 1992. See also Shiratori 1975, 1981.

44. On the Tianxin, or Heavenly Heart, ritual tradition, see Boltz 1987:33–38.

45. The status of wives rises with that of their husbands, with the wife controlling half the number of spirit generals. Skar 1992:14.

46. On the theme of the seed people, see Yoshioka 1976.

Celestial Master invites others to join the church so that they may participate in the coming age of Great Peace:[47] "Enter into my living energy and you will become a perfected. On the day of Great Peace you will fly up into the heavens. Even if you cannot fly, you will live to an old age and not die (in the attendant disasters). Then you will become a terrestrial transcendent and will get to see Great Peace." Selection was not automatic, as we see in the following passage:[48]

> The Masters of the Three Offices will select the seed people and take those who have mixed their breaths, eighteen thousand in number. How many have there been up until today? The great quota is not yet full. You should devote yourself to your body and reform your heart.

Still, participation in the Celestial Master community would seem to have been a prerequisite for consideration. This created within the movement a tremendous esprit de corps as members contemplated the devastation around them.

Building on this sort of social organization and inspired by these beliefs, the Celestial Master community was able to remain independent for over a quarter-century. Hanzhong was a rich area in a strategic position with good natural defenses, and the general strife and confusion enveloping China at the time kept attention focused elsewhere. Another factor was surely the allegiance of large numbers of Banshun Man peoples.

The Banshun, as discussed in the previous chapter, were renowned fighters who had served a series of rulers as able, fierce soldiers. They had been severely exploited by local officials who ignored the traditional *modus vivendi* the indigenous people of Eastern Sichuan had struck with the central government regarding taxes and corvée labor in their desire to maximize state and personal revenue. Driven by these exactions, the Banshun Man had repeatedly revolted against Han rule, but each time they had been brutally suppressed. The Celestial Master movement promised the security of a Chinese state that was not coercive, one founded instead on explicit ideals of egalitarianism and social welfare that resonated with their tribal lifestyle. Instead of the cold face of the imperious Chinese bureaucracy, the

---

47. *Nüqing guilü* (HY 789): 3/4b. On the dating of this scripture, see Schipper 1994:69n20, where he theorizes that it may be the earliest extant Celestial Master scripture.

48. *Nüqing guilü*, 5/1a.

Celestial Masters promised the warm, open arms of a welcoming community. Their promise of an idyllic future that would follow the current disorder and hardship appealed to many in that troubled time of warfare, famine, and plague.[49]

Historical sources tell us that Zhang Lu taught his people through a Way of Demons (*guidao* 鬼道) that pleased the non-Chinese.[50] It is tempting to dismiss this comment as the disparaging slander of a non-believer seeking to dismiss the cult, but there is at least some justification for the characterization. New converts were dubbed Demon Troopers, and we have seen that some divine figures were called Demon Soldiers. Each ordained member of the church controlled a host of otherworldly warriors who might well be considered demons or gods.[51] The purpose of these troops and of the many apotropaic charms and talismans produced by the Celestial Masters was to protect the bearer from the attack of unsubjugated demons, who were thought to roam the countryside spreading contagion, misfortune, and death. In this sense, demons were a major concern of the movement.

We know little about the indigenous religious beliefs of the Banshun Man or even of the larger Ba people. Clearly there was a tiger cult with special veneration for white tigers that was associated with the transformed Lord of Granaries.[52] Some Ba groups performed human sacrifice to this figure but when and who remain open questions. It is possible that the reborn tiger lord provided a focus for Ba rebellion

49. An intriguing parallel to this process is found among the Flowery Miao, who adopted Christianity in large numbers during the late Qing dynasty. Cheung (1995) has argued that the new faith provided a means of expressing resistance toward an oppressive social order and prompted greater social cohesion. The key difference in the two cases would seem to be that Daoism was a faith that brought the Ba into a new community shared with the Chinese, rather than in opposition to them.

50. See below, p. 120: "At the end of the Han dynasty, Zhang Lu took up residence in Hanzhong, teaching the people the Way of the Spirits. The Zong were devout believers in shamans (*wuxi* 巫覡); many went to follow him."

51. The distinction between demon or ghost *(gui)* and god *(shen)* was always somewhat hazy, as in the common term *guishen* for supernatural beings, but during the Han the situation seems to have been even more amorphous as reflected in references to the God of the Hearth (*zaoshen* 灶神) as Demon of the Hearth *(zaogui)*. SJ 28/1387.

52. The modern Tujia peoples, who are often linked to the historical Ba, worship tiger spirits who are propitiated with sacrifice but also exorcised and "driven off" lest they harm newborn babies. See *Zhongguo ge minzu zongjiao yu shenhua dacidian* 1990:578–587, esp. 582. For a more politicized reading of the weretiger theme, see Hammond 1995.

and a point of entry for Daoist millenarian doctrine.[53] Beyond this we can do little more than speculate.[54] Whatever the exact nature of their native faith, it was sufficiently similar to win their allegiance to the Celestial Master cause. Among those moving to Hanzhong were three Banshun kings, each presumably bringing the tribe over which he ruled. These kings were eventually moved to Gansu along with the Lis, and their descendants were among those returning to Sichuan among the refugees.[55]

Liu Yan 劉焉, who had been appointed Pastor of Yi Province in 188, was a convert to Celestial Master Daoism with special ties to the mother of Zhang Lu.[56] In 191 Yan sent Zhang Lu and Zhang Xiu to attack the Hanzhong region. Zhang Xiu died, either in the attack or at Lu's hands,[57] and Lu was able to establish an independent power base that combined political and religious power. When Liu Yan died, his son, Liu Zhang 劉璋, succeeded to his position and proceeded to kill Lu's mother and younger brother, but Lu was able to extend his control to the Ba region. In 215 Cao Cao made a concerted drive on the Hanzhong community. On the advice of his Merit Officer Yan Pu 閻圃, Zhang Lu first withdrew to eastern Sichuan, then surrendered. Zhang received extremely favorable treat-

53. Cheung (1995) argues that the Miao tradition of a Miao King who would appear to lead his people in their return to a perfect world of social justice provided just such a foundation for later Christian millennial beliefs.

54. HYGZ 105.6 records that pine and cypress trees were common at shrines to gods of the mountains and streams in Sichuan, perhaps reflecting an early tree cult, but this was not limited to the Ba region. Ancient trees are still common at Sichuanese cult sites and are often recorded in local gazetteers.

55. See Ren 485n1.

56. The histories record that she "had youthful features" or "possessed graceful beauty" as well as a command of the Way of the Demons, and that she often visited Yan's dwelling. Ren Naiqiang (2/74n4) maintains that this implies only that she commanded certain secrets that retarded aging and for this reason was a favorite among the members of Yan's harem, but others assume that these statements imply an illicit relationship between the two. She is never referred to as the wife of Zhang Heng, perhaps because he was already dead at this point. See HYGZ 2/17.1; HHS 75/2432.

57. The accounts of Zhang Xiu are quite confusing. He was a leader of a religious movement who rebelled first in Ba commandery in 184. HHS and SGZ say that Lu killed him and stole his following, but HYGZ reports that he died in battle with Su Gu. Moreover, one source tells us that Xiu's sect was called the Five Bushels of Rice group. Ren believes that all of the rebels of 184, including Xiu, Ma Xiang, and Zhang Jiao, were part of a single movement established by Zhang Daoling, whereas Ōfuchi argues that Xiu was head of the one Celestial Master parish in Ba commandery. This problem may not be resolvable with surviving evidence. See Ōfuchi 1991:46–49; Ren 2/74n6.

ment from Cao Cao. He was appointed Great General Quelling the South and enfeoffed as Marquis. His sons and Yan Pu also received enfeoffments. A daughter of Zhang Lu was married to a younger son of Cao Cao, and a son of Zhang's may have received a Cao daughter in marriage as well.

The Zhangs and their close followers were moved to Cao's administrative center at Ye (west of Linzhang in Henan). In the subsequent five years more than eighty thousand Hanzhong residents moved to the Ye-Loyang area of their own volition, no doubt happy to be close to the leaders of their faith.[58] Other members of the Hanzhong community were also transferred in an attempt to disperse their influence. Several tens of thousands of families, perhaps two hundred thousand to three hundred thousand individuals, were moved to the Chang'an region in this same period.[59] This group probably included Li Te's grandfather, Li Hu, and other Banshun tribesmen, who passed through the Chang'an area on their way to Gansu. There was yet another transfer of the Hanzhong population in 220, after Liu Bei regained control of the area.[60] All these movements spread the Celestial Master faith abroad.

According to Tao Hongjing 陶宏景, Zhang Lu died shortly after surrendering in 216.[61] When, in 221, a group of courtiers joined in a petition urging Cao Pi to proclaim a new dynasty, Yan Pu was among them and Zhang Lu was not, nor, as far as we can tell, were any of his sons. The administration of the movement after his death is something of a mystery. We are told that Lu's son Fu 富 succeeded him,

---

58. The laudatory biography of Du Xi 杜襲 attributes their willingness to move to Du's astute guidance. See SGZ 23/666. The grandfather of Zhao Xin would seem to have been among those who moved at this time, settling in the kingdom of Zhao (north of Ye, with its administrative center near modern Gaoyi, Hebei), but Chang Qu indicates that he moved there to follow Zhang Lu rather than because of the blandishments of Du Xi. See HYGZ 8/109.1; Ōfuchi 1991:58.

59. SGZ 15/472 records the move as at the suggestion of Zhang Ji 張既, a native of the Chang'an region who had participated in the campaign against Zhang Lu. Liu Jiusheng (1986:100) maintains that there were Ba communities who had maintained their ethnic identity in the Shaanxi area ever since the early Han. If these communities had not accepted the Daoist faith at the same time as their Sichuanese compatriots, they were likely converted by the transferred masses.

60. HYGZ 6/83.14.

61. *Zhengao* (HY1010) 4/14b. Tao relates that Zhang was buried east of Ye but revived briefly some forty-four years later when his coffin was exposed by a flood. Cf. Tang Changru 1983b:229; Ōfuchi 1991:58.

but at some point hereditary succession was broken, and it is unclear to what degree Zhang Lu's heirs maintained control of the movement. Traditional historical sources tell us little about the Celestial Masters or their followers for the rest of the third century.

There is one source for the history of the movement, however, preserved in the Daoist canon. In a Tang collection of Celestial Master texts we find the "Family Commands and Precepts of the Great Dao," a text that we can date with some certainty to 255 or shortly thereafter.[62] The text is pronounced by Zhang Lu, presumably through a medium or other mantic means. He speaks of his defeat at the hands of Cao Cao in the following terms:[63]

> When the kingdom of righteousness (yiguo 義國)[64] was toppled, those who fled or died numbered in the tens of thousands. How this broke one's heart. Ever since the movements and transfers, you have been scattered across the world. The Dao then saved your lives again and again. Sometimes it has spoken to you through the Determiner of Pneumas;[65] sometimes there were former officials and worthy ministers who rectified you, yet you still did not grant them credence. This is truly lamentable.

Zhang goes on to describe the disasters that would ravage the world before Great Peace could be established. This passage reflects a movement groping to survive in the face of physical dispersion and doubts about its message.

The Celestial Master church was, as we have seen, a tightly organized movement with clearly defined official positions and criteria for appointment to those positions. The original system of twenty-four parishes, established during its period as a purely religious movement

62. *Zhengyi fawen Tianshi jiaojie kejing* (HY 788):16b. My understanding of this text has profited greatly from a translation by Stephen Bokenkamp, to appear in his *Early Daoist Scriptures* (1997).

63. *Zhengyi fawen Tianshi jiaojie kejing* (HY 788): 14b–15a.

64. The sense of this term would seem to be that it was not a formally declared state. Cf. Tang Changru 1983b:228.

65. The Determiner of Pneumas (*jueqi* 決氣) is probably an alternate term for the Controller of Determinations (*lingjue* 領決), an official post among the Celestial Masters responsible, in cases where a man or woman has been possessed by a pneuma and transmits messages, for determining whether the pneuma is true or false and whether it is Chinese or of some other ethnic group. Presumably this passage would then refer to a spirit communication that the Controller of Determinations has certified to be from an authentic spirit. See *Sandong zhunang* (HY 1131):7/19a.

operating throughout western China, was inevitably transformed by the establishment of the theocratic state in Hanzhong, which would have had direct access to only three parishes. Zhang Lu's surrender to Cao Cao and the transfer of the Zhang family and other cult leaders to Ye must have presented new obstacles to the maintenance of cult functions. A later passage in the same document speaks of organizational difficulties:

> Ever since 231, the various officers have all appointed themselves. Appointments no longer derive from selection and promotion by the Five Pneumas, True Pneumas and Controller of Gods.[66] Sometimes they listen to the Determiner of Pneumas[67] and believe the shadowy dreams of their wives. Some employ whoever is memorialized. Some have no choice and do not follow the old ceremonies. Accepting gifts of faith, they make special explanations. Sometimes there are redundant officials for one position. Sometimes an office or parish goes unfilled.[68]

It would seem that even after the removal of Zhang Lu and his colleagues in 215 the church continued to function along traditional lines but that central control broke down in succeeding decades. It is unclear why 231 was a pivotal year in this process. There is little evidence of central direction to the sect in fourth-century southeast China, where we next find evidence for it, but it did survive and flourish, gaining converts at all levels of society. This continuity is probably to be attributed to the master-disciple relationship through which registers were conferred and scriptures transmitted from one generation to the next.

Although by the latter half of the third century Celestial Master Daoism had spread far beyond the Sichuan-Shaanxi region of its birth, that area remained a dynamic breeding ground for religious movements. Chen Rui 陳瑞 led such a movement in southwestern Sichuan:[69]

66. Of these three offices I have found only the Controller of Gods, who is said to have been "in charge of selecting worthy and virtuous and demoting the false and ugly." See *Sandong zhunang* 7/18a–b.

67. The implication here would seem to be that the appointment was made solely on the basis of a spirit communication verified by the Director of Pneumas, rather than through standard bureaucratic channels.

68. *Zhengyi fawen Tianshi jiaojie kejing* (HY 788): 17a. The sense of several of these phrases is problematic and my interpretations somewhat speculative, but the general import of the passage concerning irregularities in appointments is clear.

69. HYGZ 8/105.3–7.

In the spring of 277 the Governor [of Yi Province] Wang Jun 王
濬 executed Chen Rui, a man of Qianwei (modern Yibin,
Sichuan). Rui had at first used the Way of Demons to beguile
the masses. In his Way one first sacrificed a ladle of wine and a
fish and worshiped no other god. They esteemed freshness and
cleanliness. Those who had experienced a death, mourning, a
birth or nursing were not permitted to visit the Daoist parish
for one hundred days. Those who served as their masters (*shi*
師) were called Libationers. During mourning for a father,
mother, wife, or son, they were not permitted to rub the casket
or enter and mourn or to ask after one nursing or ill. Rui gradually became more extravagant. He made a vermilion robe, an
undyed belt, and vermilion turban and was presented with a
worthy's cap. He styled himself Celestial Master. His followers
numbered in the thousands. Jun heard of this and considered it
unfilial. He executed Rui and the Libationer Yuan Xing and
others and burned their hostels and lodges.

Chen Rui's movement was clearly inspired by the Celestial Masters
and was probably a direct offshoot of the movement. The emphasis
on ritual purity is not found, or at least not recorded, among the
Celestial Masters.

DAOISM AND THE CHENG-HAN STATE

The Daoist faith was an important factor in the fate of the Lis and
their state. The mass of refugees that entered first Hanzhong then
Sichuan at the beginning of the fourth century must have included
a sizable number of Daoists, people who had been transferred to the
Chang'an region and points west at the fall of Zhang Lu's kingdom.
The Lis gained the allegiance of these migrants by practicing along
the way the charity and magnanimity that their religion demanded.
Their motivation to offer a helping hand to coreligionists would
have been particularly strong, but there is no reason to think that
they limited their efforts to fellow Daoists. We cannot be sure why
the refugees decided to first move to the Hanzhong region, but since
there are more direct routes from Gansu into Sichuan, this choice
may well have had religious motivations, a yearning for the utopian
community of old.

Once the migrants entered Sichuan, they were repeatedly aided by
men with Daoist ties. The first person to actively assist the refugees
was Zhao Xin, the Governor of Yi Province. Xin, like Li Te, was
originally from Baxi commandery (though a different county), and

like Li Te, his grandfather had also been a member of Zhang Lu's Hanzhong community. The Zhaos, rather than moving to the northwest, followed Zhang Lu to the northeast, eventually settling in the state of Zhao, due north of Ye. There Xin came to the attention of Sima Lun 司馬倫, King of Zhao, who appointed him to a succession of posts. There may be a Daoist connection here, as well, because Sun Xiu 孫秀, Sima Lun's closest adviser, was also from a hereditary Daoist household.[70]

Faced with hundreds of thousands of starving refugees, Zhao Xin opened the provincial granaries to feed them. Perhaps any worthy Confucian official would have done the same—it is precisely what the imperial emissary Li Bi had intended when he suggested that the refugees be permitted to proceed to Sichuan and its "stockpiled reserves of grain"—but no one did. In fact, another official, Geng Teng 耿滕, complained about the "empty granaries" in reporting on Xin's intentions. Xin also had Li Xiang organize a militia from among the refugees and sent him to repress a Qiang rebellion.[71] Chang Qu, followed by later sources, sees in these actions by Xin an intention to revolt and consequently interprets his aid to the refugees as a quest for allies in sedition.[72] Ren Naiqiang rightly points out that Xin was following a central government directive, but Ren is, in my opinion, too quick to dismiss religious ties as a reason for the ready alliance struck up between Xin and the Lis.[73] Similarly, Chang Qu's assertion that Xin turned against Li Xiang because of his ethnic identity is not wholly convincing.

It is sometimes claimed that Li Te had from the beginning the intention to declare himself independent and contest for the empire.[74] His statement upon entering Sword Gate Pass about the defensibility

70. Tang Changru 1983b:221. According to Tang, when opposing forces were closing in on the capital, Sima Lun and Sun Xiu "prayed day and night" and "used spirit mediums to select the day of battle." He argues that this may in fact reflect Daoist practices. See ZZTJ 84:2657–2658.

71. Li Xiang is not explicitly named in connection with the suppression of this rebellion, but Yang Weili's argument that the honor conferred upon him for subduing the Qiang could only have been from this campaign of 298 is persuasive. See Yang Weili 1982:15, 99n23.

72. HYGZ 8/107.5. Cf. Yang Weili 1982:14.

73. See Ren 8/449n8 and note 6 to the translation below.

74. Liu Jiusheng (1986), on the basis of two popular ditties said to have circulated in Chengdu in 293, argues that Li Te had long planned to move into Sichuan and found a Daoist kingdom. The seeming occurrence in one of the rhymes of the name Li Te is suggestive, but Liu himself makes clear that the original context of these songs was probably a cult around a Sichuanese sage named Li A 李阿. Moreover, even if some connection with Li Te was intended

of the Sichuan region and especially the reference to the second ruler of the Shu-Han state (see below, p. 121) are taken as evidence for such a plan. This is not persuasive. Te was at the time a junior member of the family and hardly one to be plotting his own overlordship of west China. The statement was no doubt first recorded, if not fabricated, much later, when Li Xiong or his descendants ruled and looked back to Li Te as the valiant founder of their dynasty. Moreover, the tale might have been intended to demonstrate no more than Te's familiarity with history and with military strategy.

Whatever the intentions of the Lis at this time, there may well have been religious reasons for Zhao Xin to worry about his new compatriots. As discussed above, Sichuan had been an important focus of speculation and prophesy concerning the appearance of an avatar of Laozi bearing the surname Li, who would usher in cataclysms followed by a utopian world. Now confronted with a family of valiant, skilled, and well-educated Daoists surnamed Li and leading a huge host of followers, Zhao Xin, perhaps more than others unfamiliar with this religious background, had reason to fear them. Even if one of them was not truly the appointed savior, they could use these prophesies to gain support among both the refugees and the local population.

The murder of Li Xiang and a large number of his relatives (sources vary as to whether they were more than ten or more than thirty) did not succeed in removing the threat. On the contrary, Xin soon died at the refugees' hands, his independence having lasted only two months. Li Te's reign was also shortened by war, but Li Xiong, who eventually came to the throne, seems to have been an even more devout follower of Celestial Master Daoism.

The turning point in Li Xiong's battle for dominance in Sichuan against the new Governor, Luo Shang, was the aid of a Daoist holy man. Fan Changsheng 范長生, or Long-lived Fan, was originally from Fuling.[75] Other names associated with him were Yanjiu 延久 ("prolonged eternity") and Chongjiu 重九 ("nine-layered").[76] He is

---

by Chang Qu, it is unclear whether the songs can reliably be attributed to the year 293 or are the result of ex post facto mythologizing of Li Te, much like his reputed comments on entering Sword Gate discussed below. Further, the two rhymes are known only from citations and do not seem to occur in surviving editions of HYGZ.

75. Fan's ancestors, or Fan himself as a child, may have been among five thousand families moved from Fuling to Shu in 251. HYGZ 1/11.10.

76. HYGZ 9/120.5.

credited with the authorship of a commentary to the *Book of Changes* in ten scrolls, now long lost, under the name the Genius of Shu (*Shu-cai* 蜀才).[77] Fan had established an independent community of more than one thousand families from Fuling on the sacred Green Castle Mountain 青城山 northwest of Chengdu, later famous as the site of a paradaisical Cavern-Heaven where Daoist transcendents resided in subterranean, microcosmic splendor. Running a well-ordered community on religious principles remote from outside interference, Fan was able to produce an agricultural surplus when everyone else about him suffered famine. He resupplied Li Xiong's army just as it was about to lay siege to Luo Shang in Chengdu, thereby assuring his victory. A man of Fuling with a grudge against Luo Shang claimed to have a hand in winning Fan's support and was rewarded for it, but one consideration must surely have been a preference for supporting a coreligionist against the representative of the central government and its profane state cult.

After defeating Luo Shang and gaining control of all Sichuan, Li Xiong expressed his gratitude and reverence for the elderly recluse by first offering him the throne. Fan declined, citing his calculation that cosmic forces favored a state established by someone surnamed Li in 304, the first year of a new sexagesimal cycle.[78] A pro forma refusal to accept an honor or high position is common in the Chinese tradition, but Xiong seems to have been genuinely troubled by his moral qualifications for the throne. For a time he left the government in the hands of his cousins, sons of his immediate predecessor as head of the family, Li Liu. This was surely a reflection of the concept of sinfulness that was at the core of most of the religious movements of the day.

77. *Yanshi jiaxun huizhu*, "Shuzheng" 書證, 17/98b; Zhang Zongyuan 1936:23c–24a, 4/5061–5062; 429a, 4/5467. These commentaries seem to have disappeared in Song times, but there are at least three reconstructions of the *Changes* text, one by Ma Guohan. Fan's commentary is said to have followed, in main, the interpretations of Zheng Xuan 鄭玄 (127–200) and Yu Fan 虞翻 (167–233).

78. Chinese years are reckoned according to series of pairs drawn from ten Heavenly Stems and twelve Earthly Branches, yielding a full set of sixty. Each stem and branch is correlated with one of the Five Phases 五行, as are the directions, seasons, dynasties, and surnames. It is not stated how Fan arrived at this conclusion that the Li family should rule, but his calculations were probably similar to those made by the diviner Wang Kuang 王況 for a man surnamed Li in 21 C.E.: "Li is associated with the musical note *zhi* 徵 and *zhi* is associated with fire. You shall become the coadjutor of the Han dynasty." Adapted from Seidel 1969–70:218. Cf. Dubs 1938–1955:3, 408.

When Li Xiong did finally consent to ascend the throne as emperor in 306, he insisted on personally ushering Fan into the capital while attending him as if one of his subordinates. Fan was appointed Chancellor, at least nominally the head of government, and was awarded the designation Worthy Fan 范賢. Fan, in return, urged Xiong to take the final step and declare himself Emperor, putting himself in direct conflict with the Jin dynasty. This time Fan received a special title: Grand Preceptor of the Four Seasons, Eight Nodes, and Heaven and Earth. Preceptor or Master (*shi* 師) was a term shared by most religious leaders of the day. Zhang Daoling had been Celestial Master, and Chen Rui had claimed this title as well. Zhang Heng may have been called Celestial Master while alive, but to history he was the Inheriting Master (*sishi* 嗣師), just as Zhang Lu was Connecting Master (*xishi* 系師); Lu was commonly addressed simply as Lord Master (*shijun* 師君). Zhang Jiao, leader of the Yellow Turbans in the East, was Great Worthy and Good Master (*daxianliangshi* 大賢良師). All these titles seem related to that of Master or Preceptor of State (*guoshi* 國師) assumed by the Celestial Master in his relationship to Cao Cao.[79] Moreover, the name of the state, Cheng or Great Cheng 大成, also had utopian significance; it derives from the venerable *Book of Poetry* but was used by the Han Emperor Huan in 150 to express his own resolve to reach the sort of ideal state that rebels of the day were promoting.[80]

There are also indications that Daoist principles informed the administration of the Cheng-Han state, particularly during the rule of Li Xiong. The early Celestial Masters instituted a variety of social reforms, including a liberalized legal system, free food for the needy, a system for assuring equitable prices in the marketplaces, and equal treatment of Chinese and non-Chinese peoples. Li Te is said to have "given the people a simplified legal code (*yuefa* 約法) in three articles, granted amnesties on debts and provided emergency loans, paid courtesy calls on worthies, and transferred those on stalled career paths." To Li Xiong is attributed an abridged legal code in seven articles, leniency in using punishments and magnanimity of spirit in pardoning, among others, the killers of his mother. He also reduced taxes, established schools, and avoided warfare when possible, with the result that "The village gates were not closed and no one picked

79. Seidel 1969:82–84; *Zhengyi fawen Tianshi jiaojie kejing* (HY 788):18a.
80. Seidel 1969–70: 219; HHS 7/295; *Shijing* (H-Y Index ed.) 39/179/8. The note by Zheng Xuan, quoted at HHS 7/296n2, specifically links Great Cheng or Great Perfection to "the bringing about of Great Peace."

up lost articles on the highways. There was no one who rotted in prison and punishments were not employed indiscriminately."[81] Stein has cited as an example of Daoist influence the pact between Li Xiong and Li Li to alternate as ruler every three years and the many taboos that Li Xiong observed in burying his mother.[82] Liu Jiusheng sees evidence of Daoist prophesies concerning Li Te in several popular prophesies preserved in the *Record of the Land of Huayang*.[83]

Chang Qu was a member of the native Sichuanese aristocracy that for centuries had resolutely suppressed rebellions by both messianic religious leaders and indigenous peoples. Moreover, although he was an official of the Cheng-Han state, the *Record of the Land of Huayang* was revised and published after the fall of the state under the watchful eyes of the Jin court. As a consequence, we see little in his record of the religious faith of the Cheng rulers or the role it must have played in policy formulation and the creation of alliances, just as we are never informed of the role the ruling family's ethnic identity and ancestral origin must have had in gathering allies among indigenous peoples and men of Baxi. Indeed, after his appointment to the supreme post of Chancellor, we are told nothing about Fan Changsheng. Chang records only those events that are of such political significance that they cannot be ignored.

Still, there is an indication of the continuing importance of the Daoist faith and of the Fan family in the historical record. The *Book of Jin* notes that in a final gasp of independence after years of incompetent rule by Li Shou and Li Shi[a], the generals left in charge by the conquering Huan Wen immediately rebelled.[84] They chose to put on the throne as emperor Fan Changsheng's son, Fan Ben 范賁. Their rebellion was short-lived, but the dream of a utopian Daoist kingdom never died.[85]

81. HYGZ 9/121; cf. JS 121/3040.

82. R. A. Stein 1963:33–34. This practice of sharing rule is found in a description of a foreign state that Stein argues convincingly reflects Daoist utopian ideals, but there is no evidence for alternating leadership among the Celestial Masters. It is also unclear if the "shamans" who advised Xiong on the burial were Daoist priests, but the likelihood here seems high.

83. Liu Jiusheng 1986. The material Liu cites is intriguing but subject to other possible interpretations. At the least, it reflects expectations in Sichuan at the time of the appearance of a religious leader with the surname Li.

84. JS 98/1569, 8/193–195. See below, p. 207 n. 19.

85. Tang Changru 1983a records ten examples of later rebellions in the name of Li Hong and also discusses prophesies of a savior surnamed Li in Daoist scriptures. See also Mollier 1990.

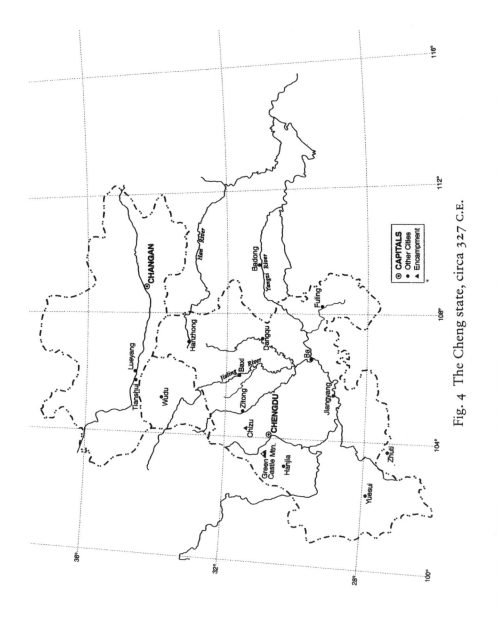

Fig. 4 The Cheng state, circa 327 C.E.

THREE

History

Ethnicity and religion were important factors in the formation, administration, and eventual defeat of the Cheng-Han kingdom, but the unique historical circumstances of fourth-century China are also vital to a proper understanding of this state. The historical experience of the Li family and the other refugees had its roots in the societal, political, and economic organization of the day, as well as the play of events in other parts of China. This chapter will contextualize the historical account of Cheng-Han in the translation below through an examination of the nature of fourth-century Chinese society and the relationship of Cheng-Han history to external political developments.[1]

By the fourth century, the Qin and Han administrative ideal of direct control of an undifferentiated, universally registered local populace through impartially chosen, centrally appointed representatives who extracted taxes and corvée labor was largely dead. Moreover, the ancient local societies that Ebrey has characterized as "relatively closed, often clan-based, socially and economically homogeneous village communities" had been rent by the economic and political changes of the Han empire.[2] When centralized government control weakened, first at the end of the Former Han, then increasingly during the latter half of the Latter Han, new modes of organization arose. The religious communities of the second century C.E. were one type of response to the need for new local structures; their function

1. The primary source for this chapter is the surviving record of the state of Cheng-Han, translated and annotated below. Other sources are the "Annals" of the *Book of Jin,* the relevant chapters of ZZTJ, and Yang Weili 1982. Below I will give characters and annotation only for matters not discussed in the annotations to relevant portions of the translation.

2. Patricia Ebrey, "The Economic and Social History of Later Han," in Twitchett and Loewe 1986: 626.

in replacing the lowest level of local administration is often noted in the historical record.

The dominant new form of social organization, however, was the local strongman or magnate. At the center of this structure was an extended family of several generations, referred to as a "great surname" (*daxing* 大姓) or "aristocratic clan" (*haozu* 豪族), that owned land, dominated the local economy, and often educated some of its sons in preparation for government service. Around this nucleus formed a large group of non-kin households who were in some sense dependent upon the great family, some as slaves, servants or tenants, but others with less formal, mutually beneficial ties of patronage and protection. From these dependents, sometimes numbering into the thousands of households, the great family was able to organize a private army or militia (*buqu* 部曲, sometimes referred to as "family soldiers," or *jiabing* 家兵). These militias were of considerable importance at the end of the Han and throughout the Period of Disunion; "official" titles like Inspector of Militias (*buqudu* 部曲督) are an attempt to grant legitimacy to the temporary assimilation of one of these private militias into governmental forces.[3]

The prevalence of militias in the history of the Period of Disunion was in part the result of large-scale population movements. The breakdown of centralized control magnified the consequences of both rebellions and natural disasters, leading large numbers to leave their homes in search of food and security. Militias formed to protect local communities against the external threats of marauding non-Chinese and desperate refugees, but when these communities were themselves overrun and forced to flee, the magnates and their militias migrated as communities of hundreds and thousands, some as big as cities, forcing in their turn the militarization and often migration of the population in areas to which they moved. This was particularly true of the early fourth century, a period when Xiang Da has estimated that two million people migrated internally, but private militias played a significant role in the period leading up to this time of strife as well.

The political and military confusion at the end of the Han dynasty facilitated the creation of regional power bases independent of the court and central government. The Daoist state of the Celestial

3. On militias, see Yang Zhongyi 1956; Tang 1990; Ch'ü 1972:132–133, 503n458. The term originally referred to military units ("division and squad") but came by the Tang to indicate a distinct social status between that of slave and commoner.

Masters was one of these newly independent centers of power, one with a special significance for the development of Chinese religion and for the Cheng-Han state. Even here the community was composed, at least in part, of local magnates and their dependents, as evidenced by the presence among them of Ba "kings" and men like Li Te's grandfather, Li Hu, who led a group of five hundred families. Other new centers, each with one local magnate at its center, were less rooted in ideology but were similar in their struggles to establish defensible borders and win legitimacy from their neighbors. Eventually these regional forces coalesced into three states, the Wei 魏 ruled by the Cao 曹 family in the north, the Shu 蜀 or Han 漢 state of Liu Bei 劉備 in the southwest, and the Wu 吳 state of Sun Quan 孫權 and his heirs in the southeast. Zhang Lu had cast his fate with the Caos and thereby ensured the diffusion of his new religion throughout north China, but Liu Bei maintained control of most of Sichuan.

The Cao family, with their eunuch origins, were administrative innovators who favored a strong central government. Their effective grasp on power, however, was short-lived. The General Sima Yiᵃ 司馬懿 (179–251), together with his sons and grandson, gradually usurped power; by 249 they effectively controlled the Wei state. Coming from the class of local magnates, they were unhappy with many of the Wei innovations. When Yi's grandson, Sima Yan 司馬炎, usurped the throne as Emperor Wu of Jin (r. 265–290), he proceeded to refeudalize the state by enfeoffing imperial princes as kings controlling powerful regions of the Jin state. His reign was peaceful and saw the reunification of the southeast into the Jin state in 280, but after his death the folly of radically decentralizing power became evident.

The 290s was a turbulent decade during which external threats from non-Chinese ethnic groups exacerbated rifts among the contending princes. The sixteen years from 291 to 306 are commonly referred to as the Disorders of the Eight Kings 八王之亂. Altogether twenty-seven members of the Sima lineage had been enfeoffed by Sima Yan, but the primary players at this time were Sima Liang, King of Runan 汝南王司馬亮; Sima Lun, King of Zhao 趙王司馬倫; Sima Yong, King of Hejian 河間王司馬顒; Sima Ying, King of Chengdu 成都王司馬穎; Sima Yi, King of Changsha 長沙王司馬乂; Sima Jiong, King of Qi 齊王司馬冏; Sima Wei, King of Chu 楚王司馬瑋; and Sima Yue, King of Donghai 東海王司馬越. Emperor Hui 惠帝, who occupied the throne throughout this period, was a weak and ineffectual ruler, often characterized as an idiot, but the court exercised a strong influence on the country during the 290s through his consort, Empress Jia 賈后 (Jia Nanfeng 賈南鳳, 256–300), who was the effective ruler of the state. In 291 she disposed of Sima Liang and Sima Wei. There was intense jockeying for power, but open warfare among the remaining six broke out only after she had left the scene.

Although the 290s did not see the sort of fratricidal warfare that characterized the following decade, it was not a peaceful age. The level of tension is reflected in an incident of 295. When the state armory caught fire, the Junior Tutor Zhang Hua 張華 feared that it was the beginning of a coup d'état; he insisted on immediately marshaling the troops and manning the defenses, thereby permitting the armory to burn, together with countless state treasures and arms sufficient to outfit two million soldiers.[4]

It was an especially unsettled time for those on the borders of the state. The Guanzhong region (southern Shaanxi province) was considered of key importance because of its strategic location, natural defenses, and historical significance. The Jin state, wary of entrusting this area to potential rivals, turned repeatedly to members of the royal house. From 291 on, Sima Lun, King of Zhao, was made Great General Quelling the West and Inspector-General for Military Affairs of Yong and Liang[a] provinces, and when in 296 he was transferred for stirring up the area, he was replaced by Sima Tong 司馬彤, King of Liang. These royal princes did not depend upon achievements for their positions and were not accountable to the central government.[5]

In 294 the Xiongnu He San 郝散 rebelled, attacking Shangdang commandery (northwest of Lucheng, Shanxi) and killing the Grand Warden. When, after crossing into the Guanzhong area (Shaanxi), he surrendered three months later, the Defender of Fengyi 馮翊 (modern Dali, Shaanxi) killed him. Two years later, in 296, He San's

4. Zhang Hua (234–300), cognomen Maoxian 茂先, was instrumental in the conquest of Wu in 280 and was a reliable senior minister providing continuity with the former court throughout the 290s. Zhang had opposed Sima Lun and in 300 died at his command. He is best known for his *Bowuzhi* 博物志, a record of anomalies, supernatural occurrences, and arcane facts in ten chapters. See *Jinshu* 36/1068–1077, esp. 1073–1074. The Junior Tutor was an irregularly appointed but extremely prestigious post as advisor to the Emperor. See Hucker 1985:entry 5097.

5. The Prefect of the Palace Secretariat Chen Zhun 陳準 made exactly this point about Sima Tong in recommending the appointment of Zhou Chu to the region in 296. ZZTJ 82/2616.

younger brother He Duyuan 郝度元 led the Qiang of Beidi 北地 (modern Yaoxian, Shaanxi), Fengyi, and Malan 馬蘭 (a mountain northwest of Baishui, Shaanxi) as well as unspecified Central Asians (*hu* 胡) from Lushui 盧水 (near modern Jingchuan, Gansu) in rebellion, killing the Grand Warden of Beidi commandery, repeatedly defeating the Grand Warden of Fengyi, and eventually overcoming the Governor of Yong Province.

Inspired by He Duyuan's victories, angered by Sima Lun's execution of dozens of Qiang chieftains, and perhaps seeking to take advantage of the recent replacement of Sima Lun by Sima Tong as General Quelling the West, the Di and Qiang of Qin and Yong provinces all arose, taking the Di chieftain Qi Wannian 齊萬年 as their leader.[6] Zhao Xin was at this time appointed Governor of Yi Province and ordered to send troops from Liang and Yi provinces to aid in suppressing the rebellion.[7] The court initially dispatched Zhou Chu 周處 to quell the rebellion, but in 297 Zhou was forced to confront a host of seventy thousand with only five thousand troops, was not reinforced by local officials, and was soon killed.[8] Meng Guan 孟觀 finally captured Qi Wannian in the first month of 299. The growing threat from non-Chinese peoples led Jiang Tong 江統 in 299 to propose the radical solution of forced transfer of non-Chinese peoples away from the borders in his famous "Argument for the Transfer of the Barbarians" ("*Xirong lun*" 徙戎論).[9]

The two years of Qi Wannian's rebellion were devastating. In 296 a famine and epidemic were reported in the Guanzhong region, and in the summer of 297 there was a great drought as well as continuing epidemic disease that raised the price of grain to ten thousand cash per bushel. Warfare, disease, famine, and drought combined to make large parts of the Shaanxi-Gansu area unlivable. One part of the populace moved southwest to Chouchi 仇池 (west of modern Chengxian, Gansu), where they took refuge under the Di leader Yang Maosou 楊茂搜.[10] A larger group moved to the southeast,

6. Sima Lun's executions are recorded only in an "Appreciation of Jin Lords" ("*Jin zhugong zan*" 晉諸公賛). See Yang Weili 1982:98n17.

7. ZZTJ 82/2617. The exact timing of this appointment is unclear.

8. Zhou Chu (240–299), the son of a famous general of the state of Wu, had a reputation for uprightness and integrity. As head of the Censorate, he had once indicted Sima Tong, earning his undying enmity. See JS 58/1569–1571.

9. JS 56/1529–1534. Jiang's primary concern was the Qiang and Di peoples living in the Guangzhong area.

10. ZZTJ 82/2617. Yang Maosou, whose native surname was Linghu 令狐, was the adopted son of his uncle Feilong 飛龍, who had held the office of General

entering the Hanzhong region. This group, numbering more than two hundred thousand, was headed by the Li family.

The local residents and officials of Hanzhong did not welcome this body of refugees. Their complaints brought a central government directive that the refugees be directed back to their places of origin, and an official was sent to enforce this decree. Whether through bribery or moral suasion (sources differ), this representative was won over and was able to convince the central government to permit the refugees to move on into Sichuan. There again local elites and officials sympathetic to them protested strongly the presence of the refugees. The Governor of Liang Province, Zhao Xin, for reasons of simple charity, common religious faith, and perhaps common ethnicity, extended aid to them and incorporated militia drawn from the refugees in his campaigns to put down local rebels.

All of this was occurring against the backdrop of considerable turmoil in the central government. Sima Lun, deprived of his army in Guanzhong in 296, had sought the post of Overseer of the Affairs of the Imperial Secretariat, only to be denied it due to the protests of Zhang Hua and Pei Wei 裴頠.[11] Emperor Hui being of limited mental capabilities, Empress Jia, together with her relatives and affines, was able to control the court. In 299 they began a concerted effort to depose the heir apparent and replace him with a more malleable, younger candidate. Eventually the Empress was able to get him drunk enough to write an incriminating letter that convinced the Emperor to depose him. Sima Lun, who now commanded the Army of the Right, first joined in a plot to overthrow Empress Jia, then leaked word of the plot to members of her party so that she would kill the former heir apparent, and finally used her action as justification for moving against her and her clique. In the fourth month of 300, in league with Sima Jiong, King of Qi, he entered the palace at the head of a body of troops and proceeded to behead the Empress, her relatives, affines, and supporters, in most cases executing all family members of each individual within three generations (i.e., all who shared the same

Pacifying the West under the first Jin Emperor. Maosou declared himself General Supporting the State (*fuguo jiangjun* 輔國將軍) and Worthy King of the Right. He seems to have been generally recognized among the Di as their leader, and Emperor Min (r. 313–317) eventually confirmed him in the position of General of Doughty Cavalry. See WS 101:2227–2228; Taniguchi 1976.

11. Pei Wei (267–300), from a renowned scholarly family, was famous as a conservative defender of traditional morality and author of the "Argument for Exalting Being" ("*Chongyoulun*" 崇有論). See JS 35/1041–1047.

grandfather, their wives, and children). Lun forged a rescript declaring himself Commissioner Bearing Credentials, Inspector-General for Internal and External Military Affairs, Minister of State, and Palace Attendant, modeling himself in this on the positions his father, Sima Yi, and elder brother, Sima Zhao, had held under the Wei dynasty when they controlled the government.

Zhao Xin had been promoted by Sima Lun but was related by marriage to Empress Jia. When, in the eleventh month of this tumultuous year 300, he was summoned back to the court to serve in a post in the Empress' retinue, he believed it a stratagem to eliminate him. The Seneschal of the kingdom of Chengdu, Geng Teng, who had been appointed to replace Zhao Xin, tried to enter the provincial capital but was killed. After the Colonel of the Western Barbarians, who controlled a key military force, had also been killed, Xin assumed the titles of Great General, Great Inspector-General, and Pastor of Yi Province. Li Xiang initially assembled a force of four thousand cavalry from among the refugees and eventually gathered more than ten thousand to fight for Zhao Xin. Xin dispatched them to block the northern road to Chang'an, whence Jin troops were likely to come.

Shortly thereafter, either at the end of 300 or the beginning of 301, Zhao Xin turned on Li Xiang and killed him together with more than ten (according to one source, thirty) of his sons, nephews, and so forth. The recorded story is that Xin's advisors urged Xin to act against Xiang because of the unreliability of non-Chinese allies. The pretext for Xiang's execution was his suggestion that Zhao Xin take to himself the title of Emperor. It is likely, therefore, that the event occurred in the first month of 301, after Sima Lun had formally deposed Emperor Hui and elevated himself to that position, further eroding the legitimacy of the Jin royal house. Li Te and Li Liu led their militia to encamp at Mianzhu. Xin sent a force of ten thousand to camp in the same area. When the Lis had gathered together a sizable force, they assaulted the camp by night and burned it, then moved on to Chengdu. Xin fled but was captured and killed, and the Lis sent an emissary to Luoyang to explain the situation.

The court named the Governor of Liang Province, Luo Shang, to replace Zhao Xin, with the titles General Quelling the West and Governor of Yi Province. As Luo entered Sichuan with a complement of centrally appointed local officials and seven thousand troops, Li Xiang[a] greeted them with rich gifts and Li Te entertained them with a sumptuous banquet. One in this retinue, the new Grand Warden of Guanghan Xin Ran 辛冉, was a confederate of Sun Xiu and an old enemy of Li Te, presumably from the period when Sima Lun was controlling military affairs in the Guanzhong area.[12]

Events were moving quickly in central China. Sima Jiong led several of the other kings in an attack on the usurper, Sima Lun. In the fourth month of 301 they took the capital and killed Lun, Sun Xiu, and all their henchmen. The sixty days of battle had left more than one hundred thousand dead. Sima Jiong made himself Grand Marshal and the effective regent, dispensing important positions to the other kings. Sima Ying, King of Chengdu, had played a key role in the attack on the capital but, fearing to share the regency with Jiong, withdrew to his base at Ye. After an abortive plot against Jiong in the eighth month, Jiong's position seems to have stabilized until the end of 302, but plotting continued, especially after the fifth month of 302, when he established an eight-year-old child as Heir Apparent with himself as Grand Tutor.

During 301 the central government took a number of actions that influenced the refugees. Two Censors were dispatched with tallies of authority to order their return to Qin and Yong provinces (Shaanxi-Gansu). Li Te acted as spokesman for the refugees, first requesting a stay until autumn, then until the following winter, reinforcing his requests with substantial bribes. At the same time, Li Te and Li Liu were appointed generals and other refugees were supposed to receive rewards for their roles in the defeat of Zhao Xin.

Xin Ran, who feared punishment for his former ties to Sima Lun and Sun Xiu, encouraged Luo Shang to expel the refugees without delay and also secreted the imperial rescript so that they did not receive their proper rewards. As the year progressed, he set up barriers on the major roads and waterways, planning to seize the possessions of the refugees. Xin Ran had wanted posters distributed that offered a rich reward for the death of the Lis. The Lis gathered the posters in their area and altered them to include among the wanted many of the most prominent refugee families as well as the Di and Sou leaders in the group. This solidified their support among the other refugees, resulting in a force of more than twenty thousand men. Troops dispatched by Xin Ran and Luo Shang to attack their camps were ambushed and routed.

This victory encouraged Li Te to declare independence. He assumed the titles of Great General Stabilizing the North and Great Inspector-

12. JS 36/1073 records an occasion in 296 when Xin Ran vouched for the conduct of his old friend Sun Xiu in Guanzhong. Xin was eventually killed by Liu Hong for political plotting. See JS 66/1766.

General and appointed family members and allies to suitable positions. He also instituted a legal reform, proclaimed an amnesty on debts, and took other actions to win the support of the populace. Luo Shang, having retreated to Chengdu, ordered that palisades be erected along a long stretch of the west bank of the Pi River and requested help from neighboring Ning and Liang provinces.

In the fifth month of 302 the central government launched a major assault against the refugees. Sima Yong, King of Hejian, sent Ya Bo 衙博 to attack from the northeast, and the court appointed a new Grand Warden of Guanghan, Zhang Zheng 張徵,[13] who encamped to the southeast. Luo Shang then sent a force under Zhang Gui 張龜 to attack from the southwest. Ya Bo was easily defeated and driven out of the area, his entire army surrendering. Zhang Zheng nearly succeeded in capturing Li Te's army in a narrow mountain defile, but a valorous attack by Te's son broke through the encirclement, and Zhang Zheng was eventually captured and killed. Zhang Gui's force seems to have been repulsed relatively easily. Li Xiang[a] and Li Liu advanced to attack Chengdu, burning one of the city gates. The new Governor of Liang Province repeatedly sent armies down from Hanzhong, but each time they were defeated.

In the eighth month Li Te's rebellion expanded dramatically when local leaders from Guizhou and eastern Yunnan arose in response, driving out the Jin-appointed Grand Wardens. Although they constituted large forces, numbering in the tens of thousands, these troops seem to have been poorly trained or led. In any case, they were quickly routed by Li Yi 李毅, the Colonel of the Southern Barbarians. As a result, Jin was able to reestablish Ning province, making Li Yi its Governor. In subsequent years this area was repeatedly the object of contention between Cheng and Jin forces. Li Yi subsequently sent Sou troops to aid Luo Shang, but they were repulsed.

Dissension among the Jin princes seems to have thwarted another central government campaign against Li Te. The Overseer of the Army Liu Chen 劉沈 was dispatched to attack the rebels but was waylaid by Sima Yong, King of Hejian, who controlled the Guanzhong area.[14] Yong was at the time planning an attack on Sima Jiong

13. ZZTJ and some editions of HYGZ give Zhang Wei. See the annotation to the translation, p. 127 n. 47.

14. The date of this campaign is problematic. ZZTJ places it in the third month of 303, but Chen's biography (JS 89/2306) makes it clear that he owed his appointment to Sima Jiong, hence he could not have been dispatched after Jiong's fall at the end of 302.

and no doubt was delighted to have the reinforcements. He assembled a force of one hundred thousand and marched on the capital, calling upon Sima Ying, Sima Xin, and especially Sima Yi, who was in the capital to depose Jiong and hand over the regency to Sima Ying, who had earlier won popular support by refusing a coregency and providing for the dead of the recent campaign to eliminate Sima Lun. As soon as word of this reached the capital, Sima Yi acted, capturing and beheading Sima Jiong. Power then devolved upon Sima Ying, who remained in his base at Ye.

In the first month of 303 Li Te moved on Luo Shang's marine forces. Advancing on Chengdu, Te took the smaller walled city. Shang barricaded himself in the larger city and sued for peace. The various fortified villages of the area submitted, and Te dispatched small forces to each but refused to take hostages. Shang then secretly contacted village leaders and arranged for a coordinated uprising on a specified day of the second month. At this time the court sent the Governor of Jing Province up from the south with a marine force of thirty thousand, and Te was forced to dispatch a sizable contingent to repel them. The concerted attack of Luo Shang and the villagers caught Te unaware. After a series of battles, Te was defeated, captured, and beheaded. Li Liu assumed his titles as Great General, Great Inspector-General, and Pastor of Yi Province.

Over the next two months, Luo Shang pressed the attack. He sent his troops from the south in a two-pronged attack that was joined by a force of commoners from Fu (modern Mianyang) to the northeast. In the midst of a concerted attack on the main encampment while two major contingents were away fighting elsewhere, the Di tribesmen within the camp turned on the Lis. Even the widow of Li Te donned armor to repel them and lost an eye in the process, but the field armies returned in the nick of time to avoid disaster. By the fifth month, Li Liu was ready to surrender and sent hostages to Sun Fu, who commanded the vanguard of the Jing provincial forces. Li Xiong convinced the refugees to mount a surprise attack on Sun Fu's camp, which succeeded. From this time on, Li Xiong became the effective leader of the refugees. Shortly thereafter the Governor of Jing Province died of illness and his troops withdrew.

The government's response to this setback was a general mobilization of the adult male populace of the Hubei-Hunan region to suppress the Lis; these men came to be known from the date of the imperial rescript as the *Renwu* (day nineteen of the sexagesimal cycle, i.e., June 10, 303) soldiers. The exactions of the local officials in assembling and supplying this force aroused great popular discontent. A Man-barbarian leader named named Zhang Chang 張昌 changed his name to Li Chen 李辰 and set up a minor official, whose name he changed to Liu Ni 劉尼, as Son of Heaven of the Han empire.[15] In this he was clearly appealing to widespread prophesies of the restoration of the Han dynasty and the Liu royal house through a coadjutor surnamed Li. Within two months, Zhang controlled most or all of five provinces, comprising the middle and lower Yangzi basin, the Huai River basin, and most of the Han River basin.

The government was further distracted from the campaign against Sichuan by the return of internecine warfare. In the eighth month Sima Yong, based in Guanzhong, and Sima Ying, based in Ye, mobilized troops and marched on the capital with the intention of removing Sima Yi from power. Their total forces approached three hundred thousand. Sima Ying's army initially met with defeat but eventually laid siege to the capital. In the first month of 304, Sima Yue led the palace guard to seize and imprison Sima Yi, who was later killed by a subordinate of Sima Ying. Ying was appointed Chancellor but returned to Ye, while Sima Yue became the Prefect of the Imperial Secretariat.

These rebellions and internal strife permitted Li Xiong to focus on Luo Shang and the conquest of Sichuan. In the seventh month, he took the walled city of Pi, on the west side of the river, but found it empty of stores. It is at this point that the Daoist leader Longlived Fan seems to have stepped in to reprovision the refugees' army.[16] In the ninth month, Li Liu died and Li Xiong formally acceded to the leadership of the refugee group, taking the same titles as Liu and Te. When Luo Shang sought to take advantage of this transition period to attack Xiong in Pi, Xiong used a ruse to lure his army to the gates of Pi, then sprang an ambush and, pursuing the retreating army, was able to retake the smaller walled city of Chengdu. After Li Xiang[a] cut off Shang's line of supply from the south, he was trapped without food in the larger city and soon absconded in the night. Xiong's army gained no stores by capturing the famished provincial capital. Such was the devastation of years of strife and

15. On the rebellion of Zhang Chang, see JS 100/2612–2614; Zhang Zexian and Zhu Dawei 1980:94–112; Ōfuchi 1991:494–495.

16. The exact date when Fan began to support the refugees' army is not recorded but can be inferred from reports of famine among the troops in the seventh month and the fact that they were able to fight spiritedly in the twelfth month. Cf. Yang Weili 1982:39.

interrupted agriculture that he was forced to lead his army to an area as yet untouched by war to dig wild taro. Luo Shang retreated to Jiangyang (modern Luzhou) and regrouped, having been assigned the revenue of three Eastern Sichuan commanderies to use in rebuilding his army. By the following winter, he moved to Jiangzhou, seat of Ba commandery, and from there was able to launch a raid on Li Xiong, capturing the wife and sons of Li Xiang[a].

Li Xiong now had uncontested control over the entire Chengdu plain, and his followers clamored for the trappings of a state. He first offered the state to the holy man Long-lived Fan, whose aid had been so pivotal in their victory. Although this may have been merely a symbolic act expressing gratitude or a calculated scheme to use the religious leader as a drawing card, much as Zhang Chang had used Liu Ni, Xiong's subsequent actions seem to indicate a genuine piety and reverence for the Daoist sage. Fan may have been more pragmatic in refusing the throne from this battle-scarred warrior; the leaders of the refugee group had been dying in rapid succession, and Fan was later offered the more secure position of Chancellor, the same post for which the Jin princes had been contesting so murderously in central China.

In the tenth month of the year 304, Li Xiong finally declared himself King of Chengdu and appointed a full complement of civil and military officers, with major posts other than the Chancellorship going almost exclusively to members of his family. There is no mention of Fan's actions as Chancellor, but the surviving record is one of generals and battles, not civil government. Li Xiong is credited with a number of reforms, including a simplification of the legal code, reductions in tax and corvée burdens, and the establishment of public schools, and these may well have been at the suggestion of Fan.

In the sixth month of 306, again at the urging of Long-lived Fan and others, Li Xiong took the imperial title, inaugurating the state of Great Perfection (Da Cheng 大成). He appointed Fan Great Master of Heaven and Earth and regularized the bureaucracy. Little is recorded about events in Sichuan during the nearly two years between Xiong's enthronement as King and his ascension to Emperor, except for a raid on Hanzhong at the end of 304. Presumably this was a period of recovery, when agriculture was resumed and stores built up. Luo Shang seems to have been unable to mount a significant offensive, and the central government was kept busy with developments in other parts of China.

The millenarian movement of Zhang Chang had been broken in late 303, but one of his subordinates continued to disrupt the lower Yangzi region well into 304, and Zhang Chang himself was not finally captured until the eighth month of that year. At court, Sima Ying had compromised his reputation for integrity by having the Heir Apparent deposed and himself appointed Younger Brother Apparent (*taidi* 太弟) in the third month. This led to an unsuccessful campaign against him by Sima Yue in the seventh month, in the course of which the Emperor himself was injured. Then in the eleventh month, Sima Ying's senior general abducted both him and the Emperor, taking them to Chang'an. Shortly thereafter Ying was stripped of his Heir's position and sent back to his fief while Sima Yong assumed direction of the military.

Soon the state was forced to focus on a renewed threat from non-Chinese peoples of the north. In the eighth month of 304, Liu Yuan 劉淵, a highly sinicized ruler of the Xiongnu peoples who had been settled in northern Shanxi province at the beginning of the first century C.E., rebelled against the Jin, taking the traditional title of the supreme Xiongnu leader, Shanyu 單于.[17] In the tenth month, relying upon the imperial surname Liu, which his ancestors had appropriated on the basis of their descent from a Han royal princess, he made a broader claim to suzerainty over China itself by proclaiming himself first King, then Emperor, of a reestablished Han dynasty, tracing his lineage through the Shu-Han state of Liu Bei and Liu Shan 劉禪. A famine in 305 impeded the growth of this power somewhat, but by late 305 Liu Yuan had assembled a formidable force including other ethnic groups and advanced into southern Shanxi province.

Meanwhile, in the seventh month, Sima Yue began collecting support in the east to return Emperor Hui to Luoyang. When, in the eighth month of 305, the Governor of Yu 豫 Province (eastern Henan and northeastern Hubei) defied Sima Yue's commands, Sima Yong and Sima Ying rallied to his defense, guarding the bridge across the Yellow River. Yue was able to force the Yu provincial forces to retreat, then led Wuhuan and Xianbei troops in an attack on Sima Yong. At the same time, the general who had defeated Zhang Chang's followers in the southeast sought to establish himself independently in the area south of the Yangzi.

17. Honey 1990 provides a translation of Liu Yuan's biography (JS 101) and a detailed study of his life.

After rejecting a peace initiative from Sima Yong, Sima Yue dispatched Xianbei troops against his base in Chang'an. In the fifth month of 306 they captured Chang'an, where they went on a rampage, killing more than twenty thousand inhabitants. They escorted Emperor Hui back to Luoyang, where Sima Yue assumed control of the government, while Sima Yong and Sima Ying both fled. Ying was captured and killed in the eighth month, and three months later Emperor Hui was poisoned. Sima Yue lured Sima Yong to the capital with a high appointment, then had him assassinated, bringing the "Disorders of the Eight Kings" to a close.

The area south of the Yangzi was finally pacified in 307, but Liu Yuan continued to gather allies and enlarge his territory across Hebei and northern Henan. In the tenth month of 308 he declared himself Emperor. Finally in the spring of 309 he was strong enough to send an army against the capital, Luoyang, but it was repulsed, as was a second force sent in the tenth month of that year.

Li Xiong took advantage of the warfare in central and north China to expand his influence toward his northeast, in the key commandery of Hanzhong, a fertile, well-populated area that controlled communications between Sichuan and the north China plain to the east and the Guanzhong area to the north. At the end of 306 Li Li 李離, his Grand Commandant, was sent to raid the area, killing the military commander for the region. In the spring of 307 a group of refugees from Guanzhong rebelled in Hanzhong; when they were besieged by government troops, they bought time through bribes and sought aid from Li Xiong. It is possible that these rebels had ties to the Li family from the period when they were all still in the northwest. Li Xiong dispatched a force that released the siege and routed the government defenders. Because Cheng could not at this time devote the resources necessary to holding Hanzhong, they settled for raiding the area, carrying off as much of the population as possible to fill the void left in Sichuan by warfare and migration. A small force of Hanzhong locals subsequently reclaimed the Hanzhong capital, but it was many years before a sizable military contingent would be reestablished there.

To the south of Cheng, Li Xiong was aided by continuing unrest among the indigenous peoples, exacerbated by the death of the Colonel of the Southern Barbarians. Although there are conflicting accounts of the reasons for this rebellion, with the *Book of Jin* citing continuing famine and pestilence whereas the *Record of the Land of Huayang* focuses on the treatment of a surrendered local leader, and even as to the results of the rebellion, there can be little doubt that this unrest effectively precluded an attack from that quarter or the supply of reinforcements to Luo Shang.[18]

Luo Shang had in the interim rebuilt his army and renewed attack. In 307, from his base at Ba commandery (modern Chongqing), Shang advanced up the Yangzi, setting up fortifications on the lower reaches of both the Min and To rivers. At the same time, he sought to retain control over and draw upon the resources of refugees from the Sichuan region by establishing "guest" (qiao 僑) counties and commanderies for them in the east and south and appointing a Military Advisor to each who would organize from them military bands for the reconquest of Sichuan. In 309 Luo Shang was strengthened by a revolt in Zitong, on Cheng's northern border. The rebels killed Li Xiong's cousin, Li Li, and Yan Shi 閻式, a former Jin official and one of the original leaders of the refugees; defeating a Cheng force sent against them, they declared for Luo Shang. At the beginning of 310 Baxi commandery (modern Langzhong, to the northeast of Chengdu) also revolted and surrendered to Shang. Shang had sent a force to Anhan, south of Baxi on the Jialing River, and now sent a general further up the Min River to a point near modern Pengshan.

This encirclement from the south, east, and northeast marked the most serious threat to the Cheng state during Li Xiong's rule. Xiong sent a subordinate with allies within the walled city of Zitong to take it by subterfuge and personally led an expedition to rout Shang's force at Anhan. Soon thereafter, in the seventh month of 310, Luo Shang died and his successor was killed by Shang's subordinates, temporarily eliminating the threat from the southeast.[19] By the beginning

18. On the varying accounts of this series of events, see the translation, Li Xiong, note 30.

19. HYGZ records the death of the new Governor, Pi Su, in the twelfth month of 310 and attributes his death to two men from the northwest who had surrendered to Shang, but when the Defender of Jianping avenged this murder, he killed the son of Luo Shang as well. The dispute seems to have centered on the treatment of Qiao Deng, who had launched a private and quite successful campaign against Cheng but had alienated Luo Shang and company by his demands for support. It would seem that the Luos had made no attempt to rescue Qiao Deng when he was under attack from Li Xiang[a] and feared punishment from the new Governor. See HYGZ 8/115.9–14, 11/210, and the discussion in the translation below, notes 40–41 to the chapter on Li Xiong. Following Pi's death, local officials were left to appoint one of their own as his successor, indicating that communication with the central government had completely broken down. Moreover, this new Governor was forced to establish his headquarters far to the east, at Badong (modern Fengjie).

of 311, Cheng had retaken all of the area lost over the previous two years.[20] They then moved to the south, taking Qianwei and attacking Jiangyang.

The year 311 saw a general breakdown in central control throughout China. In central and south China, tensions between natives and refugees led to two major refugee uprisings. The first, beginning at the end of 310 in the Nanyang, Henan, area, was led by a man from the Chang'an region named Wang Ru 王如. He gathered a large force of refugees from the Guanzhong area who refused to obey central government directives that they return. His force, driven by famine, surrendered at the end of 312. Wei Wen and Fu Cheng, two Di leaders who had betrayed Li Xiong at a critical moment, initially joined with Wang Ru, then split off, raising their own insurrection on the middle Yangzi near modern Yicheng, Hubei. They moved up the Yangzi to Badong, where they killed the Grand Warden, plundered the city, and then, driving the entire population before them, headed west to surrender to Li Xiong, who welcomed them magnanimously.

Another remnant of Wang Ru's band made its way to Hanzhong in 313. In 311 the Governor of Liang Province had been able to reoccupy Hanzhong. Now he attacked these refugees, and both groups turned to the Di King Yang Maosou of Wudu for support in the battle. Yang, nursing old resentments, pretended to aid the Governor, then turned on him in mid-battle, thus taking the provincial capital. In 314 the Di turned to Li Xiong for support and protection; Hanzhong was formally incorporated into the Cheng state, and a provincial governor was appointed. At the same time, Li Xiong made clear his greater ambitions by appointing governors for Ning province to the south (roughly modern Yunnan and western Guizhou) and Jing province to the east (modern Hubei and Hunan). At this time he also founded schools, appointed a court historian, and reduced taxes.

Du Tao 杜弢, who had once urged Luo Shang to deal leniently with the refugees, had himself migrated southeast into the Hunan area, where he became the focal point of a rebellion against local officials, who planned to kill all the local refugees rather than run the risk that they might rebel.[21] Tao soon controlled most of Hunan

20. The sequence of these reconquests and their significance are discussed in Ren 9/489n21.

21. On the rebellion of Du Tao, see JS 100/2620–2624; Zhang and Zhu 1980:131–165.

and southern Hubei. He battled back and forth with the Jin General
Tao Kan 陶侃 for several years but was not defeated until early 315.

After Liu Yuan had died in 310, his son, Liu Cong 劉聰, killed
his elder brother and ascended the throne of the Han. Sima Yue
died in the third month of 311, and the Han general Shi Le 石勒
attacked the funeral cortege, killing more than one hundred thousand soldiers and officials. In the sixth month of 311, Liu Cong
captured the Jin capital, Luoyang, and with it the Jin Emperor. Sima
Rui 司馬睿 and other officials fled south, putting Rui's nephew,
Sima Ye 業, on the throne in 313. Liu Cong also captured Chang'an,
which was by this time devastated and almost totally bereft of population, but soon abandoned it. Sima Ye acceded to the throne there
in the fourth month of 313. Liu Cong repeatedly sent his General
Liu Yao 劉曜 to attack Chang'an, and the city suffered prolonged
famine. Near the end of 316, Sima Ye surrendered and was executed
the following year, bringing to a close the Western Jin.

During this period, the Cheng state continued to expand. In 312
the Grand Warden of Yinping commandery (west of Pingwu, Sichuan)
in the northwest surrendered. Cheng gained control of the entire
Yangzi valley up to the gorges; that same year, Jin officials took
refuge for a time south of the Yangzi in Fuling (modern Pengshui),
then were captured while trying to escape down the Yangzi. In the
power vacuum of the mid-310s, officials and magnates in all directions turned to Li Xiong, including the indigenous leaders of Hanjia
(modern Ya'an, Sichuan), Shushi (modern Zhaotong, Sichuan), and
Jianning (modern Qujing, Yunnan). The Di King Yang Maosou and
a local rebel leader in Gansu also found Li Xiong preferable to the
Xiongnu and sought alliances.[22] In 316 Grand Wardens of Pingyi
(in Guizhou) and Pengle (in Guangxi) pledged themselves to Li Xiong.
In 318 the Chancellor Fan Changsheng died but was immediately
replaced by his son, Fan Ben, reflecting the continuing Daoist influence on the state.

In 319 Li Xiang[a] launched an expedition against Yuesui (modern
Xichang) and Shushi commanderies in the southwest; Grand Warden
of Yuesui Li Zhao 李釗 surrendered in 320 and was brought to
Chengdu but later fled back to his post. In 323 Li Xiang[a] launched
another campaign to the southwest, again effecting the surrender of
Li Zhao together with the Grand Warden of Hanjia. Li Zhao is said

22. The locations and identities of these allies are discussed in Ren 9/490n25.
Most of the alliances were rather short-lived.

to have become an important ritual specialist at the Cheng court. The Si-sou of Yuesui revolted later that year and were quelled only after three years. In 324 two Grand Wardens from the Yunnan area surrendered.

In 323 Cheng also sent a force to chastise Yang Nandi, who, after his surrender and subsequent return to Wudu, had attacked Cheng officials. Yang cleverly detained one arm of the Cheng force while permitting the other to advance deep into his own territory, where they were ambushed and killed. Because two sons of Li Xiong's deceased elder brother were lost in the campaign, Xiong resolved to pass the throne to this brother's eldest surviving son, Li Ban, who was formally appointed Heir Apparent the following year. This eventually led to a succession struggle for which Xiong is faulted by both Chang Qu and the *Book of Jin* editors, but given the personalities involved, such a confrontation was perhaps inevitable.

Throughout this period, the events of central China seem to have had little influence on Cheng. In 317 Sima Rui established himself in Jiankang (modern Nanjing), ascending the throne the following year as Jin Yuandi, first Emperor of the Eastern Jin, controlling the area south of the Huai and Han rivers. Han ruler Liu Cong died in 318 and was succeeded by Liu Yao 劉曜, who changed the name of the state to Zhao and established his capital at Chang'an. This state survived ten years, until Liu Yao was captured by Shi Le during an attack on Luoyang. Although Yao does not seem to have directly attacked Cheng, pressure from his forces prompted leaders in the far northwest to seek alliance with Cheng.

Shi Le 石勒 (274–333), of the Jie 羯 nationality, had served as a general under Liu Cong and was enfeoffed as King of Han by Liu Yao.[23] In 319 he claimed independence, retaining the state name Zhao, which came to be known to history as Latter Zhao, though he did not claim the title of Emperor until 330. He controlled most of northeast China throughout this period. When Shi Le died in 333, his nephew, Shi Hu 石虎, usurped the throne and reigned until his death in 349.

The Eastern Jin state was long preoccupied with internal affairs. Prime among them was the rebellion of the Great General Wang Dun 王敦 (322–324), who relied on his military power to control

23. For the Jie nationality, which may have been Turkish, see Rogers 1968:90n136; Pulleyblank 1983:456. Shi Le's biography is found in JS 104–105: 2707–2752.

the court and threatened to usurp the throne. After his death, Dun's cousin Wang Dao 王導 was the leading figure at court until his death in 339 (except for a period during 328 when Su Jun 蘇峻 was in effective control) but was unable to make significant headway in regaining lost territory. This was in part the result of a deliberate policy of government inaction, or "quietude," that may have had its roots in the Daoist-influenced Mysterious Learning (xuanxue 玄學).[24] Wang Dao was convinced that the non-Chinese enemies of the Jin state were waiting expectantly for any sign of internal confusion, such as that which might be caused by a transfer of the capital or a large military campaign, in order to invade. Further, he saw that a period of tranquillity was necessary to absorb the huge number of refugees who had followed the court south and to re-invigorate the state's agricultural base.

The Jin central government was also concerned during this period with a recurring threat from the Governor of Jing Province, whoever he might be. Jing province (modern Hubei and Hunan) occupied a strategic position upstream from the Jin capital and was heavily fortified as a bulwark against both Cheng and forces from the Guanzhong area.[25] A succession of military leaders, beginning with Wang Dun, followed by Tao Kan 陶侃, Yu Liang 庾亮, and Huan Wen 桓溫, used this position to influence the court, but doubts concerning their support at court kept these men from turning their attention to the west. During the mid-330s a major drought and famine plagued the residents of the southeast. In 339 a planned campaign to retake the north under the direction of Yu Liang failed.

In 330 a Cheng force under the command of Li Shou 李壽, eldest son of Li Xiang[a], finally captured Badong (Fengjie), driving the Jin representatives down the Yangzi to Yidu (Yicheng). The following year Shou attacked Yinping in the northwest and in 332 led a campaign against Ning province in the south. In 333, Ning province again surrendered to Cheng, and Shou was charged with its administration, eventually being enfeoffed as King of Jianning. Cheng now controlled all of modern Guizhou and Yunnan provinces. Shi Le, the ruler of Zhao, died in 333. At this time Zhang Jun 張駿 repeatedly sent envoys to Cheng, seeking transit in order to reestablish relations with Jin and urging Li Xiong to follow him in submitting to Jin.

24. See his biography in JS 65:1745–1754, esp. 1751.
25. Fu Lecheng (1977:103) points out that the military strength of Jing Province was exceptional because it was not divided among other "guest" provinces established within its borders.

In 334 Li Xiong fell seriously ill. Li Shou returned to the capital, and when Xiong died in the sixth month, he assumed the position of Regent to the new Emperor, Li Ban. Ban soon fell victim to a plot by two sons of Li Xiong, Li Yue 李越 and Li Qi 李期, who killed Ban in the tenth month of 334 and put Li Qi on the throne, with Li Yue as Chancellor. Fearing retribution, Li Qi ignored senior officials from the previous court and installed his own confidants in senior positions.

Li Shou was given exalted titles, then sent out to guard the northern borders. From there he amassed power and extended Cheng territory again into Hanzhong. In 338 he led a large force into Chengdu, deposed Li Qi, and placed himself on the throne. Because he had been enfeoffed King of Han, he changed the name of the state to Han. He appointed a new administration, giving no positions to Li family members and systematically excluding former officials of the original refugee group. A failed revolt led him to execute all surviving sons of Li Xiong. Jin was increasingly able to launch attacks on the southern and eastern borders of the state.

In 340 Shou plotted with Shi Hu, King of Zhao, to launch a joint attack on the Jin state. He assembled a large flotilla of ships with an army of seventy thousand troops and was barely dissuaded from launching them on an expedition down the Yangzi. The following year he began a major building program, expending state resources and pressing the populace into labor for the sake of palaces that would rival the splendor of Shi Hu's. Both these actions were in marked contrast to the policies of Li Xiong, who always maintained a respect for the Jin state, which his ancestors had served, and who practiced a frugality in expenditure that I have argued was inspired by Daoist teachings. He also began to entrust major power to his son Li Shi[a], who was named Great General and given control of the Imperial Secretariat.

In 343 Li Shou died and Li Shi[a] came to the throne. Historical accounts concerning Li Shi[a] are overwhelmingly negative, casting him as a dissolute, violent, and cruel ruler. It is difficult to sort from this the standard bias applied to the last rulers of dynasties, but he seems to have had few accomplishments to his name. In 344 he executed advisors who supported his younger brother Guang and compelled this brother to commit suicide. In 346 the Grand Protector Li Yi[a] 李奕 rebelled, gathering a force of several tens of thousands, but died in the attack on the capital. Cheng's position was further exacerbated by the invasion of Sichuan at this time by large numbers of Lao tribesmen, who occupied the mountains and remote valleys and harassed the Cheng-Han forces.

Huan Wen, an imperial son-in-law with great plans for restoring the Jin to its former glory, was in 345 appointed Governor of Jing Province and General Pacifying the West, with authority over all the military affairs of west China. He gathered a force and on his own authority launched a major expedition up the Yangzi in an attack on Cheng-Han. By taking an unexpected course he was able to reach the capital of Chengdu without serious opposition. Li Shi[a] surrendered and was given an honorary enfeoffment. He lived out the rest of his days in Jiankang, dying in 361. A final rebellion by Cheng-Han loyalists the following month placed on the throne Fan Ben, the former Chancellor and son of Long-lived Fan. In 349 it was put down, Fan Ben was beheaded, and Cheng-Han was no more.

The dynasty had lasted for forty-five years and controlled a sizable territory in comparative peace for most of that time. By the end of the dynasty little was left of the extended Li family. Many died in warfare, leading the charge in battle after battle. Others were the victims of internecine warfare following the death of Li Xiong. On the whole, the people of Sichuan fared better under the Lis than the inhabitants of most other parts of China at that time. This was the result of the talents of the Li family founders, the wisdom of their advisors, and the tenets of their religious faith.

FOUR

Sources of Cheng History

Any historical study is shaped and limited by its sources; this is as true for the current study as it was for each of the government and private historians responsible for the surviving record of the Cheng-Han state. This chapter will examine these authors and their compositions and assess the significance of their contributions to the historical record.

THE WRITINGS OF CHANG QU

Chang Qu 常璩 (ca. 291–ca. 361) must be central to any account of Cheng-Han history. He was a native of Sichuan, an official of the Cheng-Han state, and a prolific historian whose works on Sichuanese history were the primary source for almost all other information.

Chang Qu, whose cognomen was Daojiang 道將, was from a gentry family in Jiangyuan county, Shu commandery (near modern Chongqing[a] 崇慶, Sichuan).[1] During the troubles at the beginning of the fourth century, the Chang family elder Chang Kuan 常寬 had led many members of the family out of Sichuan to the east, where they allied with Du Tao, then further south to Jiao province in northern Vietnam. Qu, being young, remained in the Chengdu area, where he benefited from the relative peace and emphasis on learning that characterized Li Xiong's reign. When the refugees did finally return to Sichuan, Qu aided their resettlement.

Qu served in the Cheng government. The only post recorded for him is Cavalier Attendant-in-Ordinary, a literary post without formal administrative duties, but he may have had a role in the conservation

---

1. There is no surviving biography of Chang Qu, so all information must be derived from his few appearances in the historical record and from examination of his surviving writing. This account follows in large part the detailed researches of Ren Naiqiang into Chang's life, the textual history of his compositions, and their influence on later authors. See Ren 1–27.

of government records and the compilation of a history. In any case, such compilation seems to have been one of his primary endeavors. He first composed accounts of Liang, Yi, and Nanzhong provinces, which he later reworked into three regional gazetteers, the "Monograph on Ba and Hanzhong," "Monograph on Shu," and the "Monograph on Nanzhong."[2] He also composed a history of the Cheng-Han kingdom, which he initially called the *Book of the Han* (*Han zhi shu* 漢之書) or perhaps the *Book of Han in Shu* (*Shu Han shu* 蜀漢書).[3] This book, in ten chapters, was transmitted to north China and survived at least into the early Tang.[4] In the 340s Qu combined these various works into the *Account of the Land of Huayang* (*Huayangguo ji* 華陽國記). It would seem at this time to have included only the three geographical treatises and a shortened version of the history of Cheng-Han.

Following the fall of Cheng-Han in 347, Chang Qu was transferred to the capital at modern Nanjing, where he lived out his days. During this period he worked at revising his general history of Sichuan, separating the geographical treatise on Liang province into two chapters, on Ba and Hanzhong, adding short biographical notices on local notables, editing out anything that might be offensive to the Jin rulers, and changing the name of the work to the *Record of the Land of Huayang* (*Huayangguo zhi* 華陽國志).[5]

As scion of a great family with a tradition of scholarship and as a Cheng official, Chang Qu had a variety of sources at his disposal. The four geographical treatises draw upon both national sources like the *Account of the Historian (Shiji)* and regional histories like Yang Xiong's *Annals of the Kings of Shu (Shuwang benji)*.[6] For his

2. Ren (3) places these initial compositions in the early 330s and their first rewriting in 336, when Qu was in his forties. It may be that the *Huayangguo zhi* in three chapters listed in the *Jiu Tangshu*, if not a scribal error, may refer to these three chapters. See *Jiu Tangshu* 46/1992.

3. Liu Zhiji 劉知幾 (661–721) notes that this work, known to him simply as *Han shu*, was renamed *Shu Li shu* 蜀李書 when it entered the Imperial Library. See *Shitong tongshi* 12/39.

4. This work is listed under the title *Han zhi shu*, in ten chapters, in the *Sui shu* (28/963) and the *Xin Tangshu* (48/1461), and under the title *Shu Han shu*, in nine chapters, in the *Jiu Tangshu* (46/1992). The discrepancy in the number of chapters is probably to be explained by the presence or absence of a preface.

5. Following Ren. But note that, as Ren points out, the author of the *Shuijing zhu*, Li Daoyuan 酈道元 (?–527), quotes the text repeatedly as *Huayangguo ji* or simply *Huayang ji, The Account of Huayang*. It would seem that it circulated under a variety of names for a prolonged period, perhaps even into the Tang.

6. Ren (6) lists eight different "Annals of Shu" to which he believes Chang Qu had access.

history of the Cheng state his sources were more limited, but they were supplemented by his personal experiences and those of others with whom he spoke. For the early history of the state he had the writings of a senior member of his own family, Chang Kuan 常寬, who wrote a *Later Record of Shu* (*Shu hou zhi* 蜀後志) concerning events in Shu during the period from the founding of the Western Jin to the beginning of the third century. Du Gong 杜龔 continued this work up through the time of Zhao Xin and Luo Shang. Records for this first decade of Cheng history are considerably more detailed than for any later period, reflecting the value of this source. It is further assumed that Chang Qu, as a government official, perhaps even the court annalist, would have had access to the primary sources in the Cheng archives.[7] This may well be true, but if so, he drew upon these sources sparingly because the account for the period when he was in office is a mere outline with few details.[8]

The transmission of *Record of the Land of Huayang* was less than ideal, particularly during the Tang. The work occurs in catalogs beginning with the Sui in twelve chapters, but the *Jiu Tangshu* records a version in only three chapters (possibly a graphic error),[9] and the *Xin Tangshu* gives thirteen chapters.[10] Ren (7–8) lists a series of major historical works from both north and south China that made use of the *Record of the Land of Huayang* during the ensuing centuries. Among the most important of these are the *Book of Latter Han* (*Hou Hanshu*) of Fan Ye 范曄 (398–445), the *Commentary to the Record of the Three Kingdoms* (*Sanguo zhi*) by Pei Songzhi 裴松之 (372–451), and the *Commentary to the Classic of Streams* (*Shuijing zhu* 水經注) of Li Daoyuan 酈道元 (?–527). Most of the major collectanea and geographical works of the Tang and Song also drew upon the *Record of the Land of Huayang*.

The first recorded printing of the text was in 1078, by an official in Chengdu named Lü Dafang 呂大防.[11] The preface to this edition is preserved in the edition of Li Ji 李𡊀 discussed below. A Qing

7. Liu 8; Ren 5.

8. It is, however, possible that some of these records had to be expunged when HYGZ was edited in the Jin capital in order not to offend Jin sensibilities.

9. Zhang Zongyuan suggests that a "ten" (*shi* 十) may have dropped out of the text, giving thirteen chapters, but it seems equally likely that the top line of the character *san* 三 derives from an incomplete or poorly written *shi*, thus giving twelve. See *Suishu jingjizhi kaozheng*, 4970.

10. See *Suishu* 28/963; *Jiu Tangshu* 46/1992; *Xin Tangshu* 48/1461.

11. The following discussion of editions is based primarily upon the detailed analysis in Ren 8–23. Cf. Kano 1963; Zhu Shijia 1934; Liu 9–12.

edition of *Record of the Land of Huayang* with notes by He Zhuo 何焯 (1661–1722) collating this edition with the Lü text has survived.[12] Lü's edition was in a poor state, with numerous graphic errors, missing passages, and misordered text fragments. In 1204 Li Ji set about remedying this by comparing the text to surviving accounts in a variety of early sources, especially the first four dynastic histories, and correcting the text on this basis.[13] This new recension drove out the Lü edition, but its distribution was limited by the Mongol invasions, and it did not survive the Ming.

The earliest surviving editions of the *Record of the Land of Huayang* date to the Ming. Earliest is the 1564 edition of Liu Dachang 劉大昌, which is preserved in the Sichuan Provincial Library and Beijing Library. Printed in Chengdu, it is based on the Li Ji recension. The same year an edition was printed by Zhang Jiayin 張佳胤 (1527–1588). Now preserved in the Beijing Library, it is also based on Li Ji's version but lacks four pages at the end of the eighth chapter. An edition closely based on Zhang's was reprinted around 1592 in Wu Guan's 吳琯 *Gujin yishi* 古今逸史, and this, in turn, was reprinted with new pagination and even more misprints at the beginning of the seventeenth century in the *Han Wei congshu* 漢魏叢書 of He Yunzhong 何允中. This latter was reprinted in 1791 by Wang Mo 王謨 (1777 *jinshi*) and reprinted with considerable corrections around 1796 in Zhejiang, both in reprints of *Han Wei congshu*. An edition from the mid-sixteenth century by Qian Gu 錢穀 is a hand copy of the original Li Ji edition; it is reprinted in the Sibu congkan collectanea.

There are several Qing editions of note. The edition reprinted in *Hanhai* 函海 by Li Tiaoyuan 李調元 (1763 *jinshi*) is a careful collation of Qian Gu's text with four other Ming editions. The 1814 edition of Liao Yin 廖寅 (1752–1825) was based on a Song edition from the collection of the famous philologist Sun Xingyan 孫星衍 (1753–1818) and collated carefully by Gu Guangqi 顧廣圻 (1770–1839) and Gu Huaisan 顧槐三.[14] There are a number of late Qing reprints of *Record of the Land of Huayang* but none that makes a

12. Ren records a twelve-chapter edition in the private collection of the scholar Xiang Da 向達 and a partial version, comprising the first four chapters, in the Beijing University Library. On He Zhuo, see Hummel 1943:283–285.

13. Li Ji's text does not survive, but the preface is preserved at the beginning of the modern Basic Sinological Series edition and Ren 741–742.

14. An original copy of Gu Guangqi's collations is preserved in the Beijing University Library.

substantial contribution beyond those described above. Today these are all superseded by the modern collated, annotated editions of Ren Naiqiang, Liu Lin, and Taniguchi Fusao.

OTHER SOURCES OF CHENG-HAN HISTORY

The writings of Chang Qu are the primary source for all surviving accounts of the state of Cheng-Han. Among the most important of these was the *Springs and Autumns of the Sixteen Kingdoms (Shiliuguo chunqiu* 十六國春秋) of Cui Hong 崔鴻 (d. 525), historian of the Northern Wei. The work consisted of a ledger (*lu* 錄) for each of the sixteen non-Chinese states of the preceding two centuries. Cui's biography tells us that this work was substantially complete in 508 but lacked materials on Cheng-Han, which Cui obtained only in 522.[15] Cui described this newly obtained material as "the work which Chang Qu wrote concerning the time when Li Xiong and his sons occupied Shu." Only excerpts of Cui's chapter on Cheng-Han survive, but they are sufficient to conclude that the work Cui referred to is the *Han zhi shu* rather than the *Record of the Land of Huayang*.[16]

Another important source for the period is the *Book of Wei (Weishu* 魏書) of Wei Shou 魏收 (506–572). The account of Cheng-Han history in this work is brief and records only major events. Zhou Yiliang has shown that the *Shiliuguo chunqiu* was the primary source in Wei's treatment of the Sixteen Kingdoms, but the portion of the *Weishu* concerning Cheng-Han does not bear striking similarity to surviving portions of that work.[17]

By far the most important source after the *Record of the Land of Huayang* for the history of the Cheng-Han state is the *Book of Jin (Jinshu* 晉書), one of a number of historical works compiled by imperial commissions during the early part of the Tang dynasty in

15. WS 57/1504–1505. Ren (4) argues that Cui originally possessed the *Han zhi shu* but lacked the HYGZ, which he acquired in 522, but the "course of events surrounding their raising of troops and assuming a reign name," which Cui already knew of and which Ren assumes to have derived from the *Han zhi shu,* could have come from central government records or any of a number of private Jin histories.

16. Compare the passage of the *Shiliuguo chunqiu* quoted at TPYL 123/7a to the passage from the *Han zhi shu* quoted at TPYL 398/6a and HYGZ 9/ 119.8. The primary source for the *Shiliuguo chunqiu* material on Cheng-Han is chapter 123 of TPYL. Rogers (1968:20) believes that this derives from an abridged version of the *Shiliuguo chunqiu,* rather than the full one-hundred chapter edition, but this fact does not affect the validity of the comparison made here.

17. Zhou Yiliang 1963:245–254; Rogers 1968:22.

an attempt to supply official histories for the dynasties of the preceding era that did not yet possess a standard record. Tang Emperor
Taizong ordered the compilation of this work in a decree of 646,
appointing Fang Xuanling 房玄齡 (579–648), Chu Suiliang 褚遂
良 (596–667), and Xu Jingzong 許敬宗 (592–672) to direct the
work. They completed this task no later than 648.[18] As one of the
standard dynastic histories, the *Book of Jin* has enjoyed a careful
and continuous transmission to the present.

The *Book of Jin,* being a history of the legitimate ruling dynasty,
gives short shrift to the independent states that arose to contest
with Jin for the territory of China. They are treated in a series of
thirty chapters at the end of the work that are designated "illegitimate annals" (*zaiji* 載記). The Cheng-Han state is given two chapters
(120 and 121) that omit much important information available to
men of the early Tang.

An examination of the sources of the *Book of Jin* chapters on
Cheng-Han must begin by distinguishing the opening material concerning the origins and identity of the indigenous peoples of Eastern
Sichuan from the later material dealing directly with the Li family
and the Cheng state. The legend of the Lord of Granaries, or Linjun,
and other comments concerning the Ba people are closely related to
material in the *Book of Latter Han (Hou Hanshu)* of Fan Ye. The
Linjun legend itself derives ultimately from the *Generational Origins*
(*Shiben* 世本), a work that was in existence at the time of the compilation of the *Account of the Historian* (ca. 100 B.C.E.) but was expanded in later ages.[19] It is possible that Fan Ye's immediate source
was earlier compilations of Latter Han history; we cannot be sure
that any of these works contained the Lord of the Granaries legend,
but passages in the same chapter of the *Book of the Latter Han* can
be shown to derive from the *Continued Book of Han (Xu Hanshu* 續
漢書) of Sima Biao (240–306) and the *Book of the Latter Han (Hou
Hanshu* 後漢書) of Hua Qiao 華嶠.[20]

For the portions of the *Jinshu* account dealing directly with the Li
family and the Cheng-Han state, there can be little doubt that the

18. See Rogers 1968:15–16. The original decree is preserved in *Tang huiyao*
69/1091. Yang Lien-sheng (1961:119–120) believes that work on the history
was begun in 644 and that the decree of 646 merely confirmed their appointments.

19. See the *Zhengyi* commentary to *Shiji* 1/1.

20. For Sima Biao, compare TPYL 820/2b–3a; for Hua Qiao, see TPYL 808/
1b, 3b and HHS 86/2849. The TPYL quotations are somewhat abridged but
identifiable.

ultimate primary source is the writings of Chang Qu. The difficulty is in determining whether the proximate source was the *Record of the Land of Huayang* or the now lost *Han zhi shu;* since we can assume a fair amount of similarity between these works, parallel passages in *Book of Jin* and *Record of the Land of Huayang* do not prove that the latter was the source. There is at least one passage that occurs in the modern *Book of Jin* chapters and is cited elsewhere as deriving from the *Han zhi shu* but does not occur in the modern *Record of the Land of Huayang.*[21] The question is complicated, however, by the existence of the *Springs and Autumns of the Sixteen Kingdoms* account, which we know was based upon the *Han zhi shu* and which was a source for the compilation of the *Jinshu.*

We can conclude, then, that the *Record of the Land of Huayang,* coming from the hand of Chang Qu, is the most reliable surviving source for the history of the Cheng-Han state but that other sources, including the *Book of Jin,* surviving passages of the *Springs and Autumns of the Sixteen Kingdoms,* the *Book of Wei,* and even the Song compilation *Comprehensive Mirror to Aid in Government* (*Zizhi tongjian* 資治通鑑) can provide valuable, accurate information not contained in *Record of the Land of Huayang* but possibly also deriving from the hand of Chang Qu. The translation in Part 2 integrates all of these sources into a single continuous narrative history of the state and its rulers.

21. TPYL 811/7b; cf. JS 121/3040.9–10.

PART 2

Great Perfection:
The Historical Record

Li Te

李特

Li Te 李特, sobriquet Xuanxiu 玄休, was a man of Dangqu 宕渠 in the commandery of Baxi 巴西.[1] His ancestors were the descendants of Linjun 廩君 (Lord of the Granaries).[2]

Long ago Wuluozhongli Mountain[3] collapsed, revealing two caves, one as red as cinnabar and the other as black as lacquer. A man emerged from the red cave. His name was Wuxiang 務相, and his surname was Ba 巴. In all, four clans emerged from the black cave: the Yi 曎,[4] Fan 樊, Xiang 相,[5] and Zheng 鄭. These five clans emerged at the same time and all contested to be god.[6] Accordingly, all tried to pierce the cave roof with their swords, and he who could stick his

1. Dangqu was located seventy *li* northeast of modern Qu 渠. See *Dushi fangyu jiyao* 68.2953; cf. Zang 1936:449.1, which gives no exact distance. I follow Gu in placing the administrative center of Baxi commandery twenty *li* east of modern Langzhong. Zang 1936:148.3 and Morohashi 8745.60 would place it to the west of modern Langzhong, but this would indicate a location west of the Jialing River, whereas the name Langzhong, which was in use at this time, clearly indicates a place like modern Langzhong, surrounded on three sides by the winding Jialing River, also known as the Langjiang 閬江.

Huayangguo zhi (HYGZ) 9/119.1 says Te was from Linwei 臨渭 in Lueyang 略陽 but that his ancestors had originally been Zong 賨 people from Dangqu, Baxi. Linwei, eighty *li* southeast of Qin'an county in Gansu, was the administrative center of Lueyang commandery (*Dushi fangyu jiyao* 59/2596; Zang 1936:849.1, 1293.1). On the Zong peoples, whose name refers to a type of partial tax remission awarded these people, see the discussion above, p. 41.

2. Linjun literally means "lord of granaries," a curious term for the leader of a people renowned for their hunting and fishing rather than agricultural skills. The text to this point is identical with a quotation from the *Shiliuguo chunqiu* in TPYL 123/5a.

3. See the discussion of variant names for this mountain above, p. 000.

4. *Hou Hanshu* 86/2840 has *shen* 曋. TPYL 37/5b quotes a parallel passage in *Shiben* 世本 that gives Hui 暉.

5. Following HHS, *Jinshu jiaozhu* and *Shiben* as quoted in TPYL in reading Xiang 相 for Bo 柏.

6. HHS reads, "They did not yet have a ruler and together served the spirits

sword in would be made Linjun. None of the swords of the other four clans stuck, but Wuxiang's sword hung suspended there. Again they contested. They made boats from earth, carved designs upon them, and floated them on the water, saying, "He whose boat stays afloat we will take as Linjun." Again Wuxiang's boat alone floated. Thereupon they proclaimed him Linjun.

Boarding his earthen boat and leading his followers, he descended the Yi River 夷水.[7] When he arrived at Yanyang 鹽陽, the river goddess detained him, saying, "This place has both fish and salt; the land is broad and vast. I will live with you. You should stay here; do not go on." Linjun said, "I must search for a bountiful place for you.[8] I cannot stay." The salt goddess would pass the night with Linjun but always left at morning, becoming a flying insect. All the gods[9] would follow her in flight, obscuring the sun and turning daylight into dusk. Linjun wanted to kill her but could not identify her. Nor could he tell east from west or Heaven from Earth. This continued for ten days.[10] Then Linjun presented to the salt goddess a green thread, saying, "Wrap this around your neck. If it fits, I will live with you. If it does not fit, I am going to leave."[11] The salt goddess accepted it and wrapped it around her neck. Linjun stood on a multicolored (dang 碭) stone[12] and, searching for the one with a green thread on its breast, knelt and shot it, hitting the salt god-

---

(guishen 鬼神)." The Shiben reading, "They emerged together and had a contest of supernatural powers (zhengshen 爭神)," fits better with what follows.

7. Probably to be identified with the Qingjiang 清江 of southwestern Hubei province. See Tong Enzheng 1979: 9.

8. Wo dang wei jun qiu lin di 我當爲君求廩地. Another possible but less natural reading would be, "I must be lord and seek a bountiful land." Either way, the term lindi, literally, "granary land," is otherwise unattested, and my "bountiful land" is a conjecture.

9. HHS reads "all the insects."

10. HHS says "more than ten days," and the subcommentary quotes Shiben as "seven days and seven nights." See HHS 86/2840; HHSJJ 86/9a–b.

11. The Shiben, quoted in the Li Xian commentary to HHS, has an emissary who transmits the thread and message to the goddess. The goddess would seem to be in insect form when she receives this gift. The HHS says merely "Linjun awaited an opportunity and shot her to death" (adopting the textual emendation, suggested by Hui Dong, of si 思 to si 伺).

12. The Shiben reads yang 陽 for the more specialized dang of our text, but the dang stone of our text no doubt partakes of a yang nature. Hui Dong notes the variant yang 煬, "blazing." All are probably cognates of yang 暘, "sunny, clear." Li Xian cites a Map of Jing Province (Jingzhou tu 荊州圖) that (following the emendation of Hui Dong) tells of a Warm Spring 溫泉 west of Yiling (modern Yichang, Hubei) that was said to have once produced salt and which had a salty odor. West of the town there is also a mountain with a cave containing two

dess. The salt goddess died, and the many gods who flew with her all left. The heavens then opened and shone.

Linjun again boarded his earthen boat and descended to Barbarian City. At Barbarian City the stony shore curved and the spring waters also curved. Linjun, seeing that it resembled a cave, sighed, "I have newly emerged from a cave and now again will enter one. What am I to do?" Thereupon a part of the bank more than thirty feet wide collapsed, forming flight upon flight of steps. Linjun ascended them. On top of the embankment was a flat stone ten feet square and five feet high. Linjun rested on top of it and, casting lots, calculated. Each lot stuck into the rock; for this reason he established a city beside the place and took up residence there.[13] Afterward the varieties (of his people) became numerous.

When Qin unified All-under-Heaven, the territory was incorporated into Qianzhong commandery and taxed lightly, each person paying forty cash. The Ba people called the tax *zong,* and for this reason they were referred to as the Zong people.[14]

When Han Gaozu (i.e., Liu Bang) was King of Han, he enlisted the Zong people to pacify the Three Qin (southern Shaanxi). When this was accomplished, they asked to return to their native place. Gaozu, deeming their achievement equal to that of his followers from Feng 豐 and Pei 沛 (his native region), exempted them from taxes and changed the name of their homeland to Ba commandery. The earth (of their home) yields bounties of salt, iron, cinnabar, and lacquer.[15]

---

stones ten feet apart, a wet one called the yin stone and a dry one called the yang stone. Hui Dong cites an account in the *Jingzhou ji* of Sheng Hongzhi 盛弘之 that describes a mountain cave containing a *yang* 陽 stone and a yin stone that were involved in a rain-making ceremony. A man would beat the yin stone to produce rain and the yang stone to clear the skies, but this man suffered a shortened lifespan and no one dared speak his name.

13. The HHS text diverges from that of the *Jinshu* here, continuing, "Upon his death his soul (*hunpo* 魂魄) became a white tiger for generation after generation. Because the Ba clan believes that tigers drink men's blood, they sacrifice men to him."

14. HHS records an earlier stage of accommodation with these people. It relates that at the time of the Qin conquest, King Hui of Qin had made the Ba clan supreme over the non-Chinese and for generations sent Qin women to the Ba as wives. He further confirmed them in their ranks and permitted them to redeem crimes with a forfeiture of rank. The ruler was responsible for a yearly tax of two thousand sixteen cash and a loyalty tax of one thousand eight hundred cash once every three years. Commoner households paid eighty-two feet of *jia* 賨 cloth and thirty arrowheads (*hou* 鍭)-weight of chicken feathers.

15. TPYL 123/5a, quoting the *Shiliuguo chunqiu,* reads, "The earth yields the benefits of salt and lacquer and the people are enriched thereby." HYGZ 1/

The people are by nature fierce and brave as well as being adept at song and dance. Gaozu loved their dance and commanded the Music Bureau to learn it. This is what we today call the Bayu Dance.[16]

At the end of the Han dynasty, Zhang Lu took up residence in Hanzhong, teaching the people the Way of Demons.[17] The Zong were devout believers in shamans (*wuxi* 巫覡); many went to follow him. When the world fell into great disorder, they moved from Dangqu in Baxi to Yangjuban in Hanzhong, where they robbed and plundered passing travelers. The populace suffered because of them and called them the Yangju Ba.[18] When Emperor Wu of Wei (r. 220–226) conquered Hanzhong, Te's grandfather Hu 虎[19] led more than five hundred families in submitting to him. Emperor Wu appointed him general and transferred him to the region north of Lueyang.[20] They were called the Ba Di.[21]

2.3–4 gives a more exhaustive list of products for the Ba region: "The earth grows the five grains; their sacrificial victims include all six domestic animals. Mulberry trees, silkworms, hemp, ramie, fish, salt, bronze, iron, cinnabar, lacquer, tea, and honey, the divine turtle, the great rhinoceros, long-tailed pheasant, silver pheasant, shimmering golden fabrics and bright cosmetics, all these they offer as tribute."

16. Yu 渝 is an old name for the Qu 渠 River. The SLGCQ continues, "Their descendants increased and divided into dozens of clans" (TPYL 123/5a). HYGZ 1/4.2 has a parallel passage, in which Gaozu also remarks, "This is the song sung when King Wu attacked Zhou (the last Shang ruler)."

17. Hanzhong commandery was in southeastern Shaanxi province, with its headquarters in modern Nanzheng. On Zhang Lu, see the discussion above, pp. 76–79. On the Way of Demons, see above, p. 75.

18. This is a place in Hanzhong. A certain Li Hei 李黑 from Yangju was among the Ba leaders who moved to Lueyang along with Li Te's ancestor Li Hu 虎.

19. HYGZ 9/119.5 and SLGCQ (TPYL 123/5a) agree in inserting the name of Li Te's grandfather, Hu 虎. Because Hu was tabooed during the Tang, JS (120/3032.4) gives his name as Wu 武. See the collation note in JS 120/3032, n. 3.

20. SLGCQ inserts at this point, "Those who were moved internally also numbered more than ten thousand households. They lived scattered through the various commanderies of Longyou 隴右 and in the Three Dependencies 三輔 and Hongnong 泓農 (=弘農)." This would indicate a substantial movement of people, perhaps fifty thousand, moving into an area stretching across northwestern Henan and southern Shaanxi into Gansu and Qinghai provinces. HYGZ 9/119 lists among those moved to the area north of Lueyang (following the textual emendations of Gu Guangqi) Du Huo 杜濩, Pu Hu 朴胡, Yuan Yue 袁約, and Li Hei 李黑 of Yangju 楊車. Ren Naiqiang argues that Li Hu is in fact Li Te's great-grandfather, as stated in this passage in HYGZ, and not his grandfather, as might be supposed from the *Jinshu*. But the SLGCQ, in TPYL 123/5a, clearly states that Hu is father of Mu, who fathered Te as the second of five sons. The JS editors have mispunctuated this passage.

21. Or the Ba clan. The Di are a Tibeto-Burman people of the Northwest

Te's father, Li Mu 穆, was Eastern Qiang Hunting Commander (*dongqiang liejiang* 東羌獵將).[22]

When young, Te held posts in the provincial and commandery administrations. Men of the day thought him remarkable. He was eight feet tall,[23] brave and martial, adept at riding and archery. Grave and resolute, he was gifted with a generosity of character.

During the Yuankang reign period (291–299), the Di tribesman Qi Wannian 齊萬年 rebelled.[24] In the area west of the passes there was confusion and disorder, and a major famine persisted for a number of years. Commoners migrated in search of grain. Several thousand households entered Hanchuan in groups.[25] When Te was about to enter Shu in this company of migrants, having reached Sword Pavilion, he squatted on the ground, took a deep breath, and, gazing about at the towering defile, said, "Liu Shan 劉禪 (207–271) had a place like this, yet he was bound in submission by another.[26] Surely he must have been a man of but common talent." Yan Shi 閻式,[27]

---

related to the Qiang (see Rogers 1968:4–6). Their name, Di 氐, is graphically very similar to *shi* 氏, "clan." Parallel passages in SLGCQ (TPYL 123/5a) and HYGZ (9/119.6) both have "Ba people" (*baren* 巴人), and both the JS and HHS accounts of the Linjun myth frequently use the term, "Ba clan" (*bashi*). The *Jinshu* editors (120/3032.4) accept this reading, arguing that the Ba people are not in fact Di. But in an area of widespread Di inhabitation, Di could easily have come to mean simply a non-Chinese, and then Ba Di would mean no more than a non-Chinese from Ba. Yang Ming (1991:63) understands the term to mean a mixed group of Ba and Di. Ba Di does occur again, at HYGZ 8/115.8. However these readings are evaluated, this passage does not indicate that the Ba or Banshunman were Di.

22. This title is otherwise unknown. It is uncertain if the Eastern Qiang describes the people Li Mu was supposed to police or the troops he was to lead. Ren Naiqiang (1987:486n2), pointing out the importance of hunting in this region, argues that this title indicates a leader of hunters and that the Eastern Qiang are in fact the Di, hence the Ba Di of our account. On the military system of this period, see Hucker 1985:21–22.

23. Approximately six feet four inches by modern measurement. All measures are converted on the basis of Wu Chengluo 1937.

24. HYGZ 8/106.11–12, placing this event in the year 298, specifies that the rebelling forces were Di tribesmen from the Guanzhong area (i.e., Shaanxi) and the Qiang of Malan 馬蘭 Mountain (sixty *li* northwest of Baishui, Shaanxi). SLGCQ (TPYL 123/5b) lists among the areas affected the commanderies of Tianshui, Lueyang, Fufeng, and Shiping. HYGZ adds Wudu and Yinping.

25. Hanchuan refers to the Hanzhong region of southeastern Shaanxi, northeastern Sichuan, and northwestern Henan.

26. Liu Shan was the last ruler of the Shu Han state established by Liu Bei. His surrender to Deng Ai 鄧艾 is recorded in SGZ 33/900.

27. SLGCQ (TPYL 123/5b) gives this name as Yan Yu 或, no doubt a graphic error. Yan Shi plays a large role in later Cheng history.

Zhao Su 趙肅, Li Yuan 李遠, and Ren Hui 任回, who were migrating with him,[28] all were impressed by this statement.

At first, when the refugees had reached Hanzhong, they submitted a memorial petitioning that they be lodged and boarded in Ba and Shu. The Court Conference denied this request and sent the Attendant Censor[29] Li Bi 李芯 bearing credentials of authority to comfort and mollify them, at the same time observing that they not be permitted to enter Sword Pass. Arriving at Sword Pavilion, Li Bi accepted a bribe from the refugees and, on the contrary, wrote a memorial, saying, "The refugees number more than a hundred thousand, more than the single commandery of Hanzhong can support. To the east toward Jing 荊 province the torrents are rapid and precipitous; moreover, they have no boats. Shu has stockpiled reserves of grain, and its people are enjoying another bountiful harvest. They should be permitted to proceed there in search of food." The court adopted this suggestion, and the migrants subsequently could not be stopped from dispersing throughout Yi and Liang provinces; they could not be prohibited or halted.

In the first year of the Yongkang (Eternal Tranquillity) reign period (300) an imperial edict summoned Zhao Xin 趙廞, Governor (cishi 刺史) of Yi Province, to be Director of the Palace Domestic Service (dachangqiu 大長秋) and replaced him with the Seneschal (neishi 內史) of Chengdu, Geng Teng 耿滕.[30] Xin consequently plotted rebel-

28. Following the collation note at 120/3032, n. 2, and SLGCQ in reading yi 移, "to migrate," for yi 夷, "barbarian." HYGZ 8/106.12, under the year 298, lists among the migrants Li Te, his younger brother Xiang 庠, Yan Shi, Zhao Su, He Ju 何巨, Li Yuan 李遠, the Di Sou 氐叟 and the Green Sou 青叟.

29. The Attendant Censor was a member of a small, elect staff of nine who supervised officialdom, reporting directly to the Censor-in-Chief and, through him, to the Emperor. See Hucker 1985:entry 5350. HYGZ 8/106.14 gives Li Bi's office as a subordinate of the local Revenue Section (hucao 戶曹), on which see Hucker 1985:entry 2798. Ren (8/448n3) argues that Attendant Censor must be correct because a low-level local official like the hucao would not have the authority to countermand a provincial directive. Liu Lin (8/617–618n2) assumes that Li moved from the hucao post to become Attendant Censor but offers no evidence for this interpretation. HYGZ 11/198.7–9 records for Li Bi only local Sichuan offices, ranging from county magistrate to commandery governor. There is no mention of a position in the Censorate. Cf. JS 4/97 (where Li Bi is called Li Mi 密). It would seem that two figures are confused, one a local official named Li Bi, the other a representative of the central government whose name was either Li Bi or Li Mi.

30. HYGZ 8/107.4 adds that Geng was also to be appointed General Foiling the Charge (zhechong jiangjun 折衝將軍) and should adopt the official attire and regalia of Xin. It continues, "At first, Xin thought that the Jin administration

lion, secretly harboring the ambition to carve out a piece of territory for himself as the Liu clan [of the preceding Shu-Han state] had done. He emptied his granary, distributing grain to the refugees in order to win the support of the masses. The members of Te's group were all from Baxi, the same commandery as Zhao Xin. Many were brave and strong. Xin treated them well, turning them into his henchmen.[31] Therefore Te and the others collected followers and devoted themselves to robbery and banditry. The people of Shu suffered at their hands.

Geng Teng secretly submitted a memorial maintaining that: "The refugees are hardened and brave while the men of Shu are cowardly and weak. The guest should not dominate the host;[32] this is certainly the first step toward disorder. They should be sent back to

---

had declined, but the *Yellow Prognostication of the Stars of Zhao* said, 'He whose star is yellow will be king.' Xin harbored plans for rebellion. The Shu territory has natural defenses on all four sides and one could find a secure place for oneself there." JS 4/97.1 gives Geng's personal name as Sheng 勝, a simple graphic error. Zhao's summons took place in the context of Sima Lun's execution of the Empress Jia. The Director of the Palace Domestic Service (or, more literally, Great Elder) was the minister in charge of the Empress' household and directed a retinue of officials beneath him. It would seem that in preparation for the coup against the Empress, Sima Lun sought to lure Zhao back to court with an exalted position responsible directly to his protector, the Empress, but events forced his hand before Zhao's return could be secured. If Hucker is correct that this is a eunuch office (as it was for most of the Han; see Bielenstein 1980:70), the proposed appointment entailed an even more fundamental change in Zhao's lifestyle. In any case, with the death of the Empress, Zhao's motivations for rebellion are clear. The Seneschal was the highest officer in a kingdom (here, that of the King of Chengdu), with a rank between a commandery's Grand Warden and a province's Governor. See JS 24/735, 737, 746; Ren Naiqiang 8/449n7; Hucker 1985:entry 4236, 5886.

31. Ren Naiqiang (8/449n8) maintains that Chang Qu is mistaken in this characterization of Zhao's intentions. He points out that Zhao's aid to the refugees was in response to Li Bi's memorial and the court's subsequent command to allow these migrants to enter the Sichuan basin. Further, their entry into Sichuan and Zhao's relief operations had begun two years earlier (in 298), whereas Zhao's actions in this case were in fact prompted by the dethroning and death of Empress Jia, to whom he was related by marriage, in 300. Ren also discounts Chang's claims concerning the common origin of Zhao and Li Te, noting that Zhao had been born and reared in Shanxi while Te and the other migrants were from the Shaanxi-Gansu region. But this ignores the fact that the Lis and Zhaos were coreligionists, part of the same well-organized movement sharing a common leader and distinctive societal organization. This surely must have influenced Zhao's willingness to open state granaries to the refugees and strengthened his appeal for their support at this critical juncture.

32. HYGZ 8/107.7 reads "guest and host cannot benefit each other."

their original home. If they are placed in a strategic location, I fear that the disaster of Qin and Long will burgeon again in Liang and Yi provinces. This is certain to bequeath to this court worries about the West."[33]

Zhao Xin heard of this and was offended. At the time, more than a thousand civil and military officials of Yi province had already gone to welcome Teng. Teng entered the provincial capital at the head of this group. Xin sent a force to oppose Teng, and they battled at West Gate. Teng was defeated and killed.[34]

Because Zhao Xin had not yet vacated the provincial capital, Teng was still in the commandery capital. Xin recruited Luo An 羅 安, *Wang Li* 王利, *and others of [Li] Xiang's* 李庠 *band to seize Geng, but they suffered a serious defeat. At Xuanhuating in Guanghan, they killed the bearer of the imperial rescript.[35] Teng argued that he wanted to enter the provincial walled city. The Merit Officer[36] Chen Xun* 陳恂 *remonstrated against this, saying, "Now both province and commandery have established administrations, and the antagonism that has developed between them grows deeper day by day. If you enter the city, there will certainly be a great disaster. It would be better to remain secure in the small city while circulating an announcement to the counties to join into fortified villages in order to prepare for the Di from Qin. [Colonel of the] Western Barbarians* (xiyi xiaowei 西夷校尉)[37] *Chen Zong* 陳總 *will soon arrive;*

33. HYGZ 8/107.7 tells us that Geng repeatedly memorialized this matter. Geng also suggests an alternative (107.8–10), "Otherwise cede to them the narrow defiles of the three eastern commanderies and observe their actions. Small beginnings cannot be permitted to grow. . . . Moreover, the granaries are exhausted and there is nothing with which to meet the exigencies of warfare."

34. JS Annals (JS 4/97.1–2) records this event under the twelfth month of the first year of Yongkang (300.12.28–301.1.25) and explicitly names Li Xiang as a participant. It also lists among those killed the Grand Warden of Qianwei Li Mi 李密 and the Grand Warden of Minshan Huo Gu 霍固.

35. Ren (8/451n12), noting that there is a Jiaohua in Chengdu, argues that the imperial representative must have stayed in a guest house in the commandery headquarters portion of Chengdu. The characters *guanghan* would then be excrescent, but Ren gives no explanation for their intrusion. Liu Lin (8/620n7) instead maintains that after Luo and Wang had failed to capture Teng, they turned to pursue the emissary now returning to the court via Guanghan.

36. The *gongcao(shi)* 功曹(史) had a general advisory role in addition to supervision of personnel at the local level. Hucker (1985:entry 3489) translates Scribe of the Labor Section.

37. The Colonel at this time was a military title of varying importance, generally ranking below a General and having special charge to police the non-Chinese of a specified region. The Colonel of the Western Barbarians was based at Minshan 汶山. See Hucker 1985:entry 2456; Rogers 1968:252n451.

we should await his actions. If not, you should retreat and occupy Qianwei, crossing over at Jiangyuan 江原 *(east of modern Chongqing* 崇慶*) so as to forestall anything unforeseen." Teng did not follow this advice.* [HYGZ 8/107.9–11]

Winter, twelfth month. Teng entered the city and climbed West Gate. Xin sent his personal advisor, Dai Mao 代茂*, to capture Teng. Mao made an announcement to him and left. Xin again sent soldiers to attack Teng. Teng's army suffered a great defeat, and he threw himself from the smaller city's wall. The clerk Zuo Xiong* 左雄*, bearing Teng's son Qi on his back, hid in the house of the peasant Song Ning* 宋寧*. Xin offered a reward of a thousand pieces of gold [for Qi], but Ning did not turn him in. Xin's search failed, and they were able to escape. All the commandery clerks fled into hiding. Only Chen Xun presented himself to Xin with his hands tied behind his back, asking for the corpse of Teng. Xin, considering him dutiful, did not kill him. Xun and the Administrator of the Revenue Section (hucao yuan* 戶曹掾*)*[38] *Chang Chang* 常敞 *joined in preparing a coffin and burial mound, then buried him.* [HYGZ 8/107.12–14]

Xin also sent an army to counter Chen Zong. Zong, reaching Jiangyang 江陽 *(modern Luzhou), heard of Xin's intention to rebel. His Recorder*[39] *Zhao Mo* 趙模 *advanced and said, "Now the province and commandery are at odds. There will certainly be a great disturbance. You should move swiftly. Our headquarters (fu* 府*)*[40] *is of strategic military importance. If you aid the loyal and assault the refractory, none of them will act." Zong tarried along the road. When he reached the Yufu Ford* 魚涪津[41] *in Nan'an, he encountered Xin's army. Mo advised Zong, "Dispense money to recruit troops in order to repel them. If you are victorious over the provincial army, then you can take the province. If you are not victorious, retreat downstream and you will certainly suffer no harm." Zong was unable to do this and said instead, "Zhao of Yi province was angry at Marquis Geng. That is why he killed him. He has no enmity for me.*

38. The Administrator was in charge of the Revenue Section, which supervised fiscal matters, at each level of the administration. Hucker 1985:entry 2798.

39. The Recorder (*zhubu* 主簿) was usually third in command at each level of the local administration. See Hucker 1985:entry 1413.

40. Liu Lin identifies this as Zong's headquarters as Colonel of the Western Barbarians.

41. Three *li* west of Jiajiang county. Zang 1936:871.3. Liu Lin (8/621n2) gives the location as thirty *li* north of Nan'an (modern Leshan). There are a number of variants for the second character of this place-name, suggesting a non-Chinese origin.

Why should I act in this manner?" Mo said, "Now that the province has embarked on this course of action, they will certainly want to establish their authority. Even if you do not fight, it will do you no good." He spoke until he cried, but Zong would not listen. His troops broke ranks, and he fled into the weeds. Mo, wearing Zong's clothing, met the attack. Xin's soldiers killed Mo, then, seeing he was not Zong, sought out Zong and killed him. [HYGZ 8/107.14–108. 4]

Xin proclaimed himself Great Inspector-General (*dadudu* 大督都), Great General (*dajiangjun* 大將軍), and Pastor (*mu* 牧) of Yi Province.[42]

He named the Prefect of Wuyang Du Shu 杜淑 *of Shu commandery, the Mounted Escort* (biejia 別駕) *Zhang Can* 張粲, *Zhang Gui* 張龜 *of Baxi, The Marshal of the Western Barbarians Gong Ni* 龔尼,[43] *and the Prefect of Jiangyuan Fei Yuan* 費遠 *of Qianwei as his Senior Aides of the Left and Right, Marshal, and Military Advisors* (canjun 參軍).[44] *He transferred the Grand Warden of Qianwei Li Xiang* 庠 *to be General Intimidating Bandits* (weikou jiangjun 威寇將軍) *and summoned the Prefect of Linqiong* 臨邛 *Xu Yan* 許弇 *of Fuling to be Commander of the Serrated-Flag Gate. None of the princedom officials[45] that he summoned dared to ignore the summons. He further appointed as Army Libationers[46] the Grand Warden of Guanghan*

42. Great Inspector-General was a title awarded irregularly to one in charge of a provincial army at the time of a major expedition, later often appropriated by regional warlords. It was first awarded to Sima Yi[b] 司馬毅 in 230 at the time of a campaign against Shu-Han. Hucker 1985:entry 6096; Rogers 1968:245n391; *Tongdian* 32/185c. Pastor was an ancient title that came to be used for the head of a province, alternating with Governor (*cishi* 刺史). The office of Governor originated in a censorial office of middle rank (600 bushels) and only gradually developed into a full administrative office in the local hierarchy. During the Han, the title Pastor, when used, indicated that these figures were accorded higher rank (2,000 bushels) and for this reason was preferred by men like Xin trying to establish an independent power base. Bielenstein treats this alternation in rank as a function of choosing younger or more senior figures for this censorial role, but it seems likely that a difference in duties and in relations to other members of the local administration were involved as well. Hucker 1985:entry 4041; Rogers 1968:229n261, 303; Bielenstein 1980:90–91.

43. The Liao edition gives this surname as Xi 襲.

44. This statement is misleading. From other references we know that Du Shu and Fei Yuan became Senior Aides, and Zhang Can was Marshal. Zhang Gui and Gong Ni must have been named Military Advisors.

45. That is, officials of the Prince of Chengdu, Sima Ying, who had never actually come to Chengdu.

46. This post, *jun jijiu* 軍祭酒, is otherwise unknown but would seem to be a largely honorific designation for senior counselors. Cf. Hucker 1985:entry 542.

Zhang Zheng 張徵,[47] *the Grand Warden of Minshan* 汶山 *Yang Bin* 楊邠, *and the Prefect of Chengdu Fei Li* 費立.[48] [HYGZ 8/108.5–7]

Te's younger brother Xiang, together with his siblings, his brother-in-law Li Han 李含, Ren Hui, Shangguan Jing 上官晶,[49] Li Pan 李攀 of Fufeng, Fei To 費佗 of Shiping, and the Di Fu Cheng 苻成 and Wei Bo 隗伯, led four thousand mounted troops to ally with Xin. Xin appointed Xiang General Intimidating Bandits and sent him to block the northern road. Xiang had formerly been Worthy Commander of the Eastern Qiang 東羌良將 and was conversant with military strategy.[50] He made no use of flags and banners (for relaying commands); instead his troops would form ranks at the raising of a lance. He executed three men under his command for disobeying orders, and thereafter there was no dissension in the ranks. Xin, hating the order and precision of Xiang's troops, wanted to kill him but had not yet spoken of it.

The Senior Aide (*zhangshi* 長史) Du Shu and the Marshal Zhang Can said to Xin, "The *Tradition of Zuo* records that the five great officers should not be located on the borders.[51] You, sir, have just taken up arms, yet you dispatch Li Xiang to command a strong force in the field. This benighted one is dismayed by this. Moreover, 'if he is not of our race (*zulei* 族類), his heart must be different.'[52] I think it impermissible to turn one's halberd end-for-end and give it to another. I ask that you consider this." Xin, with a sober expression, replied, "Your words accord perfectly with my intentions. One could say, 'It is Shang who can bring out my meaning.'[53] This is Heaven sending you to bring my affair to completion."

Before long, Xiang appeared at the gate, requesting an audience

47. The Qian, Hanhai, and Liao editions give Zhang Wei 微 here, as does JS 4/99, but the name occurs correctly in 11/194.12, 195.2, 12/242.10. Ren (451n18) accepts this identification with the son of Zhang Yi but still maintains that Wei is the correct reading. Cf. JS 120/3030n11.

48. Ren Naiqiang 451n18 points out that the posts mentioned in connection with these three men were not those they currently occupied.

49. Emending the JS reading of Shangguan Dun 惇 to Jing following JS 120/3032n6 and HYGZ 8/108.7. HYGZ specifically mentions the siblings Li Liu and Li Xiangᵃ.

50. For "military strategy" (*junfa* 軍法) HYGZ 107.8 has "military formations" (*junchen* 軍陳).

51. *Chunqiu Zuozhuan yinde* 376/Zhao 11/4; Legge 1861–1872:V, 635.

52. A quote from *Zuozhuan* 220/Cheng 4/7, which Legge (p. 355) translates as, "If he is not of our kin, he is sure to have a different mind."

53. A quotation from *Lunyu* 7/3/8. Bu Shang 卜商, better known as Zixia 子夏, was a disciple of Confucius. Cf. Legge 1861–1872: I, 157.

with Xin. Xin was delighted and summoned Xiang to see him. Xiang wished to observe Xin's intentions. Bowing twice, he advanced, saying, "Now the Central Kingdom is in great disorder and the mainstays of government exist no longer. The house of Jin will probably prove impossible to restore. The Way of my enlightened lord (i.e., Xin) extends to Heaven and Earth and your Virtue blankets the various regions. The circumstances of Tang and Wu (founders of the Shang and Zhou dynasties) are truly present here today. You should respond to the heavenly timing and accord with the people's hearts by rescuing the hundred surnames from the mud and ashes and giving the people's sentiments something to rally around. If you do so, the empire can be subjugated, not merely Yong 庸[54] and Shu." Xin angrily said, "How can these be the proper words for a subject?" He commanded Du Shu and the others to debate it. Shu and others thereupon indicted Xiang for treason and blasphemy (*dani budao* 大逆 不道). Xin subsequently killed him together with his sons, nephews, and clansmen, more than thirty in all.[55] Worried that Te and the others would make trouble, Xin sent someone to explain the situation to them, saying, "Xiang said something improper and his offense merited execution. It does not extend to his brothers." He returned Xiang's corpse to Te and appointed Te and his brothers as army commanders in order to pacify his (Xiang's?) troops.[56]

The Commander of the Serrated-Flag Gate Xu Yan requested that he be made Overseer of the Army (*jianjun* 監軍)[57] for Badong. Du Shu and Zhang Can obstinately refused to agree to this. Yan was angered by this and with his own sword killed Shu and Can in Xin's council chamber. The subordinates of Shu and Can killed Yan. All of them were Xin's intimate advisors.[58]

54. An ancient term for the Hanzhong region.

55. HYGZ 8/108.9 says that Xin executed Xiang and more than ten others, including his elder brother's son Hong 弘. Xiang had two elder brothers, Fu and Te, but Te's three sons were named Shi, Dang, and Xiong, hence this must have been Li Fu's son. HYGZ 8/108 roughly parallels the JS account but omits the conversation with Xin, saying instead, "Xiang urged him to declare himself Emperor of Han 漢. Xiang's subordinates were unrestrained and troublesome. Xin and the others feared them."

56. Ren (8/451–452n20) expresses dissatisfaction with the JS account of the events leading up to Li Xiang's death. He further points out the dissimilarity of this section of the JS to Chang Qu's style and wonders about the ultimate source of this information.

57. A rank, lower than Inspector-General, in command of an army on campaign. Hucker 1985:entry 815. Cf. Rogers 1968:244n380.

58. HYGZ has "both (presumably Du Shu and Zhang Can) were Zhao Xin's intimate advisors."

Te and his brothers, because they bore enmity toward Xin, withdrew with their troops to Mianzhu 綿竹.

That night Te and Liu withdrew their force and, dispersing, regrouped at Mianzhu. Xin sent the former Prefect of Yinping Zhang Heng 張衡 and Fei Shu 費恕 to placate Te and regain his allegiance. Both were killed by Te. [HYGZ 8/108.10–11][59]

Xin, fearing that the court would attack him, sent the Senior Aide Fei Yuan, the Grand Warden of Qianwei Li Bi, and the Protector-General (*duhu* 督護) Chang Jun 常俊, at the head of more than ten thousand men, to cut off the northern road. They bivouacked at Shiting 石亭 in Mianzhu. Te secretly gathered together a force of more than seven thousand[60] and launched a night raid on Yuan's army. Yuan was routed. They set fire to the encampment, and eight or nine out of ten died.

Te advanced and attacked Chengdu. When Xin heard that the soldiers had arrived, he was terrified and did not know what to do. Li Bi, Zhang Zheng, and others cut through the gate crossbar at night and fled.[61] Civil and military officials all scattered. Xin, accompanied only by his wife and children, fled in a small boat to Guangdu, where he was killed by an underling, Zhu Zhu 朱竺.[62] When Te reached Chengdu, he set his troops loose to plunder, slayed the Military Protector of the Western Barbarians (*xiyi hujun* 西夷護軍)[63] Jiang Fa 姜發, and killed Xin's Senior Aide Yuan Qia 袁洽 as well as the guard commanders appointed by Xin.[64] Te sent his [Commanders

59. In HYGZ this passage regarding Te's response to Li Xiang's murder precedes the tale of Xu Yan killing Du Shu and Zhang Can.

60. HYGZ 8/108.12 reads "over seven hundred." ZZTJ 84/1654 follows JS. Ren Naiqiang (8/452n24) argues that since the migrant could only raise a force of four thousand before, seven hundred is quite appropriate and the "seven thousand" is the work of Tang and Song editors. But when Li Xiang raised troops before, he assembled four thousand cavalry, indicating it was an elite corps of well-trained and well-equipped horsemen. The seven thousand here could represent foot soldiers assembled from local migrants.

61. HYGZ 8/108.13 also lists among those fleeing the Palace Squire (*zhonglang* 中郎) Chang Mei 常美 and Fei Yuan. Some editions of HYGZ again give Zhang Wei for Zhang Zheng. See HYGZ 265.1.

62. HYGZ 8/109.2 adds, "His eldest son, Bing 昺, who was in Luoyang, was also executed.

63. I have found no other instance of this title. It is, however, unrelated to the central government posts described in Hucker 1985:entry 2775–2779. Rather the title would seem to be related to the Protecting Army first assigned to keep watch over the Di in the early third century. See Rogers 1968:82n12.

64. Most editions of JS have *zhi* 治 for *qia*, clearly a graphic mistake. HYGZ 8/109.2 has Qia but gives as his office Prefect of Chengdu (following the Hanhai

of the] Serrated-Flag Gate Wang Jiao 王角 and Li Ji[a] 李基 to Luoyang to set forth Zhao Xin's crimes.

Previously, Emperor Hui had appointed the Governor of Liang[65] Province Luo Shang 羅尚 to the post of General Quelling the West (*pingxi jiangjun* 平西將軍), Concurrent Colonel of the Western Barbarians, and Governor of Yi Province. Leading the Commander of the Serrated-Flag Gate Wang Dun 王敦, the Defender (*duwei* 都尉) of Shangyong Yi Xin 義歆,[66] the Grand Warden of Shu commandery Xu Jian 徐儉, the Grand Warden of Guanghan Xin Ran 辛冉, and more than seven thousand men, he entered Shu.[67] When Te and the others heard that Shang was coming, they were terrified and sent Te's younger brother Xiang[a] 驤 to greet him on the road and offer precious objects of tribute. Shang was delighted and made Xiang[a] his Cavalry Inspector (*jidu* 騎督). Te and his younger brother Liu also feasted Shang with a bull and wine at Mianzhu. Wang Dun and Xin Ran both sought to persuade Shang, saying, "Refugees like Te do nothing but rob and steal. They should be eliminated quickly. You should take advantage of this opportunity to behead him."[68] Shang did not adopt this suggestion. Ran had known Te previously, so he said to him, "When old acquaintances meet, if it is not auspicious, then it will be inauspicious." Te had a deep sense of foreboding.

Shortly thereafter a tally was sent down to Qin and Yong provinces

---

edition and Liu Lin). Cf. JS 120/3030n8. HYGZ also lists among the killed Gong Ni.

65. Following JS 120/3033n9 in emending Liang[a] 涼 to Liang 梁 in accordance with HYGZ 8/109.2 and Shang's biography in JS 57/1552.12.

66. Ren (455n2) argues persuasively that the JS editors have erred in reading *yibu* 義部, "volunteer militias," as the personal name Yi Xin. Liu (625n2) assumes instead that the character *xin* dropped out of the HYGZ text because of its graphic similarity to the character *bu*, but a personal name seems out of place in this sentence. Moreover, Yi does not otherwise occur as a surname in either JS or HYGZ.

67. HYGZ 8/109.5 gives a more detailed breakdown of his forces. In addition to a tally of authority, Shang received one thousand "tally-guarding" troops, two thousand troops assigned to Liang province, and one thousand five hundred members of volunteer militia, with the remainder of the seven thousand being under the command of Wang Dun. Xu Jian is said to have moved from the Grand Wardenship of Zitong 梓潼 to the General Arousing Ardor (*yanglie jiangjun* 揚烈將軍) for Shu commandery. JS here follows SLGCQ (TPYL 123/6a).

68. HYGZ 8/109.7 attributes these words (with minor variations) to Wang Dun alone. Xin Ran is said to have concurred in this advice in order to make up for his own involvement in Zhao Xin's government, but the text is problematic and the episode occurs later in the HYGZ account.

ordering that in all cases where refugees had entered Hanchuan (Hanzhong), a tally was to be sent to their present location, summoning them to return.

The Censors (yushi 御史) Feng Gai 馮該 and Zhang Chang 張昌[69] *were appointed Retainers (congshi 從事) for Qin and Yong provinces, in charge of the return of the refugees. More than ten thousand households were moved.* [HYGZ 8/109.9–10]

Te's elder brother Fu 輔, who had remained in their native village, came (to Te) on the pretext of escorting his family back. When he arrived in Shu, he said to Te, "The Central States are in disorder. They are not worth returning to." Convinced by him, Te resolved to occupy Ba and Shu by force. In recognition of his achievements in chastising Zhao Xin, the court appointed Te General Who Spreads Intimidation (*xuanwei jiangjun* 宣威將軍) and Marquis of Changle Township 長樂鄉侯 and appointed Li Liu General of Aroused Intimidation (*fenwei jiangjun* 奮威將軍) and Marquis of Wuyang 武陽. When the sealed document of investiture came down to Yi province, it ordered that those refugees from the Six Commanderies who had joined with Te in chastising Xin be listed in order that they might be rewarded and enfeoffed. At the time, Xin Ran had been summoned to court out of rotation and did not wish to comply with the summons. He also wished to take Zhao Xin's destruction as his own accomplishment, so he "slept on" the court command and did not report the true situation. All the people hated him for this.

Luo Shang sent a Retainer to urge the refugees on their way, giving them until the seventh lunar month to get on the road. Xin Ran was by nature avaricious and cruel. He wished to kill the leaders of the refugees and seize their possessions, so he sent around a circular (*xi* 檄) ordering their departure. He also commanded the Grand Warden of Zitong Zhang Yan 張演 to set up barriers at various strategic locations and search them for valuables.[70] Te and the others were insistent in their requests, asking an extension until the fall harvest.[71]

---

69. This is presumably not the same Zhang Chang who revolted in 303. The latter had held only the lowly post of clerk. See JS 100/2612.

70. HYGZ 8/109.14–110.1 reads, "Xin Ran and Li Bi further informed Luo Shang that during the time of Zhao Xin's disorders the refugees had wrongfully seized many goods and that he should take advantage of their transfer to erect barriers in order to confiscate these goods."

71. The JS text here seems confused. HYGZ 8/110.1–2 places the establishment of the barriers in the seventh and eighth months, thus after the fall extension had been granted. JS also makes no reference to the refugees' request for a further extension until winter.

Te repeatedly dispatched Yan Shi of Tianshui to Luo Shang requesting a delay in the enforcement of the command and a temporary extension until autumn. He also presented bribes to Shang and Feng Gai, who approved this request. In the autumn, he requested another extension until winter. Xin Ran and Li Bi thought this impermissible and were determined to transfer them. Shi explained to the Lieutenant Governor Du Tao 杜弢 the pros and cons of forced transfer. Tao also wanted to grant the refugees a one-year reprieve, but Xin Ran and Li Bi objected and Shang followed their advice. Tao turned in his "Flowering Talent" tablet[72] and returned home because he knew his plans would not be employed.

At the time there was a white rainbow that stretched over the Greater Walled City (of Chengdu), with its head in a small village and its tail in Eastern Mountain. The Retainer Administering the Palace (zhizhong congshi 治中從事) Ma Xiu 馬休 asked Yan Shi, "What omen is this?" Shi replied, "The prognostication says that below (the rainbow) the breaths of ten thousand corpses are pressing upon the city. This is not an auspicious portent. Do you think that heavenly cataclysms can be trifled with? If the General Quelling the West (i.e., Shang) can be lenient with the scattered people, the disaster will dispel of itself." [HYGZ 8/109.10–14]

The refugees were scattered through Liang and Yi provinces, working as hired laborers. When they heard that the province and commanderies were pressing them to leave, all were troubled and bitter, at a loss as to what to do. Knowing that Te and his brothers had repeatedly requested a reprieve, all were moved by this and put their faith in them. Moreover, the rains were about to begin and the grain crop had not yet matured. The refugees had nothing to use as provisions for their journey, so they flocked to Te. Te then established a large encampment at Mianzhu to house the migrants and went to Xin Ran to plead for leniency. Ran was furious and sent people to post wanted posters for Te and his brothers on all major thoroughfares, offering a large reward. Seeing them, Te was greatly alarmed.

72. This is an official pronouncement recorded on a wooden board declaring Du's selection as a "Flowering and Talented," as described by Liu Lin (4/374n4). Liu assumes that Luo was responsible for Du's nomination, but his JS biography (JS 100/2612.1) implies this came at the very beginning of his career, as one might expect. Ren (456n8) points out that Tao's father had been Military Protector of Lueyang and for this reason was sympathetic to the refugees' case. Tao eventually migrated to the Central Yangzi region, where he became involved in another rebellion of refugees.

Collecting them and taking them back, he and Xiang[a] changed the terms of the reward to read, "He who can send the head of one of the leaders from the six commanderies, Li, Ren, Yan, Yang, or Shangguan, or the Marquises and Kings of the Di-sou[73] are to be rewarded with one hundred rolls of silk."[74] Since the refugees were already unhappy about the transfer, all went to ally with Te. Galloping their horses and donning quivers, with one voice they gathered like clouds. Within a fortnight to a month the multitude numbered more than twenty thousand. Li Liu also gathered together a force of several thousand. Te then divided them into two camps, with Te occupying the northern camp and Liu occupying the eastern one.

Te sent Yan Shi to see Luo Shang and petition for an extension of the deadline. When Shi arrived, he saw that Xin Ran was barricading and fortifying strategic points and thoroughfares, planning to plunder the refugees. He sighed, "If someone walls a city in the absence of bandits, there must be a grudge preserved therein. Now he hurries the preparations; disorder is imminent!"[75] Knowing that Xin Ran and Li Bi would prove impossible to dissuade from their plans, he took leave of Shang to return to Mianzhu. As he was leaving, Shang said to him, "Announce my intentions to the refugees. I accede to their request for leniency." Shi replied, "Your excellency has been deceived by treacherous words. I fear there is no chance for leniency. The common people may be weak, but they cannot be treated lightly. When pressured unreasonably, the anger of the masses is not easily transgressed. I fear the disaster you create will be considerable." Shang said, "But I do not deceive you. You should go now." When Yan reached Mianzhu he said to Te, "Although Shang said this, he

73. It is unclear whether Sou here is to be taken as a name of a distinct ethnic group or as a generic suffix for non-Chinese peoples, i.e., "kings and marquises of the Di barbarians." HYGZ 2/23.1 and 2/23.12 both mention individuals said to be Di-Sou, hence there at least *sou* parallels *yi* 夷 in that it is appended to the name of an ethnic group with no apparent change in meaning.

74. HYGZ 8/110.2 gives a longer version of the altered poster: "Anyone who can send in one of the major clans from the six commanderies, Yan, Zhao, Ren, Yang, Li, or Shangguan, or the Di Sou (see the preceding note), or the Liang 梁, Dou 竇, Fu 符, Kui 隗, Dong 董, or Fei 費 families, will receive one hundred rolls of silk per head."

75. HYGZ 8/110.3 places the fortification of the cities and Yan's comment in the eighth month of 301. The bounty incident and Te's establishment of the two camps in the ninth are preceded by the record of an army dispatched to Mianzhu, ostensibly to cultivate wheat but actually to capture any refugees who might seek to flee.

cannot necessarily be believed. Why? Shang has not enforced awe-inspiring punishments, and Ran and the others each control a powerful body of troops. If one day they should rebel, they will be more than Shang can control. We must prepare ourselves." Te accepted this advice.

Xin Ran and Li Bi plotted together, saying, "Marquis Luo is avaricious but indecisive. Day by day the refugees are able to unfold their treacherous schemes. Li Te and his brothers all have heroic qualities. We are going to be enslaved by stableboys. We should devise a decisive strategy. We need not ask (Shang) about it again." They then sent the Defender of Guanghan Commandery Zeng Yuan 曾元 and the Commanders of the Serrated-Flag Gate Zhang Xian 彰顯 and Liu Bing 劉並 to secretly lead thirty thousand infantry and cavalry in an assault on Te's camp. Luo Shang heard of this and also sent the Protector-General Tian Zuo 田佐 to aid Zeng. Learning of the attack in advance, Te repaired his armor and sharpened his weapons, maintaining his troops on alert while awaiting them. When Zeng Yuan and the others arrived, Te lay peacefully on his back and made no move. When half their troops had entered, he struck, springing the ambush. Casualties were extremely heavy; Tian Zuo, Zeng Yuan, and Zhang Xian were slain and their heads sent on to show Luo Shang and Xin Ran.[76] Shang said to his staff, "These caitiffs were as good as gone, but Guanghan (i.e., Xin Ran) would not listen to me, thereby increasing the bandits' power. Now what are we going to do?"

Thereupon, the people of the six commanderies proclaimed Te their leader. Te ordered the Inspector of Militias for the People of the Six Commanderies (*liujunren buqudu* 六郡人部曲督) Li Han 李含, the Prefect of Shanggui 上邽 Ren Cang 任藏, the Prefect of Shichang 始昌 Yan Shi 閻式, the Grandee Remonstrant (*jianyi dafu* 諫議大夫) Li Pan 李攀, the Prefect of Chencang 陳倉 Li Wu[a] 李武, the Prefect of Yinping 陰平 Li Yuan 李遠, and the Defender Commanding Troops (*jiangbing duwei* 將兵都尉) Yang Bao 楊褒 to submit a memorial nominating Te to be Great General Stabilizing the North (*zhenbei dajiangjun* 鎮北大將軍), assuming the administration and appointing and enfeoffing in accordance with the precedent of Liang

76. HYGZ records that Shang sent Tian Zuo to assist only after Zeng Yuan had attacked and been killed. Ren (457n14) explains that the JS here must base itself upon the *Sanshiguo chunqiu* of Xiao Fang, which in turn relied upon the elite patrons of Luo Shang and Xin Ran in Chengdu and Guanghan, respectively, for this confused version of events.

Tong 梁統 serving Dou Rong 竇融.[77] His younger brother Liu was to carry out the duties of General Stabilizing the East (*zhendong jiangjun* 鎮東將軍) so as to aid in the stabilization and unification.

Te then advanced troops to attack Xin Ran at Guanghan. Each time Ran sent out his forces, Te defeated them. Luo Shang sent Li Bi and Fei Yuan at the head of a force to rescue Ran, but they feared Te and dared not advance. Ran, his wisdom and strength exhausted, fled to Jiangyang.[78] Te entered and occupied Guanghan, appointing Li Chao 李超 as Grand Warden. Advancing, he attacked Shang in Chengdu. Yan Shi sent Luo Shang a missive reprimanding him for giving credence to slanderers and wishing to attack the refugees; he also set forth the achievements of Te and his brothers on behalf of the dynasty in pacifying the Yi region.

Luo Shang wrote a warning admonishing Yan Shi. Shi replied, "Xin Ran resorts to all sorts of treachery; Du Jing(wen)[79] explodes like a madman. Zeng Yuan is a mere lackey, and Tian Zuo cannot control his blood-lust. Li Shuping (Li Bi) has talents suitable to administering a court position but does not have the heart to be a military commander. They might be said capable of bettering Qiang tribesmen already beaten into exhaustion, but no more. I previously discoursed for you upon the pros and cons of transferring the refugees versus letting them stay. All men long for their native land; who would be unwilling to go? However, when they first, in search of food, took up positions as hired laborers, their families were scattered in five directions. Moreover, they encountered torrential rains, and when they requested an extension until the winter harvest, they were refused. It is no wonder they fight like a cornered deer fending

77. During the disorders preceding the foundation of the Latter Han, a group of local officials in the Shaanxi-Gansu region gathered together and elected one of their number, Dou Rong, to act as temporary leader with the title of Great General until an effective central government was reestablished. See HHS 23/796–797, 34/1165.4. HYGZ 8/110 records Te's assumption of this position as well as that of Pastor of Yi Province under the tenth month of 301 but mentions the Dou Rong story only after the capture of Guanghan.

78. Modern Lu 瀘 county in Sichuan. HYGZ 8/110.8 says that Xin Ran, after blaming the defeat on the Prefect of Mianzhu, Qi Bao 岐苞, and beheading him, fled to Deyang 德陽, southeast of modern Suining. This location seems more probable.

79. That is, Du Tao. Du's occurrence in this letter does not accord with what we have been told so far concerning his actions. Liu Lin, citing the omission of this comment concerning Du from ZZTJ's paraphrase (86/2667) as evidence of a textual problem, suggests that Du Jing is a graphic error for Zhang Xian 張顯. See Liu 8/630n8.

off a tiger. I fear only that you will correct them too severely, forcing these people to refuse to stretch forth their necks and await the blade. The worry lies in the future. If you had listened to my words and given them time to pack, they would have gathered together by the end of the ninth month and happily hit the road in the tenth. When sending a command down to townships and villages, how can you do it like this! Making no reference to the approval already granted, you followed importunate counsels. Now Xin Ran has absconded like a slave and Li Shuping has fled. In this process of dissolution and fragmentation the danger will eventually devolve upon yourself. This is what is meant by "If you do not know to bend the chimney-pipe and move away the firewood, you will end up with burned guests." [HYGZ 8/110.9–13]

Upon reading the letter, Luo Shang realized that they would have have great ambitions, so he barricaded himself in Chengdu and requested help from Ning and Yi provinces.

Te then proclaimed himself Commissioner Bearing Credentials (*shichijie* 使持節), Great Inspector-General, and Great General Stabilizing the North, assuming the administration and appointing and enfeoffing in accordance with the precedent of Dou Rong 竇融 in Hexi (the Shaanxi-Gansu corridor).[80] His elder brother Fu became General of Doughty Cavalry (*piaoji jiangjun* 驃騎將軍); his younger brother Xiang[a] became General of Spirited Cavalry (*xiaoji jiangjun* 驍騎將軍); his eldest son Shi 始 became General of Martial Intimidation (*wuwei jiangjun* 武威將軍);[81] his second son Dang 蕩 became General Stabilizing the Army (*zhenjun jiangjun* 鎮軍將軍); his youngest son Xiong 雄 became General of the Van (*qian jiangjun* 前將軍). Li Han became Colonel of the Western Barbarians; Han's sons Guo 國 and Li Li, Ren Hui, Li Gong 李恭, Shangguan Jing 上官晶, Li Pan, and Fei To became commanders (*jiangshuai* 將帥).[82] Ren Cang, Shangguan Dun, Yang Bao, Yang Gui 楊桂, Wang Da 王達, and Qu Xin 麹歆 became his minions (*zhuaya* 爪牙). Li Yuan, Li Bo 李博, Xi Bin 夕斌, Yan Cheng 嚴檉, Shangguan Qi 上官琦, Li Tao 李濤, and Wang Huai 王懷 became bureaucrats (*liaoshu* 僚屬).[83] Yan Shi became Master of Counsels (*mouzhu* 謀主).

80. HYGZ 8/110.4 does not record assumption of the offices of Commissioner Bearing Credentials and Great Inspector-General. Moreover, it places all of these appointments in the tenth month, before the attack on Guanghan.

81. HYGZ omits Li Shi and describes Li Dang as Te's eldest son, perhaps because Shi was not the issue of Te's primary wife.

82. HYGZ gives their office as "general."

83. In HYGZ (8/110.4–6) Li Yuan, Li Bo, and Xi Bin are included in the

At the time, Luo Shang, being avaricious and cruel, had become the bane of the common folk, whereas Te had given the people a simplified legal code (*yuefa* 約法) in three articles, granted amnesties on debts and provided emergency loans, paid courtesy calls on worthies, and transferred those on stalled career paths. Both the military and the civil administration were well-ordered. The common people made up a ditty about him, that went:

Li Te is still preferable,
Luo Shang kills us.[84]

Shang had been repeatedly defeated by Te. Now he interposed a long blockade, erecting palisades along the river from Du'an 都安 to Qianwei, holding Te at bay for more than seven hundred *li*.[85]

First year of Taian (302). Spring. Luo Shang's Commander of the Serrated-Flag Gate Xia Kuang 夏匡 *assaulted Li Te at Lishi* 立石,[86] *but was unsuccessful.* [HYGZ 8/110.14–111.1] King Yong of Hejian 河間王顒 sent the Protector-General (*duhu* 督護) Ya Bo 衙博 and the Grand Warden of Guanghan Zhang Zheng 張徵 to chastise Te.[87] The Colonel of the Western Barbarians Li Yi 李毅 also sent five thousand troops to aid Luo Shang. Shang sent the Protector-General Zhang Gui to encamp at Fancheng 繁城 (northeast of modern Xinfan), so as to attack Te from three sides.

Ya Bo had just sent the Military Advisor Meng Shao 蒙劭 *to persuade Li Te to surrender. Shang sent Bo a letter, saying, "Long ago I*

---

preceding group, there labeled "advisors" (*canzuo* 參佐); Yan Cheng, Shangguan Qi, Li Tao, and Wang Huai are omitted altogether. A further category of "retainers" (*bincong* 賓從) is added, comprising Yan Shi, He Ju, and Zhao Su.

84. Luo's biography (JS 57/1552–1553) adds the lines: "The General Quelling the West / On the contrary creates disaster."

85. Du'an was east of modern Guan county. Qianwei is modern Pengshan, not the current Qianwei. HYGZ 8/110.13 records that Luo had forded the Pi River 郫水, the current term for the main course of the Yangzi as it flows through the Chengdu region. It would seem then that Luo was trying to dig in on the west and south side of the Yangzi. Te and company set themselves up in Guanghan (HYGZ 8/110.13).

86. Lishi (Standing Rock) is not recorded in standard sources, but Ren (460n1) suggests that it may have been near Xindu, in the vicinity of which are found monoliths thought to mark the tombs of the former kings of Shu.

87. HYGZ 8/111.1 tells us further that Ya Bo encamped at Zitong and that Zhang Zheng, who was in fact being reappointed to his former office, occupied Deyang.

88. There is no other mention of such a correspondence. Ren (460n3) speculates that it was a letter sent to Shang by Liu asking for a reprieve when Shang and Xin Ran were advancing upon Mianzhu.

received Li Liu's missive expressing an earnest desire to surrender.[88] *Because of his adherence to my awesome power at that time, he was able to return to his status as bandit. I have heard that Te puts his faith in lowly clerks*[89] *yet daily Li Liu and Li Xiang[a] lead seven or eight thousand troops in raids upon us. Their perfidious treachery is unfathomable cunning. You must use great care in holding them at bay."* Bo did not follow Shang's suggestion and consequently was defeated by Te at Yangmian 陽沔.[90] *The Grand Warden of Zitong Zhang Yan 張演, abandoning his stores, fled to Baxi.* [HYGZ 8/111.2–4]

Te ordered Dang and Xiong to make a surprise attack on Ya Bo. Te personally struck at Zhang Gui, and Gui's force suffered a great defeat. Dang engaged Ya Bo in battle for several consecutive days; as his defeats accumulated, Bo's dead came to number more than half. Dang pursued Bo to Hande 漢德,[91] whence he fled to Jiameng 葭萌.[92] Dang advanced and plundered Baxi. The Vice-Administrator (*cheng* 丞) of Baxi commandery Mao Zhi 毛植 and the Five Officials (*wuguan* 五官) Xiang Zhen 襄珍 surrendered the commandery to Dang.[93] Dang looked after those who had first allied themselves with him, and the common people placed their trust in him. Advancing, Dang attacked Jiameng, and Bo again fled far away, his troops all surrendering to Dang.

89. Liu Lin (632n5) takes this as a reference to Meng Shao and, indirectly, Ya Bo. Ren (460n3) understands it as a more general reference to officials.

90. Yangmian Outpost was north of Zitong. Liu 633n6.

91. Northeast of modern Jiange in Sichuan. Zang 1936:1105.2.

92. Jiameng had been named Hanshou 漢壽 under the Shu-Han regime and Jinshou 晉壽 under the Jin. It reverted to its ancient name of Jiameng under Cheng-Han rule, then was restored to Jinshou after the Jin reconquest of Sichuan. *Dushi fangyu jiyao* (68/2924–2925) places Jiameng northwest of modern Guangyuan, and differentiates it from Jinshou to the east of Guangyuan. Zang (1936:1058.3) gives a location fifty *li* southeast of Zhaohua, presumably the location Gu Zuyu calls Jinshou. Ushioda (1954:24) places the Han site at modern Zhaohua. Cf. ZZTJ 84/2669.

93. HYGZ 8/111.5 inserts the statement, "Ya Bo's talents encompassed civil and military arts. The Great General of the Western Expedition, the King of Hejian, prized him highly. When he had previously been Grand Warden of Yinping, he was cashiered at the instigation of the Retainer Mao Fu 毛扶 of Ba commandery. He bore a grudge against men of Liang province. . . . Before the bandits had arrived, Bo heard a crane call and withdrew. Bo wanted to place the blame on [the Governor] of Liang Province, but the [Retainer] Administering the Palace reported the affair, and Bo was charged with a crime. Jin then used Xu Xiong as Governor of Liang Province in his place." Some editions of HYGZ give Xiang's given name as Ban 班, doubtless a graphic error for Zhen. The Liao collation suggests that the characters Baxi preceding Mao Zhi's name are extraneous and that he was in fact the Vice-Administrator of Zitong commandery, a position ably refuted by Ren Naiqiang (461n4). Cf. Ren 461n5; Liu 633n9.

First year of Taian (302).[94] Te proclaimed himself Pastor of Yi Province, Inspector-General of the Military Affairs of Liang and Yi Provinces, Great General, and Great Inspector-General. He changed the reign name to Jianchu 建初 (Establishing a Beginning) and pardoned all within the realm.

Te then advanced and attacked Zhang Zheng. Occupying high, strategic positions, Zheng held off Te for a number of days. At the time, Te and Dang had separated into two camps. Zheng waited until Te's camp was empty, then sent infantry through the mountains to attack him. Te was not successful in repelling the attack, and, hemmed in by mountain defiles, his troops did not know what to do. Luo Zhun 羅準 and Ren Dao 任道 both exhorted Te to retreat, but Te was convinced that Dang would certainly arrive and therefore would not permit it. Zheng's troops arrived in increasing numbers. Since the mountain road was extremely narrow, allowing only one or two people to pass at a time, Dang's force was unable to advance. Dang said to his Marshal (sima 司馬) Wang Xin 王辛, "My father is deep in the midst of the bandits. This is my dying day." Then, donning a second layer of armor and grasping a long lance, with a great yell he drove straight ahead. Wielding his blade as if intent upon death, he killed more than ten men. Zheng's troops came to the rescue of their comrades, but Dang's army to a man fought to the death, and Zhang Zheng's army ultimately was shattered.

Te argued for allowing Zheng to return to Fu 涪 (modern Mianyang). Dang and Wang Xin submitted a memorial that said, "Zheng's army has endured successive battles; his troops are wounded and mutilated, both wisdom and courage exhausted. You should take advantage of this fatigue to seize him. If you release him and treat him leniently, he will tend to his wounded and gather those who have fled. When the remnants of his army are reunited, it will not be easy to deal with him." Following their advice, Te again advanced to attack Zhang Zheng. Zheng broke through the encirclement and fled. Dang pursued him by land and water and in the end killed him. He captured Zheng's son Cun 存 alive and sent him home with Zheng's corpse.

Jian Shi 騫碩 was named Grand Warden of Deyang and conquered territory as far as Dianjiang 墊江[95] in Ba commandery.

94. SLGCQ, ZZTJ, and *Sanshiguo chunqiu* all place this assumption of titles and new reign name in the second year of Taian, i.e., 303. See JS 120/3033n12, ZZTJ 85/2677.

95. Modern Hechuan. The Hu Sanxing commentary to ZZTJ 84/2679 says that *dian* should here be read *die*. Both readings are listed in the *Guangyun* as

When Te was attacking Zhang Zheng[96] he sent Li Xiang[a] with Li Pan, Ren Hui, and Li Gong to encamp at Piqiao 毗橋[97] in order to ward off Luo Shang. Shang sent a force to do battle, but Xiang[a] and company defeated it. Shang again sent several thousand men to fight, and Xiang[a] again trapped and defeated them, capturing a great amount of arms and armor while attacking and burning his gate. Li Liu advanced and camped north of Chengdu. Luo Shang sent the Commander Zhang Xing 張興 to feign a surrender to Xiang[a] in order to determine his true situation. At the time Liu's troops numbered no more than two thousand; Zhang Xing returned by night to inform Luo Shang of this. Shang sent ten thousand elite troops[98] holding sticks in their mouths (to insure silence) under Xing's command to surprise Xiang[a]'s camp by night. Li Pan died fighting to repulse this force. Xiang[a] fled with his troops and officers to Liu's palisades. There they combined forces with Liu and struck back at Shang's army. Shang's army was set in disorder and defeated; only one or two in ten returned.[99] The Jin Governor of Liang Province Xu Xiong 許雄 sent an army to attack Te, which Te defeated.

The General of the Western Expedition (Sima Yong) then sent the Overseer of the Army (jianjun 監軍) *Liu Chen* 劉沈 *to lead the western expedition. Because of events in central China, it did not succeed.*[100] *The Colonel of the Southern Barbarians* (nanyi xiaowei 南夷校尉) *Li Yi dispatched Sou troops to aid Luo Shang. His army was defeated, and Li Te's position daily grew stronger.*

Second year (303). Spring. First month. First day. [HYGZ 8/111.9–10]

Advancing to the attack, Te destroyed Shang's marine force and went on to plunder Chengdu.[101] The Grand Warden of Shu Com-

readings for place-names in Ba. See *Shiyun huibian*, pp. 254, 311; Zang 1936:1084.1.

96. HYGZ 8/111.7 places this event in the eighth month of 303.

97. Ten *li* south of modern Xindu, Sichuan.

98. HYGZ 8/111.8 specifies "Sou troops" with no indication of their number.

99. HYGZ notes that they fled, abandoning their armor and weapons.

100. The account in Liu Chen's *Jinshu* biography (JS 89/2306) gives a different version of events. There we read that Liu Chen had been dispatched by the court, then under the control of Sima Jiong, to lead Luo Shang and Xu Xiong in a concerted attack on Li Liu, but that Liu Chen was detained in Chang'an by Sima Yong, who proposed to send Xi Wei 席薳 on in his place. It would seem that the troops under Liu's command remained in Chang'an and were eventually seized by Sima Yong. Cf. ZZTJ 85/2679, which relates this affair under the third month of 303 and refers to Liu Chen as Palace Attendant (*shizhong* 侍中).

101. HYGZ 8/111.10 gives two locations where Te and his troops crossed

mandery Xu Jian surrendered the small city of Chengdu to Te. Te
named Li Huang 李璜[102] Grand Warden of Shu Commandery in order
to pacify the city. Luo Shang sealed himself within Chengdu. Liu
advanced and camped west of the River.[103] Shang was frightened and
sent an emissary to sue for peace.

At this time the people of Shu, fearing for their safety, erected
village fortifications and requested Te's commands. Te sent people
to comfort them.

*Li Xiong sent a missive remonstrating that Te should take hostages
and not disperse his elite troops. Li Liu also remonstrated to this
effect. Te said angrily, "The great affair is already settled, but we
should pacify the people. Why should we act out of suspicion and
kidnap without cease?"* [HYGZ 8/111.12–13]

The Retainer of Yi Province Ren Ming 任明 (i.e., Ren Rui)[104] advised
Shang, saying, "Li Te has not only treacherously rebelled, assaulting
and terrorizing the common people. He has also dispersed his followers throughout the many fortified villages. He is arrogant, neglect-
ful, and unprepared. Thus has Heaven destroyed him. You should
inform the various villages and, secretly arranging a date, strike him

---

the Yangzi, Angdi 益底 and Chishui 赤水, or Red River. Ren (462n9) would
place the first at Taihechang 太何場, near the confluence of the Pi River 郫江
and the Pi River 毗河, and identifies the Red River as the Huanglongxi 黃龍溪,
or Yellow Dragon Stream.

102. Following ZZTJ 85/2678 and below, JS 120/3029.3 and 121/3036.5
in reading Li Huang 李璜 for Li Jin 李瑾. The characters are easily confused,
and the name Li Jin does not occur elsewhere. Cf. JS 120/3034n14.

103. Liu Lin (635n3) understands this to be Pi River, in the area of the
modern Pi, Shuangliu, Wenjiang, and Chongqing 崇慶 counties. HYGZ 8/111.11
further specifies the place as Jianshang 檢上, which Liu identifies as a location
near the Jian River, the modern Zoumajiang, but Ren (462n9) would place it in
Wenjiang county.

104. HYGZ 8/111.13 gives this name as Ren Rui 任叡, and the *Jinshu*
biography of Luo Shang (57/1553) reads Ren Rui 銳. ZZTJ 85/2678 follows
the HYGZ reading, further identifying him as the Retainer of the Weapons
Section of Yi Province, Ren Rui of Shu Commandery. JS here follows SLGCQ
(TPYL 123/6a). Ren (462n11) argues that Chang Qu originally wrote Rui 叡 in
his *Shu Li shu* but changed the name to Ming when compiling HYGZ in the Jin
capital in order to avoid the taboo name of Sima Rui 司馬睿 (?–322), Emperor
Yuan of Jin. This Ming was adopted by the JS editors but was then changed
back to Rui by some anonymous collator in late Tang or early Song times. This
account does not explain why SLGCQ, which used the *Shu Li shu* directly,
reads Ming, unless this is the result of editing on the part of the TPYL editors.
Still, Ming is on semantic grounds a likely substitution for a tabooed Rui, and
this is confirmed by the Luo Shang biography reading, clearly a phonetic error
for this same Rui. Cf. JS 120/3034n15.

from within and without; you are certain to defeat him." Shang followed this advice.

Letting Ren Rui down over the city wall with a rope, Shang sent him to transmit his order to the various villages, arranging that they would together chastise Te on the tenth day of the second month (March 14, 303). He personally wrote a second message, "By the Willow Stream."[105] [HYGZ 8/111.14–112.1]

Ren first pretended to surrender to Te, and when Te asked of the situation within the city, he replied, "The rice and grain are almost exhausted. All that is left is goods and silk." He then asked leave to visit and check up on his family. Te permitted this. Ren Ming secretly persuaded the various villages, and all of them accepted his orders. He returned and reported to Shang, who agreed to dispatch his troops at the appointed time. The villages also agreed to arrive simultaneously.

Second year (303).[106] Emperor Hui sent the Governor of Jing Province, Song Dai 宋岱,[107] and the Grand Warden of Jianping 建平, Sun Fu 孫阜, to rescue Shang. Sun Fu had already taken up a position in Deyang, and Te sent Li Dang overseeing Li Huang to aid Ren Cang in repelling him. Shang sent a large force to surprise Te's camp. The battle continued for two days, but Te's force, being smaller, was no match for Shang's and he suffered a great defeat. Gathering together and regrouping what remained of his troops, he withdrew to Xinfan 新繁.[108] When Shang's force sought to return (to Chengdu), Te again pursued them and they battled back and forth over a distance of thirty-odd *li*. Shang sent forth a great army to repulse Te, and Te's army suffered a severe defeat. Li Te, Li Fu, and Li Yuan

---

105. Ren (463n12) would read *yang* 揚 for *yang* 楊, yielding "By that rising stream." He explains that the character can be decomposed into the date of the planned attack, deriving "month" from the bottom half of the phonetic *yang* 昜 and "day" from the top, then separating the "hand" radical into a "ten" 十 and a "one" 一, with the second line of the "two" coming from the line separating the two halves of the phonetic. This explanation seems a bit forced and certainly not readily apparent unless accompanied by an explanation, but no other interpretations have been proposed. Liu (636n10) simply says that it "cannot be explained."

106. ZZTJ 85/2677–2678 follows HYGZ in placing Li Te's capture of Chengdu in the first month of 303 and his death in the second.

107. This passage along with JS 43/1241.12, 57/1553.3, and 60/1634.3 originally read Zong 宗 for Song 宋. The JS Annals and HYGZ both read Song. Cf. JS 4/112n22, Ren 466n2.

108. An anachronistic term for what was at this time still Fancheng, northeast of modern Xinfan. Zang 1936:1287.2.

were beheaded, their corpses burned and their heads transmitted to Luoyang.[109]

Te reigned for two years. When his son Xiong arrogated to himself the title of King *(wang)*, he posthumously canonized Te as King Jing 景王. When he usurped the title of Emperor, he posthumously honored Te as Emperor Jing, with the temple name Shizu 始祖 (First Patriarch).

---

109. HYGZ 8/112.3 adds at this point that Luo Shang did not follow up on this victory, sending only a mobile brigade against Li Dang.

Li Liu

李流

Li Liu 李流, sobriquet Xuantong 玄通, was Li Te's fourth younger brother. He was fond of learning when young and adept at archery and riding. The Colonel of the Eastern Qiang (*dong Qiang xiaowei* 東羌校尉) He Pan 何攀, claiming that he had the courage of a Meng Ben 孟賁 or a Xia Yu 夏育,[1] selected Liu to be Inspector of the Eastern Qiang (*dong Qiang du* 東羌督). When he sought refuge in Yi province, Governor Zhao Xin esteemed him highly. When Xin had Li Xiang gather together a personal army, Liu also summoned the young men from his native region, amassing several thousand. When Xiang was killed by Xin, Liu aided Li Te in settling the migrants, defeating Chang Jun at Mianzhu and subduing Zhao Xin at Chengdu. The court, having assessed his merit, named Liu General of Aroused Intimidation and enfeoffed him as Marquis of Wuyang.

When Li Te assumed the reins of government, he appointed Liu General Stabilizing the East. Occupying the eastern camp, he was referred to as Protector-General of the East (*dong duhu* 東督護). Te often put Liu in command of elite troops in order to hold off Luo Shang. When Te reduced the smaller walled city of Chengdu, he ordered the refugees of the Six Commanderies to divide into groups and enter the city through different entrances while the strong and brave among them were sent to inspect and command the fortified villages. Liu said to Te, "Your Excellency possesses a miraculous martial talent and has already conquered the small city, but the produce of the mountains has not yet been collected and our foodstores are not plentiful. You should take the sons and younger brothers of the great clans of the provincial and commandery capitals as hostages

1. Both these men of the Warring States era were renowned for their courage. Meng Ben is said to have been unafraid of crocodiles, rhinoceri, and tigers; Xia Yu was known for having frightened three armies through his voice alone. See the text and commentaries to *Shiji* 79/2407, 101/2739; *Wenxuan* (Liuchen ed.) 8/24b; *Zhanguoce* 5/47.

and, sending them to Guanghan, hold them in two camps, then, gathering together crack troops, establish strict defenses." He also wrote a letter to Te's Marshal, Shangguan Dun, expounding at length on the proposition that surrender should be accepted as if entertaining one's enemy. Te would not accept this advice.

After Te died, most of the people of Shu rebelled and the refugees were very frightened.[2] Liu and his nephews Dang and Xiong collected their remaining forces and returned to Chizu 赤祖.[3] Liu guarded the eastern camp while Dang and Xiong guarded the northern one. Liu proclaimed himself Great General, Great Inspector-General, and Pastor of Yi Province.

At the time, Song Dai and a marine force of thirty thousand were encamped at Dianjiang. Sun Fu, in the van, reduced Deyang, capturing the commander of its defense appointed by Te, Jian Shi; the Grand Warden Ren Cang and company retreated to Fu.[4] Luo Shang sent the Protector-General Chang Shen 常深 to encamp at Piqiao and the Commanders of the Serrated-Flag Gate Zuo Fan 左氾, Huang Hong 黃訇, and He Chong 何沖 to attack the northern camp from three sides.

Third month. Luo sent the Protectors-General Zhang Gui, He Chong, and Zuo Fan to establish a base at Fancheng; Mianzhu surrendered. Yao Shen 藥紳 and Du A 杜阿, commoners from Fuling,[5] arose in response to Shang. Shang also sent the Protector-General Chang Shen to establish a base at Piqiao, but he was repelled by Li Liu and Li Xiang[a]. Li Dang and Li Xiong attacked Yao Shen.[6] Chang

2. HYGZ 8/112.3 adds at this point that Li Xiong appointed Li Li 李離 to be the Grand Warden of Zitong (modern Zitong county). This statement, which implies a preeminent role for Xiong when Liu was supposedly the leader of their group, is omitted from JS.

3. Northeast of modern Mianzhu. *Dushi Fangyu Jiyao* 67/2894.

4. Following HYGZ 8/112.5. JS reads Fuling 涪陵, which was east of modern Chongqing, clearly impossible given Song's position in Dianjiang and an unlikely retreat in any case since it would have taken his troops further away from the main refugee forces north of Chengdu. Fuling must be a mistake for Fu county, near modern Mianyang. In his commentary to ZZTJ, which follows JS in reading Fuling, Hu Sanxing maintains that Fuling in fact refers to this Fu and that the name remained in popular use in his day, but Ren scoffs at this assertion. See Ren 466n2.

5. Ren (466n3) maintains that Yao and Du were part of a group of five thousand families that had moved from Fuling to western Sichuan a century earlier, noting that Yao is recorded as a major clan of Quren.

6. Ren (466–467n4) argues that this sentence should be moved forward to before the preceding sentence. This improves the flow of the discourse, but Ren's suggested emendation has no textual support.

Shen defeated Xiang[a], killing Li Pan. His younger brother Li Gong assumed command (of Pan's troops). Zuo Fan and Huang Yin 闇 *(i.e., Hong) closed upon and attacked Te's northern encampment. The Di and Qiang within the encampment, led by Fu Cheng, Wei Bo, and Shi Ding* 石定, *rose in rebellion in response to Zuo Fan and Huang Yin, attacking Li Dang and Li Xiong. Li Dang's mother, Madame Luo, donned armor and went to inspect the ranks. Wei Bo personally wounded Madame Luo, injuring her eye, but her resolute spirit became all the more ardent. At the time, Fu Cheng and Wei Bo battled within the camp while Zuo Fan and Huang Yin attacked it from outside. This began in the morning and by midday the encampment was on the point of defeat. Just then, Liu, having defeated Chang Shen, and Xiong and Dang, having defeated Yao Shen, returned. They ran right into Fan and Yin and defeated them soundly. Cheng and Bo, at the head of their factions, broke through the encirclement and went to Shang.* [HYGZ 8/112.5–9]

Liu personally led Dang and Xiong in an attack on Chang Shen's fortifications. Overwhelmed, Shen's troops scattered like stars. They pursued them to Chengdu, where Luo Shang shut himself up behind the gates. Galloping to pursue and strike them, Dang ran into a lance planted in the ground at an angle (*yimao* 倚矛), was wounded, and died.

Dang was whipping his horse on in pursuit of the retreating army when he was impaled on a Sou long lance and died. Madame Luo and Xiong concealed this fact and observed no mourning in order to quiet the hearts of their followers. [HYGZ 8/112.9]

Because Li Te and Li Dang had both died and Song Dai and Sun Fu were pressing him again, Li Liu was extremely frightened. Moreover, the Grand Warden Li Han urged Liu to surrender, and Liu was about to follow his advice. Li Xiong and Li Xiang[a] remonstrated one after another, but Liu would not accept their advice. He sent his son Shi[b] 世 and Li Han's son Hu[a] 胡 as hostages to Sun Fu's camp. Li Hu's elder brother, Li Han's son Li 離, hearing that his father wanted to surrender, returned at a gallop from Zitong in hopes of remonstrating but did not arrive in time. He withdrew and plotted with Li Xiong to surprise Sun Fu's camp, saying, "If we succeed, I agree to alternate with you every three years as ruler."[7] Xiong said, "We can

---

7. No further mention is made of this pact. R. A. Stein (1963:34) cites this as an example of the practice of Daoist ideals of egalitarianism. He specifically links it to practices reported among the aborigines and attributed to the state of Da Qin 大秦. Da Qin, in turn, is a projection of the Daoist vision of utopia.

decide our plans now, but if the two old men do not agree, what will we do?" Li replied, "We should deal with them now. If we cannot control them, we should carry out the big plan (i.e., usurpation). Although the old gentleman is your uncle, the situation leaves us no choice. My father will be under your command; what more can he say?" Xiong was delighted. He then attacked Shang's army.

Xiong then sought to persuade the men of the Six Commanderies, inciting them with accounts of Luo Shang's incursions against them, frightening them with the prospect of suffering the disasters of the people of Shu, and explaining how this was the time to attain wealth and status through a surprise assault on Luo Shang. With their aid, he was able to defeat Sun Fu. Large numbers of Shang's army were killed; when Song Dai died of illness, the Jing province army retreated, and they turned to attack Shang. Ashamed of his own shortcomings, Li Liu entrusted military affairs to Li Xiong. [HYGZ 8/112.12–14]

Shang took refuge in the larger walled city (of Chengdu). Xiong forded the (Yangzi) river and killed the Grand Warden of Minshan Chen Tu 陳圖,[8] thereby entering the walled city of Pi. Liu moved the encampment to occupy it.[9] The people of the three provinces of Shu all had constructed fortifications at strategic locations. The cities and towns were all empty. Liu could find nothing to plunder; his officers and soldiers were hungry and straitened.

Fan Changsheng 范長生, a man of Fuling, had led more than a thousand families to settle on Green Castle Mountain.[10] Shang's Military Advisor Xu Yu 徐轝 of Fuling sought to become Grand Warden of Minshan, with intentions to enlist the aid of Fan Changsheng and attack Li Liu on two fronts. Shang did not agree (to this appointment), and Xu Yu resented it. He asked to be sent west of the (Yangzi) river and subsequently surrendered to Li Liu. He persuaded Fan Changsheng to supply Liu's army with foodstores. Changsheng agreed to this, and Liu's army was thereby restored.[11]

Li Liu had always esteemed Xiong as having the virtue of an

8. HYGZ (8/113.3) originally read Chen Shi 岩.

9. HYGZ 8/113.3–4 places the death of Chen Tu in the sixth month and his entry into Pi as well as Liu's transfer of the encampment in the beginning of the seventh month.

10. Fifty *li* southeast of Guan county in Sichuan. This mountain has special significance for religious Daoism. It is the fifth Cavern-Heaven and the subject of a book by the Tang mythographer Du Guangting 杜廣庭 (850–933). *Dushi fangyu jiyao* 66/2830.

11. HYGZ 8/113.7, which writes Xu's personal name 轝, records here his appointment to the post of General Pacifying the West under the rebels.

elder. He always said, "It is certainly this man who will raise our house." He ordered his sons to honor and serve him. When Liu's illness became critical, he said to his military commanders, "The General of Spirited Cavalry (i.e., Li Xiang[a]) is lofty and benevolent and in his knowledge and decisions has many stratagems. He is certainly capable of carrying out great affairs. However, the General of the Van (i.e., Xiong) is brave and martial and seems to be the choice of Heaven. You should all take orders from the General of the Van and make him King of Chengdu." He then died. At the time he was fifty-five years of age. The commanders joined in establishing Xiong as ruler. When Xiong usurped the imperial title, he posthumously honored Liu with the title King Wen of Qin 秦文王.

Li Xiang

李庠

Li Xiang 李庠, sobriquet Xuanxu 玄序, was Li Te's third younger brother. When young, he was known for his ardent spirit. He served at the commandery level as Investigator (*duyou* 督郵) and Recorder (*zhubu* 主簿); in both cases he was commended for being appropriate for the position. In the fourth year of the Yuankang reign period (294) he was named Filial and Pure (*xiaolian* 孝廉) but did not respond to the summons.[1] Later, because he was adept at riding and archery, he was recommended for the position of Worthy Commander (*liangjiang* 良將) but again did not accept the appointment. Because his talents encompassed both civil and military virtues, the province recommended him as Accomplished Prodigy (*xiuyi* 秀異), but he steadfastly refused the honor on pretext of illness. The province and commandery would not heed him and submitted his name. The Capital Protector (*zhonghujun* 中護軍) summoned him insistently; he had no choice but to respond and was made Cavalry Inspector of the Central Army (*zhongjun duji* 中軍督騎).[2] He was adroit and nimble, possessing above-average strength; people of his day compared him to Wen Ang 文鴦.[3]

Because Luoyang was in a state of disorder, he left this position

1. The Grand Warden of a commandery and other local officials were responsible for recommending to the central government individuals who exhibited virtuous conduct and hence were suitable for holding office. This practice was instituted by Han Wudi. Filial and Pure was the highest level of recommendation they could accord. See *Tongdian* 13/73.3; Hucker 1985:entry 2418; Mather 1959:67n12.

2. The Capital Protector led one of two armies stationed at the capital. See Hucker 1985:entry 1564. The Cavalry Inspector is otherwise unknown. In this case, it was a central government post, but Li Xiang[a] had received appointment to this post from Luo Shang. See JS 120/3025.1.

3. A man renowned for his physical strength. See JS 104/2725 and the Pei Songzhi commentary to SGZ 28/766.

citing illness. He was by nature chivalrous and enjoyed aiding those in difficulty. Men of his native place vied to ally themselves with him. When he sought refuge in Liang and Yi provinces in the company of the refugees from the Six Commanderies, if he met someone on the road who was starving or ill, Xiang would invariably protect and nurture them, giving them succor. He distributed bounty to the impoverished, thus winning the hearts of the masses.

When Li Xiang arrived in Shu, Zhao Xin esteemed him highly and in discussing military tactics with him would always praise his views. Xin would often remark to his intimates, "Li Xuanxu is the Guan Yu or Zhang Fei of today."[4] When Xin was about to turn to treason, he entrusted Xiang with a position of utmost intimacy. He then memorialized, naming Xiang Inspector of Militias (*buqudu* 部曲督) and had him gather together the strong and brave men from the Six Commanderies; he assembled more than ten thousand. In recognition of his achievement suppressing the rebellion of the Qiang, Zhao Xin memorialized that he be made General Intimidating Bandits, be permitted use of a red banner and curved canopy,[5] be enfeoffed as Marquis of Yangquan Post 陽泉亭侯, and be presented with one million cash and fifty horses. On the day that he was executed, none of the men of the Six Commanderies failed to shed tears for him. He was at the time fifty-four.

4. Guan Yu and Zhang Fei were famous generals who served the Shu Han state of Liu Bei.

5. These were the ceremonial regalia appropriate to a General or Governor. See the Li Shan commentary to *Wenxuan* 57/7b.

Li Xiong

李雄

Li Xiong 李雄, sobriquet Zhongjun 仲儁, was Li Te's third son. Once his mother, Madame Luo 羅氏, dreamed of a pair of rainbows ascending to Heaven from their door, with one of the rainbows stopping midway. Soon thereafter she gave birth to Li Dang. Later, when Madame Luo was drawing water she suddenly fell into a sleep-like state and dreamed of a huge snake encircling her body. She became pregnant as a result and fourteen months later gave birth to Xiong. She would often say, "If one of my two children dies first, the other will certainly attain great status." In the end Li Dang died first. Xiong was eight feet three inches tall (approximately six feet seven inches) and had a beautiful appearance.

A physiognomist examined him and said, "This man will become important. There are four signs of this: his eyes are like storied clouds, his nose is like a turtle or dragon, his mouth is square like a vessel, and his ears seems to face each other. He is destined to be a man of importance, and his rank will undoubtedly surpass that of the Three Dukes. [TPYL 123/7a]

When young, Xiong was known for his ardent spirit, and each time he would make the rounds of his native place, men of discernment would value him highly.

When Xiong was young, Xin Ran physiognomized him and said that he was destined for greatness. [HYGZ 9/119.8–9]

There was a certain Liu Hua 劉化, a Daoist magician, who would always tell others, "The men of Guanzhong and Long (Shaanxi and Gansu) will all migrate south. Among the sons of the Li family only Zhongjun has an extraordinary appearance; in the end he will be a ruler of men."[1]

---

1. The text to this point, except for the comment about Xiong's "ardent spirit," is quoted in TPYL 398/6a, where it is attributed to the *Shu Li shu*. It was also used in SLGCQ (quoted in TPYL 123/7a), where we do find the "ardent spirit" comment.

When Li Te raised troops in Shu and assumed control of the government, he made Xiong General of the Van.[2] When Li Liu died, Xiong proclaimed himself Great Inspector-General, Great General, and Pastor of Yi Province with his capital at the walled city of Pi 郫 城. When Luo Shang sent a commander to attack Xiong, Xiong struck and routed him.

Luo Shang launched repeated assaults on Pi. Li Xiong sent Pu Tai 朴泰 *of Wudu to deceive Shang, saying, "Due to their famine-ravaged, isolated, perilous situation, every day Li Xiang^a and Li Xiong fight and blame each other. Xiang^a wants to lead the people west of the river in search of grain. If an army were to come under cover, with me inside the city to respond, the city could be taken."* *Luo Shang thought this true and offered him huge amounts of gold and jewels. Pu Tai said, "I have not succeeded yet. It will not be too late to claim my reward after I have brought results." He also asked that a man be dispatched to accompany him and keep watch on him, to which request Luo Shang acceded. Pu Tai agreed to light a fire, upon which Wei Bo and the other forces would assault Pi. Li Xiang^a set an ambush along the road. Tai provided a long scaling ladder for Bo's army to ascend. When Bo's army saw the fire, they all scrambled to ascend the ladder. Xiong then sent his troops to strike them, inflicting a great defeat on Shang's forces.[3] Li Xiong immediately pursued the retreating army, arriving that night at the city wall (of Chengdu). With shouts of "Long live!" and cries of "The walled city of Pi has already been taken!" he entered the smaller city. Only then did Luo Shang realize the situation and barricade himself within the larger city. Xiang^a, in a separate action, attacked Qianwei, cutting off Shang's line of supply and capturing the Grand Warden Gong Hui* 龔恢 *of Wuling. When Gong Hui had previously been Prefect of Xi* 西 *county in Tianshui, Ren Hui had been his*

2. Cf. JS 120/3027.3.

3. Here I follow the paraphrase in ZZTJ 85/2686–2687 in interpreting this laconic passage. Ren (469n18) argues that the territory surrounding Pi is flat plains, leaving no possibility for an ambush, and that a scaling ladder left leaning against the wall would be too obvious a ploy, sure to arouse Shang's suspicions. He suggests instead that the text should be emended to read "Xiang^a arranged for a hidden guide" (*shi she fudao* 使設伏導) and that it was this guide who supplied them with a scaling ladder. There is no textual support for such an emendation, nor can we be certain about the terrain in the fourth century. Moreover, it was precisely Xiang^a's ambushing troops that proved decisive in this battle. Without them, what would be the purpose in encouraging Luo Shang's attack? JS does not record this event.

clerk. Ren asked him, "Do you recognize your old clerk or not?"
Gong Hui replied, "I recognize you; that is all." The commandery
clerks scattered like stars; only the Merit Officer Yang Huan 楊渙
attended upon him and protected him. Ren Hui said to him, "You
are a man of duty. I fear my power is insufficient to save him and
that Master Gong will not be able to escape (death). You should go
quickly!" Huan replied, "To turn my back on my lord in order to
preserve my life, how can this be as good as dying in the mainte-
nance of duty?" Consequently both were killed.[4]

Li Pu 李溥 *was named Grand Warden of Qianwei.*

Xiong captured Wei Bo alive but knew he was mortally wounded.
Wei Bo's daughter was the wife of Liang Shuang 梁雙, *who was*
employed by Xiong, and for this reason he did not have Bo killed.

Intercalary twelfth month. [HYGZ 8/113.7–14]

Shang's army was suffering a severe famine and was being attacked
spiritedly. Leaving the Commander of the Serrated-Flag Gate Zhang
Luo 張羅[5] to maintain the defenses, Luo Shang abandoned the city,
fleeing into the night. Zhang Luo opened the city gates and received
Xiong; thus Chengdu fell. At the time, famine was severe among
members of Xiong's army, and he led his troops to Qi 郪 in search
of grain. There they dug wild taro and ate them.[6] The people of Shu

4. Ren (469n20) suggests that all this material was omitted from JS because
it originated in a biography of Li Xiang[a] that Chang Qu included in the *Shu Li
shu*, but which was not adopted into JS.

5. The proper form of this figure's name is problematic. JS gives Luo Te 羅特.
HYGZ 8/114.1 reads, "He left the Commander of the Serrated-Flag Gate Zhang
Luo 張羅 to hold (*chi* 持) the city through the night. When Xiong awoke, he was
long gone. In his haste he lost his staff of halberd of authority. Luo Te (variant
chi) following behind, picked them up." There are no variants to the first occurrence of *chi,* and only the Yuanfeng and Liao editions read *te* for the second, but
the second *chi* is difficult to construe (Liu suggests "holding the credentials"),
and if the man is indeed Zhang Luo, it may be excrescent. Zhang Luo is mentioned
repeatedly in HYGZ (8/115.8, 116.3, 6; 9/120.7, 11) as a Jin official, and the
modern JS editors are reluctant to conclude that this same Zhang Luo, having
surrendered Chengdu to Li Xiong, could have gone on to such an illustrious
career, nor is he mentioned again in JS. According to HYGZ, however, he did
not surrender the city but merely abandoned it. ZZTJ (85/2691) follows HYGZ
in the matter of the name but still has Zhang Luo opening the city gates and
surrendering to Li Xiong. Cf. JS 121/3050n1, Ren 469n22, Liu 462n2.

6. Qi was south of modern Santai county. Stuart (1911:29) identifies this
"wild taro" (*yeyu* 野芋) as *alocasia macrorhiza.* HYGZ 9/119.10 reads, "Xiang
then led them to eat grain and taro at the walled city of the King of Qi (*Qiwang-
cheng* 郪王城)." A textual variant would read "Qi and Five Cities counties" (*Qi
Wucheng* 郪五城), Wucheng being a neighboring county. Ren's collation note

scattered, descending to Jiangyang in the east and entering the seven commanderies to the south.[7]

Because the Governor of Liang Province Xu Xiong had not made progress in his campaign against the "bandits," he was summoned to the imperial jail in a caged cart. Only the Military Protector Zhang Yin 張殷, *the Grand Warden of the Han Kingdom (i.e., Hanzhong) Du Mengzhi* 杜孟志, *the Chief Battle Leader (duzhanshuai* 都戰帥*) Zhao Wen* 趙汶, *and the Grand Warden of Baxi Zhang Yan* 張燕, *and Jing Zi* 荊子 *of Zitong were left to guard Hanzhong.[8]*

First year of Yongxing (304). Spring, first month. Luo Shang arrived in Jiangyang. The Provost of the Army (junsi 軍司*) Xin Bao* 辛寶 *proceeded to Luoyang to submit a report. An imperial rescript gave Luo Shang temporary control of the three commanderies of Badong, Ba, and Fuling with the right to supply himself with their military taxes.[9]* (HYGZ 8/114.1–5)

Because Fan Changsheng 范長生 of Xishan 西山 lived in seclusion pursuing the Dao and cultivating his spirit,[10] Xiong wished to invite

---

(483) argues that the abandoned ancient royal city, being in a remote area, was more likely to have still had grain and taro; Liu 663n1, on the other hand, thinks it unlikely they would limit themselves to a single site. The JS compilers seem to have agreed with Ren, since they make no mention of Five Cities county.

7. The commentary to HHS 23/800, quoting a "Treatise on Geography," lists these seven commanderies as Cangwu 蒼梧, Yulin 鬱林, Hepu 合浦, Jiaozhi 交止, Jiuzhen 九眞, Nanhai 南海, and Rinan 日南.

8. This passage in all editions of HYGZ is extremely confused, with the names Zhang Yin, Zhang Yan, and Jing Zi as well as the place-name Baxi having dropped out of the text before the Song dynasty. Ren (470n22) is able to supply all of these through a careful comparison with ZZTJ and with other passages in HYGZ. He further concludes that the unusual title Chief Battle Leader designated the individual coordinating the Battle Leaders of the commandery and of Baxi commandery, which was being administered from Hanzhong at the time. Ren's identification of Jing Zi in place of the text's "Jing Province" is the least certain of his proposed emendations but does make sense of an otherwise unconstruable passage. Ren notes that the name Jing Zi (or perhaps Jingzi?) does not seem to be a Han name but then makes the unwarranted assumption that his family must have been among the refugees from the Six Commanderies; Sichuan at this time still had an ample supply of native non-Chinese inhabitants.

9. As Ren (472n2) explains, these three commanderies originally belonged to Liang province, but were temporarily placed under Luo Shang's command because the one remaining commandery of Yi province still in Jin hands was insufficient to support his army.

10. SLGCQ (TPYL 123/7a) reads "seeking the resolution to guide and culti- vate (the *qi*)." The JS reading is preferable. Xishan is to be identified with Qing-

him and establish him as lord, serving him as an official. Changsheng adamantly refused.

He said, "If one projects forward to the Grand Beginning, the five phases converge in the jiazi 甲子 *year (304). The throne will come to the Li clan. It is not the proper time for me to rule."* [SLGCQ, in TPYL 123/7a][11]

Xiong, strongly deprecating himself, did not dare to assume control of the government. All affairs, no matters how minor, were decided by the brothers Li Guo 李國 and Li Li 李離. Guo and the others served Xiong even more diligently.

All of the military commanders insistently requested that Xiong assume the throne. In the first year of the Yongxing reign period (304) he usurped the title of King of Chengdu, proclaimed a general amnesty within his territory, and inaugurated the reign title of Jian-xing 建興 (Establishing the Rise).[12] He abolished the Jin legal code and created an abridged code in seven articles. He appointed his uncle Xiang[a] as Grand Tutor (*Taifu* 太傅), his elder brother Shi as Grand Protector (*taibao* 太保), the General Foiling the Charge Li Li as Grand Commandant (*taiwei* 太尉), the General Establishing Intimidation (*jianwei jiangjun* 建威將軍) Li Yun 李運 as Minister over the Masses (*situ* 司徒), the (Colonel of the) Reserve Army (*yijun [xiaowei]* 翊軍校尉) Li Huang as Minister of Works (*sikong* 司空), and the (Colonel of) Skilled Officers (*caiguan [xiaowei]* 材官校尉) Li Guo as Grand Steward (*taizai* 太宰); others received appropriate appointments. He posthumously honored his great-grandfather Hu

---

chengshan 青城山. JSJZ 121/2b says that the name, literally, West Mountain, derives from its position to the west of Jiangyuan 江原 county.

11. HYGZ 9/119.10–11 reads, "Xiong sent tokens of his faith (*xin* 信) to offer to and welcome Worthy Fan, wishing to place Fan above himself. The worthy did not permit this, instead exhorting Xiong to place himself on the throne." Ren 486n6 maintains that in encouraging Xiong to *zili* 自立 ("establish himself") Fan referred to establishing some sort of religious community rather than positioning himself as a "feudal ruler," but this ignores the highly political nature of the early Celestial Master tradition and reads into it a Marxian class consciousness that is totally inappropriate.

12. HYGZ 9/120.1 gives the name of this reign title as Dawu 大武. This seems to be a mistake for the name of the state established in 306, Great Cheng 大成. JS gives Taiwu 太武 as the reign period beginning with the establishment of this state, but this is again a mistake for Great Cheng. The proper reign name there is Yanping 晏平. The HYGZ text would seem to be the result of an early (according to Ren, pre-Song) emendation based upon the JS entry for 306. See JS 121/3036.8, 3050n4; ZZTJ 86/2720; Ren 488n10.

虎[13] with the title of Duke Huan of Pa Commandery 巴郡桓公, his grandfather Mu with the title of King Xiang of Longxi 隴西襄王, his father Te with the title of King Jing of Chengdu 成都景王, and his mother Madame Luo with that of Queen Mother (*wang taihou* 王太后).

He also bestowed the posthumous title of King Lie of Qi 齊烈王 on his eldest uncle, Fu; that of King Wu of Liang 梁武王 on his uncle Xiang; that of King Wen of Qin 秦文王 on his uncle Liu; and that of Duke Zhuangwen of Guanghan 廣漢壯文公 on his eldest brother, Dang....[14] Yan Shi was appointed Prefect of the Imperial Secretariat (shangshu ling 尚書令), Yang Bao 楊褒 as Archer-in-Waiting (puye 僕射), Yang Fa 楊發 as Palace Attendant (shizhong 侍中), Yang Gui 楊珪 as Imperial Secretary (shangshu 尚書), Yang Hong 楊洪[15] as Governor of Yi Province, Xu Yu as General Stabilizing the South (zhennan jiangjun 鎮南將軍), and Wang Da 王達 as Army Preceptor (junshi 軍師). He appointed a full complement of officials. [HYGZ 9/119.12–120.1]

Fan Changsheng came to Chengdu from Xishan riding in a white cart. Li Xiong welcomed him at the gates and, holding a minister's tablet, led him to his seat. He appointed Fan his Chancellor (*chengxiang* 丞相) and honored him with the title Worthy Fan (Fan Xian 范賢). Changsheng exhorted Xiong to assume the imperial title, and Xiong thereupon usurped the imperial throne, proclaiming a general amnesty within his territory and changing the reign name to Yanping 晏平.[16] He posthumously honored his father Te as Emperor Jing 景帝 and his mother Madame Luo as Empress Dowager (*taihou* 太后). He augmented Fan Changsheng's title to Grand Preceptor of Heaven and Earth (*tiandi taishi* 天地太師) and enfeoffed him as

13. JS originally read Wu 武, which is regularly substituted in Tang texts for the tabooed Hu. The Liao and Gu Guanguang editions of HYGZ (9/119.12) read Hu, whereas later editions give Yong 庸, no doubt a graphic error for Hu.

14. In HYGZ the preceding passage, describing the offices given his living relatives follows here, then continues with the positions granted Yan Shi, Yang Bao, and others.

15. Ren (487n9) argues that when the surname is omitted, as in this case, it is because the name has already occurred, yet no one named Hong occurs in the text, and therefore the character *hong* must be incorrect. He further theorizes that the figure in question is in fact Li Pu 李溥, who has occurred once before. It would seem, however, that the operating principle in the current passage is the omission of the surname when it is identical to that of the preceding person mentioned in a list, and that must here mean Hong's surname is Yang. This interpretation is followed by Liu 664n7 and Taniguchi 1973:82.

16. JS originally read Taiwu. See above, note 12.

Marquis of Xishan,[17] exempting his followers from military conscription and granting him all their taxes.[18]

The Worthy's name was Changsheng. One source gives the name Yanjiu 延久 *as well as the name Jiuchong* 九重. *Another source says Zhi* 支, *with the sobriquet Yuan* 元. *He was a man of Danxing* 丹興 *in Fuling.* [HYGZ 9/120.2–4]

Winter. Luo Shang moved and encamped at Ba commandery. He dispatched an army to raid Shu, beheading Li Xiong's grand-uncle Ran 冉 *and capturing Li Xiang*[a]*'s wife Madame Zan* 昝 *and his sons Shou and others.*[19]

Twelfth month. Li Xiong's Grand Commandant Li Li attacked Hanzhong, killing the (Chief) Battle Leader Zhao Wen. [HYGZ 8/114.4–5]

In the first year of the Guangxi reign period (306) Xiong proclaimed himself emperor and changed the reign name to Yanping. [HYGZ 9/120.5]

At the time, Li Xiong had just made a rough beginning in establishing the state, and since he had heretofore lacked a legal code and ceremonies (*fashi* 法式), the various commanders relied on personal favor in contesting for position and rank. His Prefect of the Imperial Secretariat Yan Shi submitted a memorial saying, "In establishing a state's bureaucratic system, it is always[20] preferable to follow past precedents. Under the old system of the Han and Jin dynasties only the Grand Commandant and the Grand Marshal (*dasima* 大司馬) commanded troops. The Grand Tutor and Grand Protector are offices for those like a father or elder brother, positions for the discussion of moral questions. The Minister over the Masses and the Minister of Works are in charge of the five teachings and the differentiation

17. HYGZ originally read "Great Preceptor of the Four Seasons, Eight Nodes and Heaven and Earth" (*sishi bajie tiandi taishi* 四時八節天地太師). The first four characters have been omitted from the current HYGZ but were present in the eleventh century at the time of the composition of ZZTJ. See the editorial notes (*kaoyi* 考異) to ZZTJ 86/2721. HYGZ 9/120.3 places this welcome of Fan Changsheng to Chengdu in 304, after Xiong's assumption of the title "king." WS 96/2111 agrees with JS and ZZTJ in the matter of dating but records the rank granted Fan as King of Xishan.

18. On exemptions from taxes and corvée during this period, see Tang Changru 1990.

19. The text reads "Li Shou and his brother(s)." This probably refers to Shou's younger brother Fu 福, but he also had an adopted half-brother You 幽. Below we find them in the control of Qiao Deng (HYGZ 9/120.9–10), and it was perhaps he who made this raid.

20. Reading *dong* 動 for the graphically similar *xun* 勛. Cf. JSJZ 121/3b.

of the nine soils.[21] The Qin dynasty (221–206 B.C.E.) established the office of Chancellor to have overall control over the myriad affairs. Toward the end of the reign of Han Wudi (140–86 B.C.E.) the Great General was elevated above others to control the government. Now the state has just been founded and the various offices are not completely filled. The ranks of ministers of state and great commanders go up and down and all clamor for appointments. This is not in accord with classical precedents. It would be appropriate to establish regulations in order to provide a framework (for assigning positions)." Xiong followed this advice.

First year of Yongjia 永嘉 *(307). Spring. Luo Shang established barriers and outposts* (guanshu 關戍) *as far as Han'an* 漢安 *(modern Neijiang, on the To River) and Bodao* 僰道 *(modern Yibin, on the Min River).*

At the time, the people of Yi province had migrated to Jing and Xiang 湘 *provinces as well as Yuesui and Zangke (commanderies). Luo Shang established[22] commanderies and counties in their present locations and appointed a Military Advisor to each village.*

Third month. The refugees from the Guanzhong region Deng Ding 鄧定, *Hong Di* 訇氐, *and others rebelled, occupying Chenggu* 成固 *and plundering Dongchenshi* 東辰勢 *in Hanzhong.[23] The Grand Warden of Baxi Zhang Yan*[a], *leading the Commander of the Serrated-Flag Gate Wu Zhao* 武肇 *and the Vice-Administrator of Hanguo Commandery Xuan Ding* 宣定, *sent troops to besiege them. Hong Di sought rescue from Li Xiong.*

Summer. Fifth month. [HYGZ 8/114.1–7]

Li Xiong dispatched Li Guo and Li Yun to plunder Hanzhong.[24]

21. The five relationships are those obtaining between father and son, ruler and subject, husband and wife, elder and junior, and between friends. See *Mencius* 20/3a/4. The nine types of soil, including hard dark-orange, salty, dried marsh, and so forth, are listed together with the type of nightsoil appropriate to each in *Zhouli* 16/7a–b.

22. Following the Liao edition commentary in emending *shu* 書 to *shi* 施.

23. The phrase "occupying Chenggu" is supplied from ZZTJ 86/2728. It is not preserved in any extant edition of HYGZ but seems necessary to make sense of the siege below. Cf. Ren 473n8.

24. HYGZ 8/114.7–8 records that Li Li, Li Huang, Li Yun, and Li Feng were sent on this mission but makes no mention of Li Guo. ZZTJ 86/2728 mentions only Li Li, Li Huang, and Li Yun but tells us that their army numbered twenty thousand. JS 57/1564 specifies that the city in which Deng Ding was besieged was Chenggu (eighteen *li* northwest of the modern Chenggu in Shaanxi). Dongchenshi is otherwise unknown. Ren 473n8 speculates that it is Liangzhou Mountain 梁州山, eighty *li* east of Nanzheng. Ren, following HYGZ, believes that the besieged city was this Dongchenshi rather than Chenggu.

When Du Mengzhi heard of Li Li's arrival, he ordered Zhang Yan to release the siege and protect the provincial capital. Originally when Zhang Yan[a] had first attacked, Ding's troops were starving, and he pretended to surrender, presenting Yan with a gold vessel which Yan[a] accepted. Seven days later, Hong Di arrived and Deng Ding returned to Dongchenshi. Zhang Yan[a] advanced and besieged him, disregarding Du Mengzhi's instructions. When Li Li arrived, he first attacked the camp of Wu Zhao, defeating him. He next attacked Xuan Ding, also defeating him. Zhang Yan[a] was afraid to do battle and fled at the head of one hundred cavalry. Li and company inflicted a great defeat on the provincial army. The Commander of the Serrated-Flag Gate Cai Song 蔡松 retreated and announced to Du Mengzhi, "The provincial army has already been defeated. The bandits are numerous; we cannot face them." Mengzhi was frightened. The Military Protector[25] wanted to make a stand in the walled city. He said to Mengzhi, "Although the bandits come in great numbers, theirs is the common bravado of a visitor.[26] That insignificant Li (Xiong) is pressed on the southeast. He will certainly not divide his troops and station them outside his territory. He only intends to rescue Deng Ding and Hong Di." Du Mengzhi replied, "Not so. Li Xiong has dared to proclaim himself emperor, hoping to gain control of the empire. Having dispatched a large force, he will certainly take Hanzhong. Although we have a well-fortified city, the courage of the people has been broken. We cannot face the bandits with them." Du Mengzhi then opened the city gates and withdrew. The Military Protector returned to the north. Du Mengzhi entered Great Mulberry Valley.[27] With several thousand families and thousands of carts accompanying him, Du could only advance a few dozen li *each night. Because his father had had a dispute with Du Mengzhi, Jing Zi of Zitong assembled his sons and brothers and pursued him, catching up to him at the mouth of the valley. Du fled, abandoning his son(s). Jing Zi captured his son(s) as*

25. Ren (473n10) maintains that this Military Protector was in fact Zhang Yin, who was functioning as Governor of Liang Province in the absence of the recalled Xu Xiong and is mentioned as Governor in the ZZTJ account (85/2728) of these events.

26. This expression is based upon *Zuozhuan* 451/Ding 8/3, which Legge (1861–1872:V, 769) translates, "All behave like visitors." The sense is that because they are not defending their home territory their courage is transitory.

27. Otherwise unknown. The biography of Zhang Guang 張光 (JS 57/1564) records that Du Mengzhi fled east to Weixing 魏興 (northwest of Ankang in Shaanxi). Thus Ren's speculation (473n10) that it was a valley to the northwest of the Bao-Ye valley is incorrect.

well as more than a thousand families of retainers and peasants. Only the Merit Officer of Hanguo commandery Wu Jian 毌建, *with a staff on his shoulder, said, "Although I am unworthy, I am the great officer of one state and when that state perishes, I cannot survive. I will refuse to serve the bandits to my death." He starved to death in that valley. After ten-odd days, Li Li and the others pulled out. Ju Fang* 句方 *and Bai Luo* 白落, *commoners from Hanzhong, led the clerks and commoners back to guard Nanzheng.* [HYGZ 8/114.8–115.1]

The Governor of Liang Province, Zhang Yin, fled to Chang'an. Li Guo and the others captured the city of Nanzheng and moved all of the inhabitants of Hanzhong to Shu.

Second year (308). An imperial rescript acknowledged Luo Shang's merit in chastising Li Te and supplemented his official positions with Cavalier Attendant-in-Ordinary (sanji changshi 散騎常事) *and Inspector-General for the Two Provinces (of Liang and Yi), at the same time advancing him to the title of Marquis of Yiling* 夷陵侯. *Since his eldest son, Yu* 宇, *held the post Defender of Chariots* (ju duwei 車都尉), *his second son, Yanshou* 延壽, *was appointed to that of Defender of Cavalry* (ji duwei 騎都尉).

Liang province had been laid in ruins by Li Xiong. Jin now named Huangfu Shang 皇甫商 *to be Governor of Liang Province; however, he was unable to assume this office.*[28] *The Seneschal of Shunyang, Zhang Guang* 張光 *of Jiangxia* 江夏, *was instead made Governor, with his seat of government at Xincheng* 新城.[29]

Earlier the southern regions had been ravaged by successive years of famine and pestilence; the dead numbered in the hundreds of thousands. The Colonel of the Southern Barbarians (nanyi xiaowei 南夷校尉) Li Yi 李毅 steadfastly maintained his position and refused to surrender. Li Xiong induced the Jianning barbarians 建寧夷 to attack him. When Li Yi died of illness, the city fell; more than three thousand brave soldiers died and over one thousand wives and daughters were sent to Chengdu.[30]

28. JS 60/1638 records that Huangfu Shang, after having been defeated by the forces of Zhang Fang, was sent incognito carrying a rescript in the Emperor's hand to the Grand Warden of Jincheng 金城 but was captured and executed by Sima Yong, King of Hejian. JS 4/101 places Shang's defeat in the ninth month of 303, so he must have died in late 303 or early 304.

29. Xincheng is far to the east, near the modern Fangxian in Hubei.

30. This version of events differs considerably from that recorded in HYGZ 4/52–53. There the reason for the rebellion is said to have been the failure to

Third year (309). Winter.

At the time, Li Li was occupying Zitong. His brigade commanders Luo Yang 羅羕 and Zhang Jin'gou 張金苟 and others[31] killed Li Li and Yan Shi, submitting with the city of Zitong to Luo Shang.

The Grand Tutor Li Xiang^a, Li Yun, and Li Huang attacked Luo Yang. They were defeated, and Li Yun and Li Huang were killed. Yun and Huang were Li Xiong's first cousins and held the positions of Minister over the Masses[32] and Minister of Works.

Twelfth month. Hong Qi and company sent Li Li's mother and son(s) to Luo Shang. Shang beheaded them and divided up Li Li's family possessions. [HYGZ 8/115.4–5]

Shang sent his commander Xiang Fen 向奮 to encamp at Yifu 宜 福 in Anhan 安漢 (north of Nanchong) in order to press Li Xiong. Xiong led a body of troops to attack Fen but was unsuccessful.

Fourth year (310). [HYGZ 8/115.6]

At the time, Li Guo was stationed in Baxi. His subordinate, Wen Shi 文碩,[33] killed Guo and surrendered Baxi to Luo Shang.

Originally Qiao Deng 譙登 of Baxi had gone to request troops of the General Stabilizing the South. The General Stabilizing the South had no troops but memorialized recommending Deng for the positions of General Rousing Ardor (yanglie jiangjun 揚烈將軍) and Seneschal of Zitong so that he might recruit volunteers from the people of the Three Ba (commanderies), Shu, and Han(zhong) in order to reconquer territory. He first launched an expedition against Dangqu, killing

---

keep a promise of clemency for Li Rui 李叡, who had taken refuge among the barbarians. Further, it is recorded that the city did not fall, with Li Yi's daughter Xiu 秀 taking her father's place until her brother Zhao 釗 arrived. The only mention of Li Xiong in this account is to say that his revolt prevented reinforcements from arriving. HYGZ places Li Yi's death in the third month of 306. Ren (256n9) seeks to reconcile these accounts by claiming that it was Laixiang 倈降 (modern Qujing, Yunnan), the seat of the Inspector-General, that fell, and not the provincial seat of Yunping 雲平 (east of modern Xiangyun, Yunnan). Communications between the southwest and the capital at this time were extremely difficult, as is evident from the three years it took Li Zhao to travel there from the capital, and accounts of events there must have been equally unreliable. The HYGZ version merits credence. Cf. JSJZ 121/4b.

31. HYGZ 8/115.4 also mentions Hong Qi 訇琦 of Tianshui.

32. This title is added on the basis of ZZTJ 86/2746, which places these events in the tenth month. Ren (472n15) inserts a character, *qian* 遣, "to send," after Li Xiang^a's name, reading, "The Grand Tutor Li Xiang^a sent Li Yuan and Li Huang to attack Luo Yang. They were defeated and killed by him." This reading is clearer, but the emendation is not necessary to correctly construe the text.

33. Following JS and HYGZ 9/120.10. HYGZ 8/115.6 gives for his name the homophonous Shi 石.

Li Xiong's Grand Warden for Baxi, Ma Tuo 馬脫.[34] *He then withdrew and occupied Fu. The General Foiling the Charge Zhang Luo advanced and occupied Heshui in Qianwei commandery. The people of Ba and Shu made a saying which went:*

Qiao Deng is headquartered at Fucheng,
Wen Shi is at Baxi.
Zhang Luo protects Heshui.
How can the Ba Di advance? [HYGZ 8/115.6–8]

Xiong thereupon withdrew and dispatched his commander Zhang Bao to make a surprise attack on Zitong, capturing it.

The younger brother Quan 全 *of Xiong's commander Zhang Bao*[35] *was in the midst of Hong Qi's troops. Li Xiong dispatched Zhang Bao to act as a double agent, promising to appoint him to Li Li's position. Bao was by nature fierce and brave. He first killed a man, then fled to Zitong. There he secretly linked up with his intimates.*[36] *Presently Luo Shang sent an emissary on a goodwill mission to Hong Qi. When Hong Qi and company left the city to see the emissary off, Zhang Bao closed the city gates behind them. Qi and company fled to Baxi. Having obtained Zitong, Li Xiong appointed Zhang Bao Grand Commandant. Xiong personally led an attack on Xiang Fen, who fled. Li Xiang*[a] *was dispatched to attack Qiao Deng. Deng had originally seized Xiang*[a]*'s son Shou, hoping to tempt Xiang*[a] *(to surrender). Now, under fierce attack with no relief in sight, he returned Li Shou to Xiang*[a]. [HYGZ 9/120.7–10]

Shortly thereafter Luo Shang died and Ba commandery was in disorder.[37]

An imperial rescript appointed the Grand Warden of Changsha Pi Su 皮素 *Governor of Yi Province, holding concurrently the offices of Colonel of the Western Barbarians and General Rousing Ardor*

34. Qiao Deng's father had been killed by Ma Tuo and Li Xiong. ZZTJ 86/2746 makes no mention of Xiong, but perhaps Ma Tuo acted at his behest. ZZTJ largely follows the account in Qiao Deng's biography, HYGZ 11/201.5–7. Both sources record that upon killing Ma Tuo, Qiao Deng ate his liver.

35. Or "All the younger brothers of Zhang Bao. . . ." No Zhang Quan occurs in our sources.

36. ZZTJ 86/2748 seems to have interpreted this line differently, for it reads "Hong Qi and company trusted him and make him their intimate."

37. HYGZ 8/115.8–9 adds a short biographical notice: "Shang's sobriquet was Jingzhi 敬之. One source says his name was Zhong 仲 and his sobriquet Jingzhen 敬真. He was a man of Xiangyang 襄陽. He held the positions of Aide to the Imperial Secretary, Court Gentleman, and Grand Warden for the commanderies of Wuling and Ru'nan. He was transferred to Liang province and died in office."

with command over volunteer forces and the Quelling the West Army. He was to advance and take control of the Three Passes.[38] At the time, Li Xiang[a] was making a vigorous assault on Qiao Deng. Pi Su encamped at Badong. The commanders of the Quelling the West Army,[39] Zhang Shun 張順 and Yang Xian 楊顯, were ordered to rescue Qiao Deng. Luo Shang's son Yu was filled with hate and resentment and would not furnish Deng with supplies.[40] When Pi Su arrived in Fu,[41] he planned to set these officials in order and they were all frightened.

Winter. Twelfth month. Pi Su arrived in Ba commandery. Zhao Pan 趙攀 and Yan Lan 閻蘭 of Tianshui, who had surrendered, killed Pi Su by night. Su, sobriquet Taihun 泰混, was a man of Xiapi 下邳. The Defender of Jianping Bao Zhong 暴重 killed Luo Yu and Zhao Pan. Ba commandery fell into disorder and in the end Qiao Deng was not rescued. Subsidiary officials of the three ministries[42] submitted the name of the Overseer of the Army for Badong and the General Cresting the Armies (guanjun jiangjun 冠軍將軍) Han Song 韓松 of Nanyang 南陽 to be Governor of Yi Province and Colonel of the Western Barbarians, with his seat of government at Badong.

Fifth year (311). Spring. [HYGZ 8/115.9–14]

Li Xiang[a] attacked Fu, reducing the city and capturing the Grand Warden of Zitong, Qiao Deng. Riding on the tide of victory, he

---

38. This term traditionally refers to Yangping Pass 陽平關, northwest of modern Mian county in Shaanxi; Jiang Pass 江關, east of modern Fengjie and today referred to as Qutangque 瞿唐關); and Baishui Pass 白水關, northwest of Zhaohua in northern Sichuan. See Zang 1936:40.2, 957.2, 329.2, 347.3. These passes, however, are not within the bounds of Yi province. Liu (649n4) understands instead barriers as Baxi, Fu, and Heshui.

39. Following Ren (475n20). As he points out, Pi Su was given control of the army of the General Quelling the West but was appointed General Rousing Ardor, hence after Luo Shang's death there was no General Quelling the West. Zhang and Yang must therefore be commanders (jiang) and the character jun 軍 must be excrescent, as is the character jiang in the previous reference to the Quelling the West Army. Cf. HYGZ 11/201.10–11.

40. Qiao's biography in HYGZ (11/201) relates that his arrogance and bullying when demanding troops from Shang to attack Cheng positions were responsible for a general distaste for him among Shang's aides.

41. Ren (475n21) has a detailed analysis of how Pi Su could not in fact have reached Fu before his death and recommends deleting the two characters zhi Fu 至涪, but no surviving edition omits these characters. It seems far simpler to follow Liu (649n6) in understanding this phrase in the future tense.

42. These are the headquarters of the three offices held by Luo Shang: Governor of Yi Province, Colonel of the Western Barbarians, and General Quelling the West.

advanced to attack Wen Shi, killing him.[43] Xiong was delighted and proclaimed a general amnesty, changing the reign title to Yuheng 玉衡 (Jade Balance).

Jing and Xiang provinces fell into disorder.[44] The Di Fu Cheng and Wei Wen 隗文 *created disorder in Yidu* 宜都 *(northwest of modern Yidu, Hubei). They moved up west to Badong.[45] Li Xiong's force attacked Bodao, causing the Grand Warden of Qianwei Wei Ji* 魏記 *to flee and killing the Grand Warden of Jiangyang Yao Xi* 姚襲.

Second month. The Di Wei Wen and others rebelled at Badong.[46] Bao Zhong campaigned against them but did not defeat them, then killed the Governor Han Song. Song, sobriquet Gongshi 公治, *was a man of Nanyang* 南陽. *He was the grandson of the Wei dynasty Great Minister over the Masses Han Ji* 韓暨. *Bao Zhong took personal control of the affairs of the three ministries.*

Third month. The civil and military officials of the three ministries and the subordinate officials of the Grand Warden of Badong together imprisoned Bao Zhong, his wife, and son(s) at Yidu, then killed them.[47] They then joined in recommending the Grand Warden of Ba Commandery Zhang Luo to carry out the affairs of the three ministries. Zhang Luo established his seat of government at Zhi 枳

43. HYGZ 9/120.10 says that Xiang[a] sent Li Shi leading Li Feng to attack Wen Shi. See below. Qiao Deng's biography places his capture in the third year of Yongjia, that is, 309, but "three" is a common graphic error for "five," hence 311.

44. This is the rebellion of refugees from Sichuan that boke out in 311, with Du Tao 杜弢 its most prominent leader. See ZZTJ 86/2758ff.

45. The Jin Annals place the Di attack on Yidu in the eleventh month of 310. See JS 5/121. The JS text at this point is either incorrect or corrupt, reading originally Wei Bofu 隗伯苻. Ren 477n3 argues on the basis of HYGZ that the text there should read "Wei Wen, Fu Cheng." The relationship of Wei Wen to Wei Bo is uncertain, but we hear no more of Wei Bo. Ren assumes plausibly that Wei Bo is by now dead and that the leadership of his clan has fallen to Wen, presumably a son or younger brother. Cf. JS 138n13.

46. Ren (477n5) argues that Bao Zhong in fact had wanted to co-opt the Di warriors for his own benefit and only declared them rebels and attacked them when they refused to ally with him.

47. It is curious that Bao Zhong should be killed at Yidu, quite a ways downstream from Badong (modern Fengjie). Ren (478n6) believes this was because the Di were in fact in control and that it was only through their aid that Bao was defeated and captured. But he also argues that they were advancing toward the west to ally with Li Xiong; Yidu would be a significant retreat for them. Moreover, Ren argues that Yidu was in rebel hands continuously from 311 to 314. Perhaps the Di still controlled Badong, but Yidu must at this point in early 311 have still been under Jin control.

(modern Fuling). He personally campaigned against Wei Wen at Gongqi 宫圻,[48] *defeating him and obtaining his surrender. In a matter of weeks Wei Wen again rebelled, seizing the Grand Warden of Ba Commandery Huang Kan* 黃龕 *and setting him up as a puppet ruler. Huang Kan was at the end of his rope and wanted to commit suicide. The Recorder Yang Yu* 楊預 *sought to dissuade him, saying, "Wei Wen's previous evil-doings are known throughout the Sichuan and Yangzi River basin regions. When he kidnapped Your Excellency, who did not feel himself threatened? Who would believe the empty and false title (he has given you)? You should let General Zhang (Luo) know of your earnest sincerity. Why must you act rashly in this manner?" Huang Kan replied, "The bandits have already cut off the highway. How do you propose to inform him of this?" Yang Yu then wrote a missive for Huang Kan and gave it to his younger brother, so that he might flee from the Di barbarians and present it to Zhang Luo. Luo said, "I was already aware that Zixuan* 子宣 *(presumably Huang Kan) exudes sincerity." When Wei Wen heard of this, he angrily imprisoned Huang Kan and, seizing Yang Yu, questioned him concerning the circumstances surrounding the dispatch of the letter. Huang Kan said, "I did not send it." Wei Wen then interrogated Yang Yu for a day and a night, but Yu did not speak. Wen wanted to kill Kan but Yu died under the cane. Wen, moved by Yu's loyalty, spared Kan. Zhang Luo sent an army to chastise him, which returned defeated. Zhang Luo personally led a campaign against him and, suffering a great defeat, himself perished. Luo, sobriquet Jingzhi* 景治, *was a man of Liang* 梁, *in Henan. No one was left in Ba.*[49] *Wei Wen drove both clerks and commoners to the west to surrender to Xiong.*

Li Xiong's commander Ren Hui captured the Grand Warden of Qianwei Wei Ji. Civil and military officials of the three ministries

48. This place-name is otherwise unknown. Ren (478n7) speculates that it is a place along the Yangzi between modern Fuling and Fengjie.

49. Both Liu (651n10) and Ren (478n8) believe that this sentence should follow the next one relating their surrender to Xiong because it refers to Wei Wen's forced removal of the populace. Ren believes it specifically refers to Di people, all of whom accompanied Wei Wen to the west, but it is unlikely that there were any Di other than soldiers there, and they would not have to be driven (*qulue* 驅略). Another possibility would be to take it to refer to Jin officials, but it most likely refers to the people in general. It was not uncommon at this time to take the entire population of a locality and resettle them in a more securely controlled area.

joined in recommending the Marshal of the Quelling the West Army Wang Yi 王異 *to carry out the duties of the three ministries, also acting as the Grand Warden of Ba Commandery. The Governor of Liang Province Zhang Guang again established his seat of government in Hanzhong.*[50]

*Sixth year (312). The Dragon-Soaring General (*longxiang jiangjun 龍翔將軍*) and Grand Warden of Jiangyang Zhang Qi* 張啓 *together with Luo Qi* 羅琦 *of Guanghan killed Wang Yi. Yi, sobriquet Yanming* 彦明, *was a man of Shu. Zhang Qi took charge of the affairs of the three ministries while Luo Qi assumed the post of Grand Warden of Ba Commandery. Zhang Qi died of illness. Qi, sobriquet Jinming* 進明, *was a man of Qianwei. He was the grandson of the General of Chariots and Cavalry (*juji jiangjun 車騎將軍*) of the state of Shu-Han Zhang Yi* 張翼. *The civil and military officials of the three ministries again joined together in recommending the Grand Warden of Fuling Xiang Chen* 向沈 *of Yiyang* 義陽 *to fill the post of Colonel of the Western Barbarians. Leading officials and peasants, he entered Fuling to the south.*

First year of Jianxing 建興 *(313). Spring. Xiang Chen died. Many of the people of Fuling suffered from epidemic diseases. The Grand Warden of Shu Commandery Cheng Rong* 程融 *of Jiangyang, the Grand Warden of Yidu Yang Fen* 楊芬 *of Qianwei, the Marshal of the Western Barbarians Chang Xin* 常歆 *of Ba commandery, and the Prefect of Du'an* 都安 *Chang Canghong* 常倉弘[51] *of Shu commandery joined in recommending the Grand Warden of Minshan Lan Wei* 蘭維 *of Fuling to be Colonel of the Western Barbarians.*

At the time, the Central Plain had already fallen into disorder, and there were troubles east of the Yangzi, hence there was no place to look to for aid or relief. Cheng Rong and others together led the officials and commoners to exit from Zhi 枳 *to the north, hoping to*

50. Although ZZTJ (86/2760) portrays reentry into Hanzhong as a signal accomplishment founded on many years of war, Ren (478n11) argues that in fact Li Xiong had removed the populace of the region and abandoned it and that Zhang Guang's accomplishment lay in repopulating the area.

51. Liao, Gu Guanqi, and Gu Guanguang all consider the character *chang* to be excrescent. Ren points out that there are many Changs and few Cangs in Sichuan at this time and that the two-character names are not uncommon, but in the Chang clan single-character names seem to have been the rule. Ren (479n13) further points out that the titles associated with these men are not current and that they did not at the time control the administrative units this attributes to them.

descend to Badong. They were consequently defeated and captured by Li Xiong's commanders Li Gong 李恭 *and Fei Hei* 費黑.

Fifth month. The Governor of Liang Province Zhang Guang launched a campaign against Li Yun 李運 *of Fuling, a member of Wang Ru's* 王如 *clique.[52] Wang Jian* 王建 *of Baxi was erecting a mountain at Panshebian* 盤蛇便 *and (Zhang) suspected that he was going to rebel. Li Yun and Wang Jian fled, taking refuge in Gou Mountain* 枸山.[53] *Zhang Guang dispatched an army to attack and defeat them, killing them.[54] Wang Jian's son-in-law Yang Hu* 楊虎 *rebelled, taking refuge in Huangjin Mountain* 黃金山. *Zhang Guang launched a campaign against him. Yang Hu abandoned his camp by night and hurried back to the E River* 厄水,[55] *at a place forty li distant from the provincial capital. Zhang Guang dispatched his son Mengchang* 孟萇 *to chastise Hu. They battled, alternating victories with defeats. Zhang Guang sought aid from the King of the Di of Wudu, Yang Maosou* 楊茂搜. *Yang Hu also sought rescue from Yang Maosou. Originally Maosou's son Yang Nandi* 楊難敵 *had sent his*

52. This Li Yun is not to be confused with the eponymous, now-deceased cousin of Li Xiong.

53. Ren (479n14) places both these sites in Chenggu county.

54. The more detailed account in Zhang Guang's biography (JS 57/1565) gives a different slant to these events: "At that time, Li Yun and Yang Hu, remnants of Wang Ru's clique, led more than three thousand families from Xiangyang into Hanzhong. Guang sent the Military Advisor Jin Miao 晉邈 at the head of a force to repel them at Huangjin. Miao received a large bribe from Li Yun and urged Guang to accept their surrender. Guang followed Miao's advice, permitting them to take up residence in Chenggu. Then Miao, noticing that Yun possessed many goods and treasures and wanting to seize them, again spoke to Zhang Guang, saying, 'Yun's followers do not practice agriculture. They only make vessels and staffs. It is hard to know what they plan. You should overwhelm and capture them.' Guang again trusted him. He sent Miao's force to chastise Yun, but he did not succeed. Guang asked for troops from the Di King Yang Maosou. Maosou sent his son Nandi to help him. Nandi demanded goods from Guang, but Guang did not give them. Yang Hu bribed Nandi richly, saying 'All of the treasures of the refugees are in Guang's place. If you now attack me, it would not be as good as attacking Guang.' Nandi was delighted. Saying he was aiding Guang, he secretly allied with Yang Hu. Guang did not realize this and sent his son Yuan 援 to lead a force in support of Miao. Li Yun and Yang Nandi attacked Miao from both sides, and Yuan was hit by a stray arrow and killed." Zhang is said to have withstood a siege from summer until winter before dying. Cf. ZZTJ 88/2799.

55. Ren (479n14) places Huangjin Mountain on the north bank of the Han River between modern Shiquan and Yangxian; he further identifies the E River with the Xu 㳛水, northeast of modern Nanzheng, and notes that there was an outpost (*shu* 戍) there.

adopted son to trade in the Liang provincial capital, where he privately purchased the son of a good family. Zhang Guang was angered by this and had him beaten to death. For this reason, Yang Nandi hated Zhang Guang and said, "When you first came it was after a great famine and your troops and populace relied on us Di to live. Yet when a Di commits a minor offense, he can receive no leniency!" He secretly planned to launch a campaign against Zhang Guang. It was shortly after this that Zhang and Yang Hu requested rescue.

Autumn. Eighth month. Yang Maosou sent Nandi leading cavalry to enter Hanzhong, outwardly saying that he was to aid Zhang Guang but actually responding to Yang Hu's request. When he reached the provincial capital, Zhang Guang feasted him with wine and oxen. Zhang Guang then sent him together with Zhang Mengchang to chastise Yang Hu. Mengchang himself took the vanguard while Yang Nandi brought up the rear. After Mengchang had battled Yang Hu for a protracted period, Yang Nandi struck him from the rear. Mengchang suffered a great defeat and was captured alive and killed.

Ninth month. Zhang Guang died of apoplexy. The people of the commandery joined in pushing forward the Grand Warden of Shiping 始平 Hu Zixu 胡子序 to take charge of the province.[56]

Winter. Tenth month. Yang Hu and the Di attacked the provincial capital fiercely, and Hu Zixu was unable to defend it. Abandoning the city, he withdrew and fled; the Di and Yang Hu thus obtained the city. They exhumed Zhang Guang's grave and burned his corpse. Nandi, having acquired Zhang Guang's musicians and singers, proclaimed himself Governor. He led the officials and commoners into Sichuan. Zhang Xian 張咸 and other commoners of Hanzhong attacked Nandi, who withdrew. Xian reentered Sichuan. Thus all three provinces came into Li Xiong's possession. [HYGZ 115.14–117.8]

Li Xiong's mother, Madame Luo, died. Xiong trusted in the words of spirit mediums and observed many taboos, to the point where he did not want to bury her.[57] It was only when his Minister of Works Zhao Su remonstrated with him that he followed Zhao's advice. Xiong wished to observe the full three years of mourning, and though the various officials adamantly remonstrated with him, Xiong could not be dissuaded. Li Xiang[a] said to the Minister of Works Shangguan

---

56. ZZTJ 88/2799 records that Zhang Guang's younger son Mai 邁 first held this position, and it was only after he died in battle with the Di that Hu was selected.

57. Stein believes this reflects a Daoist practice. See the discussion above, p. 85.

Dun, "Just now our troubles have not yet ceased. I wish to stubbornly remonstrate so as to not permit our ruler to complete the period of mourning. What do you think about this?" Dun replied, "The observance of a three-year period of mourning extends from the Son of Heaven down to the common people. It is for this reason that Confucius said, 'Why must Gaozong be singled out; all the ancients did so.'[58] However, since Han and Wei times the world has been plagued by many troubles. The ancestral temple is of utmost importance and cannot long be left unattended. Therefore (rulers) have put aside their mourning garments of sackcloth and undyed hemp and made do with expressing their extreme grief." Xiang[a] said, "Ren Hui will soon arrive. This man is decisive in carrying out affairs, and, moreover, His Majesty often finds it difficult to oppose his suggestions. Let us await his arrival and make our request together with him." When Ren arrived, he and Xiang[a] together had an audience with Xiong. Xiang[a] removed his cap and, shedding tears, insistently implored him to abandon mourning for the good of all. Xiong, wailing and weeping, would not agree. Ren Hui, kneeling, advanced and said, "Now the royal enterprise has just been established and the myriad affairs have only seen a rough beginning. If they are without a ruler for even one day, all under Heaven will panic. Of old King Wu 武王 (of Zhou) reviewed his troops in white armor, and Marquis Xiang of Jin 晉襄侯 joined the battle wearing mourning garments stained with black.[59] How could this have been what they desired? It was because they compromised their principles for the sake of the empire that they did so. I request that Your Majesty divorce himself from his emotions and follow the exigencies of the moment. May you ever prosper and may Heaven protect you." Then he forced Xiong to his feet. Xiong shed his mourning garments and took personal control of the government.

At this time Xiong acquired Hanjia 漢嘉 (near modern Yaan, Sichuan) in the south. Men from distant regions were arriving continuously. Thereupon Xiong proclaimed a liberal policy: All those

58. See *Lunyu* 30/14/40; Legge 1862–1871:I, 291.

59. Han Fei tells us that when, the year after his father's death, King Wu, founder of the Zhou dynasty, rode into battle against the last king of the Shang, he wore armor covered with white cloth to symbolize his mourning status. *Hanfeizi jishi* 1/4. As to Marquis Xiang, the *Zuozhuan* relates how, while in mourning for his father, he took the field against the Qiang Rong in his "garb of unhemmed mourning, stained with black, and also his mourning scarf." See Legge 1861–1872:V, 225; *Zuozhuan* 143/Xi 33/3.

who surrendered would be reappointed to their former positions. He humbled himself and was loving toward others.[60] For all his appointments he found men with appropriate talents and Yi province was thereby pacified.

Afterward Deng Ding 鄧定[61] *of Fufeng, Yang Hu, and company each led several thousand families of refugees to enter Sichuan. Li Feng was named (Cheng) Great General of the Western Expedition* (zhengbei dajiangjun 征北大將軍) *and Governor of Liang Province; Ren Hui was named Great General Stabilizing the South* (zhennan dajiangjun 鎮南大將軍), *Colonel of the Southern Barbarians, and Governor of Ning Province; and Li Gong was named Great General of the Eastern Expedition* (zhengdong dajiangjun 征東大將軍), *Colonel of the Southern Man, and Governor of Jing Province. Li Xiong and Li Xiang*[a] *were diligent and sympathetic to the commoners within the state while Li Feng, Ren Hui, and Li Gong gathered in refugees outside its borders. All were praised for their achievements. The Di Fu Cheng and Wei Wen, after surrendering, had rebelled again and personally wounded Xiong's mother, but when they came to submit, Xiong pardoned all their crimes and accorded them favored treatment, making them commanders. Chen An* 陳安 *of Tianshui came to surrender, bringing the region of Longyou (primarily Gansu and northeast Qinghai). The King of the Wudu Di, Yang Maosou, offered tribute and proclaimed his allegiance. Du Tao sent an emissary from Xiang province seeking aid. The Jin Governor of Liang*[a] 涼 *Province Zhang Jun* 張駿[62] *sent a missive seeking friendly relations. King Chong* 沖 *of the Hanjia barbarians sent his son to be held as hostage. Shortly thereafter Lei Zhao* 雷炤[63] *of Shushi* 朱提 *(southwest of Yibin, Sichuan) led a group of people to surrender. Cuan Liang* 爨量 *and Meng Xian* 蒙險 *of Jianning granted Xiong their trust. Further, every day brought more adherents.* [HYGZ 9/ 120.11–121.1]

Xiong usurped the title of Empress (*huanghou*) for his wife, Madame Ren. The Di King Yang Nandi and his brothers, having been defeated

60. HYGZ 9/121.1 reads *shouren* 受人, "accepts others," for *airen* 愛人, "loves others."

61. Following Ren (490n23) in reading *ding* for *zhi* 芝, thus identifying him with the Deng Ding who had submitted to Xiong in 307.

62. Zhang Jun's family, beginning with his grandfather Zhang Gui, long had effective independence in Liang[a] province but continued to profess loyalty to the Jin dynasty and use its reign titles. See JS 86.

63. Following HYGZ 4/57.7 in reading *lei* 雷 for the graphically similar *shen* 審.

by Liu Yao 劉曜, fled to Jiameng and sent their sons as hostages. The bandit leader of Longxi, Chen An, also submitted to Xiong.[64]

Li Feng was stationed in the north and had several times effected the surrender of his opponents. Li Dang's son Li Zhi 李稚 was encamped at Jinshou[65] and felt threatened by Feng's achievements.

First year of Taixing 太興 (318). Li Feng rebelled at Baxi.[66] Li Xiang[a] was sent on an expedition against him but tarried long at Zitong, not daring to advance.[67] Li Xiong himself arrived in Fu, and Xiang[a] consequently beheaded Li Feng. Li Shou was named to replace Li Feng and given authority for affairs in the north of Liang province.

Second year (319). [HYGZ 9/120.5–7]

Xiong dispatched Li Xiang[a] on an expedition against Yuesui.

Third year (320).

The Grand Warden Li Zhao 李釗 surrendered. Xiang[a] advanced through Xiaohui 小會 and attacked the Governor of Ning Province, Wang Xun 王遜.[68] Wang sent his commander Yao Yue 姚岳 at the head of a force to repel him. Xiang[a]'s army was not successful and further encountered protracted rain. Xiang[a] withdrew his army, losing many of his troops and officers in trying to cross the Lu River 瀘水.[69]

---

64. ZZTJ 92/2918 records under the year 323 Yang Nandi's flight to Hanzhong after he learned that Liu Yao had killed Chen An. The chronological framework of this section seems to be confused.

65. That is, Jiameng. See above, Li Te, note 93.

66. Ren (493n1) places responsibility for this rebellion squarely at the feet of Li Zhi, who he claims was jealous of Feng's success. Feng, unable to match Zhi's familial relations, first avoided him by moving to Baxi then was forced into open rebellion. We have insufficient evidence to confirm or deny this interpretation of events.

67. Convinced that Zhi was at fault in Feng's rebellion, Ren (493n2) then assumes the characterization of Li Xiang[a]'s actions here is mistaken and that he did not advance because he knew of Zhi's ultimate responsibility for the rebellion. Ren would drop the character *gan* 敢 as excrescent solely on the basis of this interpretation. He thus assumes that HYGZ is a true record of events and that any deviation from the truth (as Ren understands it) is the result of textual corruption. This position is untenable. Whatever the reality, HYGZ here clearly attributes guilt to Li Feng and cowardice to Li Xiang[a].

68. HYGZ specifies that this attack occurred in the summer of 320 and further gives the place of the decisive battle as Tanglang 螳螂.

69. The chronology here is confused in both JS and HYGZ. There were two expeditions against Ning province, one in 319–320, the second in 323. Li Zhao was captured in 320 and sent to Chengdu but escaped and was reappointed Grand Warden of Yuesui. He and Wang Zai 王載 were again defeated by Xiang[a]

When Zhao arrived in Chengdu, Li Xiong treated him very generously. Court ceremony and mourning ritual were all decided by Zhao.[70]

When Yang Nandi fled to Jiameng (i.e., Jinshou) Xiong's General Pacifying the North (*anbei jiangjun* 安北將軍) Li Zhi had sought to comfort him through generous treatment and had permitted him to return to Wudu with his brothers.[71] There, relying on his strategic position, he committed many illegal acts.[72] Li Zhi requested permission to attack him. Xiong sent the Capital Captain (*zhonglingjun* 中領軍) Li Han 李含[73] and the generals Yue Ci 樂次, Fei To, and Li Qian 李乾 to attack Xiabian 下辯,[74] proceeding from Baishui Bridge 白水橋, while the General of the Eastern Expedition (*zhengdong jiangjun* 征東將軍) Li Shou led Han's younger brother Wu 玝 in attacking Yinping. Nandi dispatched an army to block him, and Shou was unable to advance, whereas Han and Zhi made a long forced march to Wujie 武街 (east of Didao, Gansu). Nandi sent some men to cut off their return route and attacked them from all four sides, capturing Han and Zhi. The dead numbered in the thousands.[75] Han and Zhi were the sons of Xiong's elder brother Dang and Xiong was sorely grieved by their fate.[76] He did not eat for several days and every time he spoke he would break into tears, severely castigating himself for his role in the affair.

Later Xiong intended to establish Li Dang's son as Heir Apparent.[77]

---

in 323 and surrendered before Xiang[a] went on to defeat at Tanglang. HYGZ 9/ 121 mentions only the expedition of 320 and mistakenly places the battle of Tanglang in the third month of that year. JS seems to refer only to the second expedition. See ZZTJ 92/2911; JS 6/195, 81/2110; HYGZ 4/54.2-4.

70. In HYGZ 11/198.9 we are told that Li Zhao was heir to a family tradition of learning.

71. HYGZ 9/121.9 and ZZTJ 92/2915 agree in reporting that Li Zhi accepted a bribe in return for this favor. ZZTJ places these events in the latter half of 323. Huang 1975:186 states that HYGZ 4 also places this event in 321, but I have found no mention of Yang Nandi in that chapter.

72. HYGZ 2/24.2 records specifically that he attacked and routed the Cheng Grand Warden of Yinping Luo Yan 羅演, who was Li Zhi's maternal uncle.

73. Following HYGZ 2/24.2 and 9/121.10, which gives Han 珆 for the homophonous Han 含, further identifying him as the Palace Attendant. He is the eldest son of Li Dang rather than Li Han 含.

74. West of Cheng county, Gansu. This place-name is more commonly written with the character *bian* 辨. Cf. ZZTJ 92/2916.

75. HYGZ 9/121.10 says the dead numbered more than one thousand and included Han and Zhi.

76. HYGZ adds that Xiong had intended upon his death to turn over the throne to Li Han, Dang's eldest son.

77. HYGZ 9/121.13 adds a key fact, that Li Ban had been adopted by the childless principal wife of Li Xiong, Madame Ren 任.

Xiong himself had more than ten sons[78] and the officials all wanted him to select one of his own sons. Xiong said, "When I first took up arms, I was merely raising my hand to protect my head. I originally had no designs on the positions of King or Emperor. At that time, when the empire was in great disorder and the ruling family of the Jin was roaming about homeless, the emotions of all were aroused to the cause of duty and to the determination to rescue the world from the muck and mire. Then those revered gentlemen were pushed to assume a position above kings and dukes. As for the foundation of this enterprise, the achievement lies with the former Emperor (i.e., Te). My elder brother was the legitimate successor, the rightful occupant of the imperial throne. Generous and virtuous, enlightened and sagacious, surely he was the chosen of Heaven. Then just as this great endeavor was nearing completion, he died in the midst of battle. Ban 班 is benevolent and filial of nature, fond of learning and precocious. He will certainly be a famous vessel."

"When Sun Quan had carved off the region east of the Yangzi, although his elder brother Ce had laid the foundation, Ce's son only reached the rank of Marquis. The Record of the Kingdom *(Guozhi 國志) considered this a cause for shame.[79] When Duke Xuan of Song cast aside his own son and established his younger brother, the 'Superior Man' thought that the Duke knew men.[80] I intend to repair the shame of the* Record of the Kingdom *and carry on the tradition of Duke Xuan's virtuous conduct."* [HYGZ 9/121.13–14]

Li Xiang[a] and the Minister over the Masses Wang Da remonstrated, saying, "The former kings' establishment of the legitimate direct descendant (*shizhe* 適者) was the means whereby they guarded against the sprouts of usurpation. You must pay heed to this. The Baron of Wu's abandonment of his son and establishment of his younger brother led to the disaster of Zhuan Zhu 專諸.[81] Duke Xuan established

---

78. HYGZ 9/121.12 tells us that Xiong had fifteen sons by concubines.

79. This refers to the *Record of the Three Kingdoms* (*Sanguozhi* 三國志). In the first chapter of the section devoted to the state of Wu, the "Comment" (*ping* 評) by Chen Shou castigates Sun Quan for precisely this point.

80. The Superior Man (*junzi* 君子) refers to moral judgments prefaced by this name and sometimes attributed to Confucius that are appended to many accounts in the *Zuozhuan*. Here the comment referred to is found at *Zuozhuan* 10/Yin 4/4.

81. Zhu Fan 諸樊, the Baron of Wu, had three younger brothers of whom the youngest was the most worthy. The Baron passed his throne on to the first younger brother, who transmitted it to the second, who the Baron expected would eventually transmit it to the youngest, Zha 札. When the time came, however, Zha refused the throne, and the son of the second younger brother

Duke Mu in the place of Yuyi and in the end there was Song Du's 宋 督 revolt.[82] You speak of your nephew, but how can he compare to your own son? I fervently hope that Your Majesty will consider this matter." Xiong did not follow this advice and in the end established Ban.[83] Xiang[a] withdrew and wept, saying, "Disorder begins from here."

First year of the Taining 太寧 *reign period (323). The Si-sou* 斯 叟[84] *of Yuesui rebelled, attacking and besieging Ren Hui and the Grand Warden Li Qian[a]* 李謙. *The General of the Southern Expedition Fei Hei was dispatched to rescue them.*

First year of the Xianhe 咸和 *reign period (326). Summer. The Si-sou were defeated.*

Second year (327). Li Qian transferred the populace of Yuesui commandery to Shu. [HYGZ 9/122.1-2]

Zhang Jun sent envoys[85] to present Xiong with a missive exhorting him to abandon the imperial title and declare allegiance to Jin. Xiong wrote in reply, "I was wrongly pushed forward by officials (to be ruler); however I originally had no desire to be emperor or king.[86] Entering (the court), I had hoped to be an official sharing in the achievement of the dynastic founding; withdrawing, I had hoped to be a commander protecting the border, sweeping out all dirt and dust in order to stabilize the imperial domain. But the Jin ruling

---

was enthroned, becoming King Liao 僚 (r. 526–515 B.C.E.). The eldest son of Zhu Fan was incensed and arranged to have King Liao killed so that he could himself assume the throne, becoming King Helu 闔廬 (r. 514–496 B.C.E.). *Shiji* 86/2516–2518.

82. Duke Xuan passed on the throne to his younger brother He rather than his son, the Heir Apparent Yuyi 與夷. This He then gave the throne to Yuyi on his own death. However, He's son Feng 馮 was sent to the state of Zheng; this together with the rival claims to the throne engendered a series of wars between Song and Zheng. These wars in turn aroused dissension within the state of Song, leading to the assassination of Yuyi by Song Du and the enthronement of Feng as Duke Zhuang. See *Shiji* 38/1622–1623; *Zuozhuan* 10/Yin 4/4, 25/Huan 2/5. This dialog seemed staged, with historical anecdotes that can neatly be turned on their heads. The JS compilers must also have thought it a bit heavy-handed, since they omitted Xiong's initial reference to the two historical anecdotes.

83. HYGZ 9/122.1 records the appointment of Li Ban as Heir Apparent under the winter of 322.

84. Otherwise unknown. See the comments concerning the Sou above.

85. HYGZ 9/122.13–123.3 records that Zhang's emissaries were the Fu Ying and Zhang Chun mentioned in the next paragraph, and in HYGZ it is they who "consider [Xiong's] words important" at the end of this paragraph.

86. HYGZ 9/122.14–123.1 adds here: "I have always admired the commander of your province, patrolling the river of sands."

house has been in decline and no reputation of their virtue resounds. I have passed months and years craning my neck looking to the east. When I was favored by your missive, your well-harmonized emotions were subtle but moving; how can I forget them?[87] I know I should follow the distant example of Chu 楚 and Han 漢 in paying homage to Yidi 義帝.[88] No principle of the *Spring and Autumn Annals* is greater than this." Zhang Jun thought Xiong's words significant and sent a succession of emissaries to appeal to him.

Ba commandery sounded an alarm, reporting that there was an army from the east. Xiong said, "I have on occasion been concerned that Shi Le 石勒 would overrun his boundaries, invading and encroaching upon the King of Langye (i.e., Emperor Yuan of Jin). The thought unsettled me greatly. I never expected that they would be able to raise troops. It makes me happy." Many of Xiong's refined remarks were of this nature.

Because the Central Plains were lost to disorder, Xiong repeatedly sent envoys to pay court and present tribute, thinking to divide the empire with Emperor Mu 穆帝.[89] Zhang Jun controlled the provinces of Qin and Liang[a]. Previously he had sent Fu Ying 傅穎 to request the right to transit Shu in order to submit memorials to the capital, which Xiong did not permit. Now Jun sent the Retainer Administering the Palace Zhang Chun 張淳 to declare allegiance to Shu, entrusting to him the task of obtaining the right of transit. Xiong was delighted and said to Chun, "Your ruler's heroic reputation is known throughout the world. His location is strategic and his troops strong. Why does he not declare himself Emperor of one region?"[90]

87. JS originally read *anshi* 闇室, "darkened room," a common metaphor for a place where one cannot be observed and hence can perform evil acts with only one's conscience as one's guide. Here I follow HYGZ 9/123.2, reading *zhi* 至 for *shi*.

88. After the overthrow of the Qin dynasty, Xiang Yu, who had proclaimed himself King of Chu, and Liu Bang, then King of Han, joined in raising King Huan of Chu to the imperial throne, with the title Yidi, or "Righteous Emperor." The next year this Emperor was killed by Xiang Yu. He was in fact never more than Yu's puppet. This strange allusion makes one wonder if Xiong is not thereby expressing certain doubts about the Jin Emperor. See *Shiji* 7/315.

89. JS reads Jin Emperor Mu, who did not come to the throne until 345, over a decade after Xiong's death. The passage seems taken from *Weishu* 96/2111.4, where it is not Jin Emperor Mu but Toba Qilu 拓跋猗盧 (?–316), later canonized as Emperor Mu of Wei, to whom reference is made. The comment is in any case placed incorrectly within JS. See JS 121/3050n6.

90. JS 86/2236.15 reads, "Why does he not declare himself Emperor and amuse himself with one region?" This portion of Zhang Jun's biography gives the background for Chun's speech. Arriving in Cheng, Chun first suggested

Chun replied, "Because, although my ruler's ancestors for generation after generation had loyal and meritorious achievements, they were not able to wipe out the empire's disgrace nor save the masses from from their imperiled state. For this reason, my ruler forgets to eat as the sun sets and, pillowing his head on a halberd, awaits the dawn. Since the King of Langye was able to restore the dynasty east of the Yangzi, my ruler lends his support over a distance of ten thousand *li*. When he is on the verge of completing the achievement of a Huan 桓 or a Wen 文, how can you mention his taking it for himself?"[91] With a mortified expression Xiong said, "My father and grandfather were also officials of the Jin. In the past when I took refuge in this place with the people of the Six Commanderies, I was pushed forward by my confederates to be ruler; if the King of Langye can restore the Great Jin dynasty in central China (*zhongguo* 中國), I also should lead my troops to his aid." Chun returned and submitted a memorial to the capital, which pleased the emperor.

At this time Li Xiang[a] died.

Third year (328). Winter. Li Xiang[a] died. He was posthumously awarded the rank of Minister of State (xiangguo 相國) *and was canonized King Xian of Han* 漢獻王. *Li Shou returned for the funeral. Li Wu was appointed Great General of the Northern Expedition and Governor of Liang Province to replace Shou. Li Ban was ordered to fill the position of General Assuaging the Army* (fujun jiangjun 撫軍將軍) *and repair the military colony at Jinshou.*

Fifth year (330). [HYGZ 9/122.2–3]

Xiang[a]'s son Shou was made Great General and Colonel of the Western Barbarians.[92] At the head of the General of the Southern Expedition (*zhengnan jiangjun* 征南將軍) Fei Hei and the General

---

that Cheng ally with Zhang Jun to attack the Di. This angered Xiong, who planned to have Zhang Chun waylaid on the road. Chun discovered these plans and confronted Xiong. Xiong then tried to persuade Chun to stay and enter his service. The speech in our text is Xiong's final address as Chun is about to leave.

91. Duke Huan of Qi and Duke Wen of Jin were two of the five Hegemons (*ba* 霸) of the Spring and Autumn period. They acted as bulwarks of the Zhou royal house, rallying the other feudal lords around the king when he was unable to defend himself and staving off threats from non-Chinese peoples. It is such a role that Zhang Chun claims here for Zhang Jun.

92. HYGZ 9/122.3–4 records the positions given Shou at this time as: "Inspector-General of Internal and External Armies, Great General, Capital Protector, Colonel of the Western Barbarians, Overseer of the Imperial Secretariat (*lu shangshu* 錄尙書), in overall command as Xiang[a] had been."

of the Eastern Expedition Ren Shao 任邵,[93] he attacked and reduced Badong. The Grand Warden Yang Qian 楊謙 retreated and fortified Jianping (modern Wushan).[94] Shou separately dispatched Fei Hei to plunder Jianping. The Jin Overseer of the Army Guanqiu Ao 毌丘奧 retreated and fortified Yidu.

Sixth year (331). Spring. Li Shou returned. Ren Shao was dispatched to encamp at Ba.

Li Xiong appointed his son Yue General of Chariots and Cavalry, stationing him at Guanghan.

Autumn. Li Shou marched on Yinping.[95]

Winter. Fu was walled.[96]

Seventh year (332). Autumn. [HYGZ 9/122.5–6]

Xiong sent Li Shou to attack Shushi, taking Fei Hei and Shao Pan 邵攀[97] as his vanguard. He also sent the General Stabilizing the South (*zhennan jiangjun* 鎮南將軍) Ren Hui on an expedition against the Muluo 木落 in order to divide the aid and supplies from Ning province.[98]

Winter. Tenth month. Li Shou and Fei Hei arrived at Shushi. The Grand Warden of Shushi Dong Bing 董炳 sealed the city. The Governor of Ning Province Yin Feng 尹奉 dispatched the Grand Warden of Jianning Huo Biao 霍彪, the aristocrat Cuan Shen 爨深, and others to aid Dong Bing. At the time, Li Shou had already besieged the city and wished to resist this force. Fei Hei said, "I expect that within the walled city they are short of foodstores. Although Huo Biao and company have arrived, they have not brought much food. You should allow them to enter the city so that they may aid in consuming the

93. JS gives for Ren's personal name 矶, which the modern editors claim is a graphic variant of *zhao* 昭. Ren (495n13) cites this passage with the name Ren Hui 任回, but it is unclear what edition of JS this is drawn from. In any case, all surviving editions of HYGZ agree on Ren Shao and this reading seems preferable.

94. JS 7/177.10 lists this event under the tenth month of 330.

95. ZZTJ 94/2927 goes on to record that Yang Nandi surrendered to Shou.

96. The Liao edition of HYGZ gives Fuling, a mistake for Fuxian (Fu county). See Ren 495n16; Liu 673n2.

97. Following HYGZ, quoted below. JS originally had Ang Pan 卬攀.

98. Ren (495n17), noting that there are no known places named Muluo, argues that this is the name of a tribe of Si-sou located in the northwest of the Yuesui commandery and that they were the Si-sou who had rebelled in 323 and been subdued in 326. HYGZ specifies that Fei Hei was acting as Marshal to Li Shou and that they entered from Nanguang (southwest of Gong 珙 county, ZZTJ 87/2984 gives Guanghan). HYGZ also specifies that it was Ren Hui's son Tiao 任調 who was sent out from Yuesui.

city's grain. I only regret that they are so few. Why should we resist them?" Huo Biao and company all entered the city. But the city held out for a long time, and Shou wished to launch an all-out assault on it. Fei Hei remonstrated, "The road to the south-central region is perilous and its people fond of rebellion. We must wait until both their schemes and courage are exhausted. We need only restrain them for a protracted period, and we will gain victory with our army intact to seek for more. Why get upset over penned-up animals?" Li Shou could not be dissuaded from doing battle, and in the end he did not gain the advantage. Afterward he entrusted all military affairs to Fei Hei.

Eighth year (333). Spring. First Month. Dong Bing, Huo Biao, and others emerged and surrendered. Our awe resounded through the thirteen commanderies. [HYGZ 9/122.6–11]

The Governor of Ning Province Yin Feng surrendered, and Xiong consequently possessed the south-central region.

Third month. Governor Yin Feng surrendered the province and sent hostages. He was transferred to Shu. Li Shou was given control of Ning province. When the southern barbarians had first been pacified, the members of his force were under strict discipline, but later they turned to oppressing and robbing the populace. [HYGZ 9/122.11–12]

Xiong thereupon declared a general amnesty and sent Li Ban to attack and pacify the barbarians *(yi)* of Ning province, at the same time naming Ban General Assuaging the Army.

Autumn. Commoners of the province of Jianning Mao Yan 毛衍 *and Luo Tun* 羅屯 *rebelled, killing the Grand Warden Shao Pan. The Grand Warden of Zangke Xie Shu* 謝恕 *declared his commandery for Jin. Li Shou chastised and crushed him.*

Ninth year (334). Spring. A portion of Ning province was cut off to form Jiao 交 *province. Huo Biao was made Governor of Ning Province and Cuan Shen of Jianning was appointed Governor of Jiao Province. Li Shou was enfeoffed King of Jianning.* [HYGZ 9/122.12–13][99]

Third month. Li Shou returned. [HYGZ 9/123.3]

99. At this point HYGZ inserts the first of the two dialogs between Li Xiong and representatives of Zhang Jun. The dating and proper ordering of these passages is problematic. Although the current passage occurs first in JS, it seems logically to follow the other two. Ren 496n23 argues on the basis of Zhang Jun's JS biography (JS 86) that there were two missions from Jun, the first, headed by Fu Ying, requesting the right to send messages through Cheng to Jin, the second, headed by Zhang Chun, actually obtained Xiong's agreement.

In the ninth year of the Xianhe reign period (334)[100] ulcers formed on Li Xiong's head and he died in the sixth month.[101] At the time he was sixty-one sui (i.e., fifty-nine or sixty years old) and had been on the throne for thirty years.[102] He was given the posthumous title of Martial Emperor (Wudi 武帝) and the temple name Grand Exemplar (Taizong 太宗). His tomb was called Tumulus of the Peaceful Metropolis (Anduling 安都陵).[103]

Xiong was by nature generous and sincere. He reduced punishments and simplified the legal code and thus achieved great renown. The Di leaders Fu Cheng and Wei Wen rebelled after having surrendered and with their own hands wounded Xiong's mother, but when they came to submit, Xiong pardoned all their crimes and accorded them favorable treatment. For this reason both Chinese and barbarian were contented and his majesty resounded through the western lands. At the time, the entire world within the seas was in great disorder, and Shu alone was without troubles; therefore people submitted to him one after another. Xiong established schools on the commandery and county levels (xuexiao 學校) and appointed official historians. In his moments of respite from the hearing of audiences and the perusal of memorials, he was never found without a book in his hand. His taxes were three hu of grain per adult male per year, with adult females paying half this amount; the household tax was no more than a few zhang of silk and a few liang of cotton. Wars were few, corvée labor infrequent, and the common people prospered. The village gates were not closed, and the people did not rob

100. Following HYGZ 9/123.4–4, SLGCQ in TPYL 123/7b, and JS 7/178 in amending "eighth" to "ninth" year. HYGZ gives the exact date as August 7, 334, whereas SLGCQ gives August 11. Songshu 23/963 places Xiong's death in the eighth month. Since the illness as described here and at the beginning of the biography of Li Ban, which immediately follows, does not seem an acute development, it may be that the illness came upon him late in the eighth year, becoming serious enough to merit the recall of Li Shou in the third month, and finished with an accumulation of liquid in Xiong's head wound, after which death followed in only six days.

101. Reading yue 月, "month," for ri 日, "day." Alternately, it might be supposed that the final stage of this illness lasted six days, as mentioned in the preceding note.

102. In accordance with our determination that Xiong's death occurred in 334, the modern JS editors believe that this figure should be emended to thirty-one. This takes the assumption of the title of Great General in 303 as its starting point. HYGZ 9/123.2 also reads thirty, but Gu Guangqi believes that Li Ji emended the text on the basis of JS.

103. The location of this tumulus is unknown. Ren (497n27) suggests that it may have been destroyed after the Jin reconquest of Sichuan.

one another.[104] However, Xiong's mind was fixed on effecting the submission of distant lands, and for this, state funds were insufficient. For this reason, when military commanders presented gold, silver, or precious jewels, they usually received office in recompense.

The Chancellor Yang Bao[105] remonstrated, saying, "Your Majesty is the ruler of the empire and should embrace and control all within the Four Seas. How can you purchase gold with offices?" Xiong dismissed him with an evasive answer. On a later occasion, Xiong got drunk, pushed the Prefect of the Palace Secretariat (*zhongshuling* 中書令), and ordered the Prefect of the Grand Provisioner (*taiguanling* 太官令) flogged. Bao advanced and said, "The demeanor of the Son of Heaven should be characterized by majesty; that of the feudal lords by gravity. How can there be a Son of Heaven who acts like a drunkard!" Xiong thereupon had (the Prefect of) the Grand Provisioner released. Xiong once went on a small outing for no reason. From his rear Yang Bao galloped past carrying a halberd. Xiong thought this strange and asked him about it. He replied, "To support all the weight of the empire is like my galloping an ill-natured horse holding a halberd. If one speeds him on, then one fears harming oneself; if one allows him to go slowly, one fears his losing his way. It is for this reason that when my horse galloped, I did not restrain him." Xiong came to his senses and returned.

Xiong ran his state without imposing ritual. His officials had no fixed emoluments.[106] Rank and seniority were not discriminated; nobility and commoners did not differ in their clothing and insignia.[107] When his armies were on the march, they made no use of commands, and when using troops he did not divide them into divisions or squads.[108] If in battle (his commanders) met with success, they did not yield to each other; if they met with defeat, they did not come to each other's rescue. In attacking a city or reducing a town, they always put the capture of prisoners and taking of plunder first. These were his failings.

104. HYGZ 9/121.3 reads, "The village gates were not closed and no one picked up lost articles on the highways. There was no one who rotted in prison and punishments were not employed indiscriminately."

105. This is the only time Yang Bao is mentioned as Chancellor. These anecdotes may originally have derived from Yang's biography in the *Shu Li shu*.

106. HYGZ 9/121.4 adds here: "Appointments and assignments piled up."

107. HYGZ 9/121.4 adds, "Bribes were transmitted openly, and rewards and punishments were not clearly articulated."

108. Instead of "squads" (*dui* 隊), HYGZ 9/121.5 has "teams of five" (*wu* 伍).

Li Ban

李班

Li Ban 李班, sobriquet Shiwen 世文.[1] He was first appointed General Quelling the South (*pingnan jiangjun* 平南將軍) and later established as Heir Apparent.[2] Humble, self-deprecating, and open to suggestions, Ban was loving and respectful toward scholars and worthies. From He Dian 何點 and Li Zhao on, Ban took all of them as teachers. He also summoned the famous scholar Wang Gu 王嘏[3] as well as Dong Rong 董融 of Longzi and Wen Kui 文夔 of Tianshui to be among his retainers and friends. He would often say to Dong Rong and the others, "When I consider King Jing of Zhou's Heir Apparent Jin 晉[4] or the Heir Apparent of the state of Wei (Cao) Pi,[5] or the Heir Apparent of the state of Wu, Sun Deng 孫登,[6] all of

1. HYGZ 9/123.6 adds, "He was Li Dang's fourth son and was adopted by Li Xiong when young."

2. HYGZ lists this event under the winter of 322, whereas ZZTJ records it under 324. See HYGZ 9/122.1; ZZTJ 93/2921.

3. I have found no record of Wang Gu, Dong Rong, or Wen Kui other than their occurrences in connection with the Cheng state. The *Yinyi* phonetic glosses to this chapter maintain that Wang's personal name should be read Jia rather than Gu.

4. Ban seems to have made a mistake here. Jin was the Heir Apparent to King Ling of Zhou (r. 571–545 B.C.E.); Jing 周景王 (r. 544–521) was Jin's younger brother Gui 貴. Jin died before coming to the throne. Ying Shao records that Jin was a precocious youth and at age fifteen had a conversation with the master musician Shi Kuang 師曠, in which Jin predicted his own death. I have found no reference to imperial patronage of worthy literati, which seems to be the point of these allusions. See *Fengsu tongyi* 2/12; *Qianfulun* 9/15b–16a.

5. Pi, the later Emperor Wen of Wei 魏文帝, was himself a famous author, although only fragments survive of his most important work, the *Dianlun* 典論. SGZ 2/88 records that he sponsored the compilation of an encyclopedia called the *Huanglan* 皇覽 in more than one thousand chapters.

6. Sun Deng was the Heir Apparent to Sun Quan, the founder of Three Kingdoms state of Wu. Deng died in 241 before coming to the throne. He had a reputation for learning. See SGZ 59/1363–1366.

them surpassingly excellent in their appreciation and knowledge of literature, I never fail to feel ashamed. How lofty and enlightened were the worthies of antiquity, how unattainable are their achievements to posterity!"[7] By nature kind to all, in everything Ban adhered to the correct path. At the time, the various sons and brothers of the Li family were all fond of extravagance, and Ban often warned and rebuked them. Every time the court held a great conference, Xiong would invariably order Ban to participate. It was Ban's opinion that, "In antiquity, when land was brought under cultivation, it was divided equally and both rich and poor obtained their proper place.[8] Today the nobility is occupying uncultivated land on a grand scale, the poor have no land on which to plant and grow crops, and the wealthy sell their surplus. How could this be the principle of the king's great impartiality!" Xiong accepted this criticism.

When Xiong was bedridden with illness, Ban waited upon him day and night. Now as his illness became severe, his scars all began suppurating and bursting. Xiong's sons Yue and the others all thought this disgusting and avoided him, but Ban would suck the pus off, with no expression of distaste. Every time he tasted medicine (for Xiong) he would cry but did not doff his official robes and cap.[9] Such was his filial piety and sincerity.

When Xiong died, Ban succeeded to the usurper's throne and made Li Shou Overseer of the Affairs of the Imperial Secretariat (*lu shangshu shi* 錄尙書事) and Regent (*fuzheng* 輔政). Ban remained in the palace observing the mourning ritual while the affairs of government were all entrusted to Shou and the Minister over the Masses He Dian and the Prefect of the Imperial Secretariat Wang Gui 王瓌.

---

7. HYGZ 9/123.8–9 has in place of the preceding quotation the unmarked quotation, "How unattainable are those men of old." The text continues, "He was proper in manner and deportment, diligent in making inquiries. He was, however, given to frivolous actions, and his failing was (an attachment to) hunting."

8. This is a reference to the so-called well-field system of land tenure, which Chinese since the time of Mencius (late third century B.C.E.) have believed was practiced during the early Zhou. Under this system a section of land was divided into nine plots, eight of which were allocated to farmers and worked individually while the central plot was farmed communally. This theory had a profound influence in this period of local magnates possessing huge estates and influenced land reform under the Northern Wei, Sui, and Tang dynasties. See Hori 1985.

9. The *Record of Rites* prescribes this activity for loyal ministers and filial sons: "When a ruler is ill, and has to drink medicine, the minister first tastes it. The same is true for a son and his ailing parent." See *Liji zhengyi* 5/15a; Legge, 1885:I, 114.

At the time, Li Yue was stationed in Jiangyang. Because Ban was not a direct descendant of Xiong, Yue thought it most unjust (that Ban should succeed to the throne). Now Yue, having returned for the funeral, secretly plotted with his younger brother Qi 期 about the matter. Li Wu exhorted Ban to send Yue back to Jiangyang and to appoint Qi Governor of Liang Province, stationed in Jiameng. Because Xiong had not yet been buried, Ban could not bring himself to send them away. Trusting of others and dwelling in liberality, his heart was without the slightest pettiness. At that time two paths of white ether (qi 氣) appeared, girding the heavens. The Prefect of the Grand Astrologer's Office (taishiling 太史令) Han Bao 韓豹[10] memorialized, "In the palace there are ethers of secret plots and weapons. Beware of someone among your relatives." Ban's eyes were not opened. In the ninth year of the Xianhe reign period (334), while Ban was crying in the hall where Xiong's body lay in state, Yue killed him. At the time he was forty-seven *sui* and had been on the throne one year.[11] Xiong's son Qi was chosen to inherit the throne from him.

Winter. Tenth month, guihai *day (December 5, 334). Li Qi and Li Yue killed Ban while he was grieving for the dead* (linci 臨次). *They also killed Ban's second eldest brother, the General Directing the Army* (lingjun jiangjun 領軍將軍) *Li Du* 李都. *His younger brother Wu fled to the Jin. Qi falsely canonized Li Ban as Fractious Heir*

10. HYGZ 9/123.14 gives Han Yue 韓約. The JS reading is no doubt the result of graphic confusion.

11. Ren (498n1) argues that this age must be incorrect because it would mean that Ban was only thirteen years younger than Xiong, his adopted father. He suggests that Ban should be thirty-seven at the time of his death, but this can be no more than conjecture (Ren is also inexplicably off one year in many of his calculations). There is clearly a problem in the statement made in HYGZ (9/122.1) that Ban was sixteen at the time he was appointed Heir Apparent in 322. This would put his birth in 307, three years after his father Li Dang's death in 304; moreover, Ban has a younger brother, Wu. It is less clear that there is any problem with the statement made here. Li Xiong's wife, Madame Ren, was childless and probably took in Ban, ignoring Dang's other four sons, only after trying many years to produce a child of her own, perhaps as an attempt to "lead in" a son. Ban would thus have been sixteen *sui* at the time of his father's death, not an inconceivable age for adoption, and Xiong would have been thirty. Madame Ren, as Xiong's primary wife, could very easily have been older than him and approaching the end of her childbearing years. This still leaves unexplained, however, the comment concerning Ban's age at the time of appointment as Heir Apparent. According to this calculation, he would have been thirty-five (thirty-three if we accept the date of 324 given in JS), a figure not easily confused with sixteen.

Apparent (litaizi 戾太子). *Li Shou posthumously canonized him as the Sorrowful Emperor* (Aihuangdi 哀皇帝). *His sons You* 幽 *and Yong* 顒 *were killed by Li Qi. Ban and his four brothers all met violent deaths. Four of them left no descendants. Li Wu under the Jin administration held successively the posts of Grand Warden of Ba, Xiangyang, and Yidu commanderies and Dragon-Soaring General. In the third year of the Yonghe* 永和 *reign period (347), in the force of the General of the Western Expedition (i.e., Huan Wen), he died in battle at Shanyang* 山陽. [HYGZ 123.10–12]

Li Qi

李期

Li Qi 李期, sobriquet Shiyun 世運, was the fourth son of Li Xiong. Discerning, wise, and fond of learning, by the time of his capping he was competent at composition. He did not esteem wealth but was fond of distributing his bounty and humbly solicited and accepted advice. When Qi had first been named General Establishing Intimidation, Li Xiong ordered his sons as well as the sons and younger brothers of the royal house to each assemble a force, relying on their past beneficence and sincerity. The others were able to gather a few hundred at most; Qi alone reached more than a thousand men.[1] Most of the people he recommended by memorial Xiong accepted, so that many of the senior administrative officials of the various bureaus had advanced through his patronage.

Having killed Li Ban, they wished to establish Li Yue as ruler, but because Qi had been reared by the wife of Li Xiong, Madame Ren,[2] and because of his many talents, Yue yielded the throne to him. He thereupon usurpingly assumed the position of Emperor and, proclaiming a general amnesty, changed the reign name to Yuheng 玉恆 (Jade-like Constancy). He executed Ban's brother Du[3] and sent Li Shou to attack Du's younger brother Wu at Fu. Abandoning the city, Wu surrendered to Jin.[4] Qi enfeoffed Shou as King of Han and

1. HYGZ 9/123.13 adds at this point, "He was appointed General Pacifying the East" (*andong jiangjun* 安東將軍).

2. HYGZ 9/123.12 explains that Madame Ren adopted Qi because his birth mother, Madame Ran 冉, was of mean birth. HYGZ and SLGCQ make it clear that it was Yue who committed or, at least, ordered the murder, then put Qi on the throne. See Ren 499n7.

3. JS refers to Du here as Ban's younger brother, but in fact he was older than Ban, being the second of five brothers, and was so characterized in the previous section.

4. HYGZ 9/124.5 records that his commanders Jiao Kuai 焦噲 and Luo Kai 羅凱 also surrendered with him.

appointed him Governor of Liang Province, Colonel of the Eastern Qiang, Capital Protector, and Overseer of the Affairs of the Imperial Secretariat.[5] He enfeoffed his elder brother Yue as King of Jianning, appointing him Minister of State and Overseer of the Affairs of the Imperial Secretariat. He established his wife, Madame Yan 閻, as Empress.

Qi's second eldest brother, Ba 霸, *was made Capital Captain and Great General Stabilizing the South. His younger brother Bao* 保 *was named Great General Stabilizing the West, Colonel of the Western Barbarians, and Grand Warden of Minshan. His senior uncle[6] Shi was named Great General of the Eastern Expedition, replacing Yue.* [HYGZ 9/124.1–2]

He appointed the General of the Guards (*weijiangjun* 衛將軍) Yin Feng to the posts of Chancellor of the Right (*you chengxiang* 右丞相) and General of Doughty Cavalry. The Prefect of the Imperial Secretariat Wang Gui was appointed Minister over the Masses.[7]

Autumn. The (Colonel) Director of Retainers Jing Qian 景騫 *was named Prefect of the Imperial Secretariat, the General of the Southern Expedition Fei Hei was named Colonel Director of Retainers, and Li Ban's maternal uncle, Luo Yan, was named Archer-in-Waiting.* [HYGZ 9/124.3–4]

Considering that he had personally planned the "great affair" (i.e., usurpation) and had brought it to fruition, Qi slighted all the former officials. Outside the palace, he trusted and employed the Prefect of the Imperial Secretariat Jing Qian, and the Imperial Secretaries Yao Hua 姚華 and Tian Bao 田褒. Bao had no other talents, but during Xiong's reign he had advocated the establishment of Qi as Heir Apparent, and for this reason he was favored most highly. Within the court, Qi trusted the eunuch Xu Fu 許涪 and company. The affairs of the administration of the state were seldom again referred to major officials; both rewards and punishments were decided by a mere handful of people. Thus the guiding ropes of government became entangled.[8]

5. HYGZ 9/124.1 adds that Shou was also appointed Great Inspector-General.

6. HYGZ originally had "elder cousin" (*congxiong* 從兄), but Shi was Li Xiong's elder brother and hence Li Qi's uncle. Cf. Liu 680n3; Ren 499n8.

7. The modern JS mispunctuates this sentence, taking Prefect of the Imperial Secretariat to be one of the posts received by Yin Feng rather than the previous post of Wang Gui. Cf. JS 121/3041.11.

8. HYGZ 9/124.6 reads, "He spurned and ignored the high officials of his father's time. The administration and penal system fell into disorder."

Li Ban's maternal uncle Luo Yan plotted with the Minister to the King of Han Shangguan Dan 上官澹 *of Tianshui to take Qi by surprise and enthrone Ban's son You. Word of the plot leaked out, and Luo Yan and Shangguan Dan were killed. Ban's mother, Madame Luo, Li Han's son Yan*[a] 礒, *and Li Zhi's wife, Madame Zan, were also executed.* [HYGZ 9/124.4–5]

The Archer-in-Waiting of the Imperial Secretariat (*shangshu puye* 尙書僕射) and Duke of Wuling Li Zai 李載 was falsely accused of plotting to rebel, imprisoned, and executed.[9]

Earlier the Jin General Establishing Intimidation Sima Xun 司馬勳 had encamped at Hanzhong.[10] Qi dispatched Li Shou to attack and reduce his position. Consequently a Warden[11] was appointed and Nanzheng was garrisoned.

Li Xiong's sons Ba and Bao both died suddenly, with no symptoms of illness.[12] Everyone said that Qi had poisoned them. At this, the great officials were all secretly fearful and the people uneasy.[13] A great fish, yellow in color, rained down from Heaven into the midst of the palace compound. Further, pigs and dogs mated in the palace.[14] Qi executed many, confiscating their wives, daughters, and possessions to fill his inner quarters. Both within and without, the people were filled with fear and on the roads and highways communicated their distress with veiled looks.[15] Remonstrators were charged with crimes, and the people were intent on avoiding misfortune by any expedient.

9. HYGZ 9/124.5 places the execution of Li Zai in 336, after Luo Yan's rebellion.

10. The Jin Annals (JS 7/180.12) record the dispatch of Sima Xun to Hanzhong in the eleventh month of 336.

11. JS uses the term *shouzai* 守宰, indicating a continuing uncertainty as to whether Hanzhong should be treated as a commandery with a Grand Warden (*taishou*) or a kingdom, specifically the Han Kingdom that was Li Shou's fief, with an appropriate Minister (*xiang*), Chancellor (*zai*), or Seneschal (*neishi*).

12. HYGZ 9/124.4 simply says that they died of sudden illnesses.

13. HYGZ 9/124.4 reads, "The great officials began to doubt their continued safety and blood relatives became estranged." JS perhaps infers from this the statement about poisoning.

14. Cf. HYGZ 9/128.3, where it is also recorded that trees blossomed in winter. All of these anomalies were portents indicating Heaven's displeasure with Qi.

15. This phrase (*daolu yi mu* 道路以目) was first used to describe the reaction of the people of the early Zhou state after the evil King Li 厲王 had passed a law banning all protest as calumny (ca. 842 B.C.E.). See *Shiji* 4/141–142; Chavannes 1895:I, 270.

Qi also poisoned his General Pacifying the North Li You[a] 李攸. You was Li Shou's adopted younger brother. Qi then plotted with Li Yue, Jing Qian, Tian Bao, and Yao Hua to make a surprise attack on Li Shou, using the burning of the Market Bridge 市橋 (four *li* east of Chengdu) as a pretense to send out troops. Qi also repeatedly sent the Palace Attendant-in-Ordinary (*zhong changshi* 中常侍) Xu Fu to Shou's headquarters to spy on his activities.

When Qi killed Li You, Shou was greatly alarmed and also became suspicious of Xu Fu's frequent comings and goings. He consequently marched on Chengdu from Fu at the head of ten thousand infantry, memorializing that Jing Qian and Tian Bao were throwing the government into disorder and saying that he (Shou) was raising the "troops of Jinyang"[16] in order to remove the evil at the ruler's side.[17] He made Li Yi[a] 李奕 his vanguard. When Shou arrived at Chengdu, Qi and Yue had not anticipated his coming and had made no preparations. Shou consequently took the walled city and camped his troops right up to the gates (of the palace).[18] Qi dispatched a Palace Attendant[19] to convey to Shou his respects. Shou memorialized that the Minister of State, King Yue of Jianning, the Prefect of the Imperial Secretariat and Duke of Henan Jing Qian, the Imperial Secretaries Tian Bao and Yao Hua, the Palace Attendant-in-Ordinary Xu Fu, the General of the Western Expedition Li Xia 李遐, and the General Li Xi 李西, all having harbored treacherous plans to disrupt the government and overturn the altars of state, were guilty of treason and that their crimes merited extermination. Qi, following this advice, thereupon killed Yue, Qian, and the others. Shou counterfeited a command from Madame Ren to depose Qi, making him Duke of Qiongdu County 邛都縣公 and secluding him in a subsidiary pal-

16. The *Guliangzhuan* (*Chunqiu jingzhuan yinde* 460/Ding 13/7) records that Shang Yang raised troops from the Jinyang 晉陽 (Taiyuan, Shanxi) region in order to eliminate the influence of Xun Yin 荀寅 and Shi Jishe 士吉射 on the ruler of Wei. This incident was later often used as justification for what were in fact rebellions.

17. HYGZ 9/124.6–7, which places this event in the fourth month of 338, says that Shou announced his purpose as the punishment of Li Yue and Jing Qian and that Qi rejected a request from Yue to purchase mercenaries for their defense.

18. Here I follow the Japanese Tokugawa-era edition (121/9b), which has "palace gates," as well as ZZTJ 96/3017. ZZTJ also records that Shou's son, Li Shi[a] 李勢, the Colonel of the Reserve Army, was inside the city and opened the gates for him.

19. This was, presumably, a eunuch serving under Xu Fu.

ace. Sighing, Qi said, "That the ruler of the empire should be reduced to the duke of a small county. It would be better to die."

In the fourth year of the Xiangkang reign period (338) Qi hanged
himself.[20] At the time, he was twenty-five *sui* of age[21] and had been on
the throne five years.[22] He was given the posthumous title Benighted
Duke (Yougong 幽公). When he was buried, he was granted a phoe-
nix carriage with nine tassels,[23] everything else following the etiquette
appropriate for a king. All of Xiong's sons were killed by Li Shou.[24]

*Fifth year (339). Li Qi's wife and sons were transferred to Yuesui.
Li Shi[a] 李勢 then sent a man to Yuesui to execute his sons.* [HYGZ
9/124.8]

20. WS 96/2111.7–8 agrees with JS in stating that Qi killed himself. However, HYGZ 9/124.7–8 and the *Jinshu* Annals (7/181.4) agree that Shou killed
him. HYGZ also notes that Shou at this time killed Li Shi. The JS Annals place
Qi's death in the fourth month, but HYGZ says the fifth.

21. HYGZ 9/124.8 gives twenty-four.

22. JS originally read "three," but Qi occupied the throne from 333 to 338.

23. The *Record of Rites* (*Liji zhengyi* 38/15b) says that nine tassels were
appropriate for the banner of the Son of Heaven, hence this is a concession to
his former imperial rank.

24. HYGZ 9/124.8 tells us that more than ten of Qi's brothers were killed at
this time. At one point, Li Xiong had fifteen sons.

Li Shou

李壽

Li Shou 李壽, sobriquet Wukao 武考, was the son of Li Xiang[a]. He was clever and fond of learning, broad in his refinement and capacity. When young, he esteemed proper demeanor, in this way differing from the other sons of the Li clan. Li Xiong considered his talent remarkable and thought him capable of bearing heavy responsibilities. He appointed Shou General of the Van, giving him charge of the military affairs of Baxi, then promoted him to General of the Eastern Expedition. At the time Shou was nineteen *sui* of age. He recruited the recluse Qiao Xiu 譙秀 to be his retainer so as to get the full benefit of his counsel. Shou's majesty and graciousness achieved renown in Baxi. When Li Xiang[a] died, Li Shou was promoted to Great General, Great Inspector-General, and Palace Attendant, was enfeoffed as Duke of Fufeng, and was made Overseer of the Affairs of the Imperial Secretariat.

From the time when he replaced his father as commander, his fixed ambition was to achieve merit and fame. Therefore, whether on an expedition against the east or marching on the south, he always achieved results. [HYGZ 9/124.9]

On an expedition against Ning province, by assaulting and besieging for more than a hundred days he completely pacified the various commanderies. Li Xiong was extremely pleased and enfeoffed Shou as King of Jianning. When Li Xiong died, it was his dying wish that Li Shou act as regent.[1] When Li Qi ascended the throne, Shou's title was changed to King of Han, he was granted the revenues of the five commanderies of Liang province for his living expenses, and was named Governor of Liang Province.

1. HYGZ 9/124.9–10 records that when Li Xiong fell ill, Shou waited in attendance upon him and that Xiong entrusted affairs (*jituo* 寄託) to Shou but makes no explicit mention of a regency.

When Li Qi killed Li Ban, Li Shi originally wanted to ally himself to Shou and plot together to chastise Qi. Shou did not dare to do this. Li Shi then angrily sought to persuade Li Qi to seize Shou. Qi feared Li Wu in the north and wished to make use of Shou to chastise him; for this reason, he would not permit it. Having been enfeoffed with Han, Shou marched north on Wu. Shou set out for Wu the benefits of leaving and offered him safe passage. Li Wu was thus able to descend the Yangzi eastward to Wu (i.e., Eastern Jin). [HYGZ 9/124.10–11]

Li Shou's awesome reputation was felt afar. Li Yue, Jing Qian, and others deeply feared him, which caused Shou great worry. He replaced Li Wu in occupying Fu. Whenever he was due to attend court, he would announce that there was a threat of incursions and the border could not be left unguarded; thus he would avoid attending.[2] Noting that Li Qi, Li Yue, and their brothers, more than ten men in all, were all just at the peak of their manhood and that, moreover, they all controlled strong contingents of troops, Li Shou feared for his own safety. He repeatedly called upon and made respectful overtures to Gong Zhuang 龔壯 of Baxi. Although Gong did not respond to these offers of employment,[3] he did pay several calls on Shou. At the time, Mount Min had collapsed and the waters of the Yangzi had dried up. Li Shou considered these evil signs[4] and would always ask Gong Zhuang about methods whereby to secure his own safety. Because Li Te had killed his father and uncle, Gong Zhuang wanted to borrow the hand of another to avenge them but had not yet had the opportunity. Consequently he counseled Shou, saying, "If Your Excellency is able to discard the small in order to pursue the great, to trade safety for danger, then you may found a state and carve out a territory. You could have a long rule as a feudal lord, your fame would be greater than the Dukes Huan or Wen, and your reputation

2. HYGZ 9/123.12 refers to these required court appearances as *chaojin* 朝覲, which designates the ceremonial visits of a vassal upon his lord in the spring and autumn, respectively. See *Zhouli zhengyi* 18/12a–b. This HYGZ passage also provides more information concerning Shou's excuse, saying that he would "fabricate an urgent missive from the commander in charge of the protection of Hanzhong, Zhang Cai 張才, reporting an alarm concerning bandits from foreign lands."

3. HYGZ 9/123.12 adds here, ". . . he feared he would be harmed and, left with no choice, ..."

4. HYGZ 9/124.14 specifies that Shou's opinion of these signs was founded in a pronouncement by Liu Xiang (77–6 B.C.E.), but I have been unable to discover exactly what was intended.

would be transmitted for a hundred generations." Shou, following his advice, secretly joined with the Senior Aide Luo Heng 羅恆[5] of Lueyang and Xie Siming 解思明 of Baxi in plotting to occupy Chengdu and declare allegiance to Jin.[6]

Presently Shou's adopted son returned from Chengdu ill and died on the way. Shou then claimed that Li Yue had poisoned him. In order to delude his [own] followers, he forged a letter from Ren Tiao saying that Li Qi and Li Yue should depose Shou. They believed him. [HYGZ 9/125.2–3]

Shou then swore his followers, military and civil, to an oath of allegiance.[7] Having obtained several thousand men, he fell upon Chengdu, capturing the city.

His son Shi[a] acted as his agent within the city, opening the gates. Shou thus captured Li Qi and Li Yue and executed more than ten of their relatives. [HYGZ 9/125.4]

Shou allowed his troops to take prisoners and plunder. They went so far as to violate the daughter(s) of Li Xiong and the wives of the various members of the Li family. The casualties were many, and the plundering ceased only after several days.[8]

Luo Heng and Xie Siming, together with Li Yi[a], Wang Li 王利, and others urged Shou to proclaim himself General Stabilizing the West, Pastor of Yi Province, and King of Chengdu, thus announcing his allegiance to Jin.[9] However, Ren Tiao together with the Marshal Cai Xing 蔡興, the Palace Attendant Li Yan 李艷, and Zhang Lie 張烈 urged him to declare his independence. Li Shou ordered that the matter be submitted to milfoil divination. The diviner said, "You may be Son of Heaven for a few years." Ren Tiao said happily, "One

5. The Bona edition (121/6a) and the Tokugawa edition (121/10a) both read Luo Huan 桓. HYGZ has Heng. See JS 121/3052n14.

6. Liu 683n6, citing Song geographical and biographical sources, argues that Xie should in fact be Xian 鮮. Clearly some Song source had Xian, but all extant versions of HYGZ and JS read Xie. There is enough graphic similarity between the two characters to suspect that a more cursive form of one of the characters could be mistaken for the other. Xie is certainly the more common surname. Xian as a single surname does not otherwise occur in JS.

7. HYGZ 9/125.3–4 adds, "promising to reward them with the spoils within the city."

8. HYGZ 9/125.5 inserts "many were slain and maimed." SLGCQ would seem to be the direct source for this section, since JS follows it closely. See TPYL 123/8a.

9. HYGZ 9/125.5–6 adds, "Zhuang would be appointed Senior Aide and Shou would make an announcement to the people concerning his allegiance to Jin. They also urged that Shou order Li Qi sent to Jin."

day would be enough, how much more a few years." Xie Siming said, "How can being Son of Heaven for a few years compare with being a feudal lord for a hundred generations?" Shou replied, "'If a man in the morning should hear the right way, he may die that evening without regret.'[10] Marquis Ren's suggestion is the best plan."[11]

Consequently, in the fourth year of the Xiankang reign period (338), he usurped the counterfeit throne, declared a general amnesty, and changed the reign name to Hanxing 漢興 (Rise of the Han).[12] He made Dong Jiao 董皎 his Minister of State, Luo Heng and Ma Dang 馬當 his right-hand men (gugong 股肱), Ren Tiao and Li Hong his minions, and Xie Siming his Master of Counsels. Shou tried to recruit Gong Zhuang to be Grand Preceptor with a comfortable carriage and a roll of silk,[13] but Zhuang persistently refused. He was granted special permission to attend court in a white silk cap and belt[14] and was permitted to occupy the position of a teacher or friend. Selecting those who had been passed over or had come to dead ends in their careers, Shou placed them in the front ranks (of officialdom). He posthumously honored his father, Li Xiang[a], as Emperor Xian 獻帝 and his mother, Madame Zan 昝, as Empress Dowager, establishing his wife, Madame Yan 閻, as Empress and his eldest son, Shi[a], as Heir Apparent.

Luo Heng was named Prefect of the Imperial Secretariat; Xie Siming became Grand Warden of Guanghan; Ren Tiao became General Stabilizing the North, Governor of Liang Province in Charge of Northern Affairs, and Colonel of the Eastern Qiang; and Li Yi[a] was made General Stabilizing the West and Colonel of the Western

10. A quotation from the Analects of Confucius. See Lunyu 6/4/8; Legge 1861–1872:I, 164.

11. Ren (504n9) argues that this passage, which does not occur in HYGZ, derives from the lost Sanshiguo chunqiu and is ultimately based on legends and rumors that circulated among Jin literati.

12. At this point he also changed the name of the state to Han, basing this name upon that of his former fief. See WS 96/2111.11.

13. The Record of Rites states that when a great officer has reached the age of seventy, he should be summoned with a "comfortable carriage" (anju 安車). The Ceremonies and Rites says that a great officer should be summoned with a roll of silk. A roll (shu 束) was five ounces (liang 兩). See Liji zhengyi 22/12a; Yili zhengyi 22/12a.

14. These are mourning garments. See Liji zhengyi 29/17a. In JS 94/2442 we read that after Gong's father and uncle(s) were killed by Li Te, he maintained mourning for many years afterward. This must be the significance of the present apparel.

Barbarians. The various commandery officials and court officials were all replaced with his own retainers and aides. Jiao province was abolished, and Shou's nephew Li Quan 李權[15] was made General Stabilizing the South, Colonel of the Southern Barbarians, and Governor of Ning Province. From this time on, the various scions of the Li clan in Chengdu no longer controlled troops or power. The old officials of Li Xiong's day and men of the Six Commanderies were all cast aside.

Autumn. Seventh month. [HYGZ 9/125.7–9]

Someone indicted the Grand Warden of Guanghan Li Qian for plotting with the great officers to depose Shou.[16] Shou ordered his son Guang and the great officers to convene a conference in the front audience hall.[17] He transferred Li Qian to become Grand Warden of Hanjia 漢嘉. There was a great wind and a violent storm; lightning struck the main gate to the palace. Li Shou reproached himself severely and commanded the various officials to exhaust their loyal counsels without fear or taboo.

Eighth month. The heavens poured down a continuous stream of rain, harming the crops. The common people suffered from famine and pestilence. The servant without office (caomangchen 草莽臣) *Gong Zhuang submitted a sealed memorial which read, "Your servant has heard that hidden virtue will certainly have its manifest reward. For this reason when Yu Gong* 于公 *adjudicated cases, he raised the village gate to await enfeoffment.[18] In my humble opinion, Emperor Xian (i.e., Li Xiang*ª*) was generous, benevolent, and full*

---

15. Ren (505n9), noting that Quan's father is never named, speculates that he was one of the distaff sons of Li Xiangª.

16. HYGZ 9/125.10 reads, "Li Yiª's elder cousin Qian plotted together with the great officers to dethrone Shou," thus substantially agreeing with JS. ZZTJ 96/3023, however, has "The Grand Warden of Guanghan Li Qian, elder cousin of Li Yiª of Han, reported that the great officers were plotting to depose Shou," thus placing Li Qian in a totally different light. Here we follow JS and HYGZ.

17. HYGZ 9/125.9–10 continues here, ". . . and establish a pact of brotherhood with them. Li Hong was promoted to General Stabilizing the East and Governor of Jing Province and transferred to garrison Ba commandery."

18. Yu Gong was a local magistrate under the Han who is said to have always resolved his cases fairly and to the satisfaction of those concerned. Once when the gate to his village toppled over, he had it rebuilt high enough to permit an official's carriage to pass, so sure was he that the otherwise unrecognized and hence "hidden" virtue (yinde 陰德) of his principles in the administration of justice would result in Heaven-sent rewards for his family. In fact, his descendants held the rank of Marquis for generations. See HS 71/3041, 3046.

of grace; he pardoned many offenses. His numinous virtue was vast and penetrating, and this has been passed down to Your Majesty. Your Majesty is innately loyal and earnest. When you received the dying command to erect your standard,[19] your intentions were equal to those of Zhou Bo 周勃 or Huo Guang 霍光.[20] Your sincerity had penetrated to the divine spirits. However, the hearts (of Li Qi et al.) ran counter to reason, and they overturned the bequeathed instructions. 'Guan' and 'Cai' having arisen,[21] slanderers and flatterers multiplied. Great principles supersede blood ties. To rectify disorder and bring salvation in this time of danger, you pointed to the starry chronograms above and made clear declaration to Heaven and Earth, then, establishing a covenant with your troops by smearing the blood of a sacrificial victim on your lips,[22] you declared the allegiance of your state to Jin. Heaven responded (with auspicious portents) and the people were delighted. A white fish jumped into your boat,[23] booming thunder served to increase your majesty, and a violent wind accorded with the righteous course. Your divine sincerity was honest and forthright, more brilliant than the sun and moon. However, your advisors did not comprehend this and created an administration according to the exigencies of the moment. Incessant rains have inundated our territory for nearly one hundred days and the crops have been harmed. On top of this there has been famine and epidemic. The common people hope desperately for relief. Perhaps Heaven seeks in this way to hold a mirror to Your Majesty. Moreover, the actions taken the previous day(s) will do no more than avert calamity.[24] Your Majesty in your earnestness originally had no aspirations to imperial power, but the present situation has long continued unchanged. Who within the empire can discern this and know of Your Majesty's original intentions? Further, the prognostication concerning

19. Or perhaps, "to establish virtue" (*jianjie* 建節). Jie can refer to either a tally of authority or a standard of virtue.

20. Zhou Bo and Huo Guang were officials who acted as regents to assure continuity after the deaths of Emperors Gaozu (in 195 B.C.E.) and Wudi (87 B.C.E.) of Han respectively. See HS 40/3051–3052, 68/2931–2958.

21. The Dukes of Guan and Cai were brothers of the Duke of Zhou who rose in revolt during his regency. See *Shangshu zhengyi* 17/1a-4b; Legge 1861–1872:III, 487.

22. This was the traditional way of sealing an oath. See *Zuozhuan* 16/Yin 7/1.

23. When King Wu was crossing the Yellow River, a white fish jumped into his boat. This was thought to portend his eventual defeat of the Shang. See *Shiji* 4/120. The other portents given below may have similar origins, but the references are too vague to permit identification.

24. It is uncertain what actions are intended.

the Mysterious Palace[25] is difficult to understand, but you have in fact gone contrary to your sworn covenant. If one morning there should be an emergency in your territory, both those within the court and without would rise in riot. You must think deeply on long-range plans and make lasting provisions for your descendants. I humbly maintain that you should accord with your former covenant and establish ties with Wu-Gui (Jiankang)[26] in order to draw near to the Son of Heaven. He will certainly honor and esteem you and enfeoff you and your descendants for generations. Although you will thus be demoted in rank one grade, your numinous virtue will linger eternally, your ancestral temple will be maintained, and you will enjoy unlimited blessings. Above, the accomplishments of ruler and minister will be inscribed; below, the common people will enjoy peaceful repose. Thus you will penetrate the lofty principles of the empire and promote the fair precepts of truthfulness and circumspection. Bowing with clasped hands before the south-facing (emperor), chanting poems and performing rites, above you will compete with Dapeng 大彭 and Shi Wei 豕韋 for excellence while below you will rival the virtue of Duke Huan of Qi and Duke Wen of Jin.[27] Would this not be auspicious? Some of your advisors say that if the people of the two provinces (i.e., Liang and Yi) ally themselves to Jin they will certainly be honored, but the people of the Six Commanderies will not find it advantageous. Of old, when Liu Bei entered Shu, the people of the Chu region were honored; in the time of Gongsun Shu, the migrants were aided and given repose.[28] However, when Han invaded Shu, casualties numbered more than half the populace, and when Zhong

25. The Mysterious Palace (*xuangong* 玄宮) refers to the two Jupiter stations belonging to the north, also known as the Palace of the Mysterious Warrior (*Xuanwu gong* 玄武宮). A prophesy by Qiao Zhou predicted internal strife when counter-Jupiter was in this part of the sky, that is, the years *ren* 壬 or *gui* 癸, which in this period would be 332–333 or 342–343. Cf. Ren 518n9.

26. Jiankang was the seat of government of the Eastern Jin regime. Wugui refers to Wu 吳 (modern Suzhou) and Guiji 會稽 (modern Shaoxing) and was a common term for this region.

27. Dapeng (or perhaps Great Peng) and Shi Wei were two officials who propped up the Shang royal house near the end of its reign. See *Fengsu tongyi tongjian* 1:4. For Duke Huan and Duke Wen, see above, p. 176 n91. *Fengsu tongyi* lists all four as among the five hegemons 五伯.

28. Liu Bei founded the state of Shu in the Sichuan region during the Three Kingdoms period, bringing with him many followers from Jing Province, the ancient area of Chu. Gongsun Shu had an independent state in the region in the interregnum between the Former and Latter Han. A number of his officers also came from outside Sichuan. See Liu 688n21.

Hui 鍾會 and Deng Ai 鄧艾 campaigned against Liu Bei, they re-
leased their troops to plunder; at that time, who took cognizance of
whether a man was from Chu or Shu? Some of your advisors, not
understanding the foundations of safety and security, are jealous of
their titles and positions. The feudal lords of antiquity had their own
Chancellors, Ministers over the Masses, and Ministers of Works.
Whether Song 宋 or Lu 魯, all had them.[29] *As for the outlying*
kingdoms of the Han, they also had Ministers of State. If you now
loyally submit to the Jin, they will only exalt and esteem you. How
could it be the case that they would diminish your position? In an-
cient times, the reason why the Wardens of commanderies, Prefects,
and Chiefs served only in the provinces and commanderies was that
the state perished and the ruler was replaced. If today you loyally
submit, the ruler will flourish and the officials will have something
on which to rely. How can you mention these two prospects together?
Some of your advisors say that I should act as Fa Zheng 法正 did.[30]
Your Majesty covers me like Heaven and nourishes me like Earth,
indulging me with those things that give me repose. As to fame and
glory, I would not enter official service, whether it be under the
(Cheng-)Han or the Jin. Why should I imitate Fa Zheng? Some of
your advisors say that Jin will certainly demand hostages and ask
what we will say when they demand troops to campaign against the
northern barbarians. In my opinion, Jin is not worried about a foot-
long sword (i.e., an insignificant force). When the whole state submits,
Jin's majesty will encompass the four seas and its territory will be
enlarged ten thousand li. Why should they demand hostages? The
barbarians in the north are our problem as well. Now we constantly
have a threat to the northeast. Even if Jin summons troops, it will
only be to reinforce the Han River. This will still be two sides less at
risk that at present.[31] *The responsibilities placed upon your servant*
are extremely heavy. Forgetting the defilements of my own exhaus-
tion and illness, I am truly grateful for my favorable treatment. I
hope that my insignificant words may serve to supplement in some

29. Song, settled by descendants of the Shang dynasty, and Lu, founded by
the Duke of Zhou and the quintessential repository of Zhou culture, are used
here to represent dramatically different states. The point here is that even should
Shou accept a fief from Jin, his staff will be able to find positions in his service.

30. Fa Zheng convinced the Governor of Yi Province Liu Zhang 劉璋 to give
his support to Liu Bei. Gong Zhuang's enemies compared him to Fa Zheng in
that his true sympathies lay not with Li Shou but with Jin. See SGZ 37/957.

31. Presumably this refers to Jin troops to the east and south.

small way an illustrious era. My constant fear is that I shall die without having expressed my foolish thoughts, thus criminally turning my back on the grace and consideration you have accorded me. Reverently I advance and, kneeling, request my punishment." Li Shou was displeased but was constrained by his former words and hid his feelings.

Ninth month. The Archer-in-Waiting Ren Yan 任顏, *Li Xiong's wife's younger brother, plotted rebellion. He was executed, and Xiong's son Li Bao^a* 李豹 *and company were also killed.*[32]

Fifth year (339). Spring. Second month. A Jin commander attacked Ba commandery, capturing Li Hong. Hong was Li Gong's son. Originally Li Shou had promised to give Hong all the territory east of Niubi 牛髀 *(west of modern Jianyang, Sichuan) but gave up the idea when those in charge of the administration objected. Shou also did not reinforce his troop strength, and it was for this reason that Hong was captured. Li Hong's younger brother Yan* 豔 *bore a grudge over this, causing a rift between him and the officials of the court. At the time Li Shou was gravely ill. Luo Heng, Xie Siming, and others again urged him to submit to Jin. Presently Ba commandery fell, and Shou thought that if he allied himself with Jin now, they would think it due to their military might. For this reason, he was unable to come to a decision, and the plan was dropped.*

Third month. Li Yi^a was appointed General Stabilizing the East, replacing Li Hong.

Summer. The Grand Warden of Jianning Meng Yan 孟彥, *leading the people of the province, bound the Governor of Ning Province Huo Biao and sent him to Jin, surrendering Jianning to Jin. The General of the Right Li Weidu* 李位都 *chastised him. At the time, Li Quan was in Yuesui.*[33]

Autumn. The (Jin) Imperial Secretary Li Shu 李擄 *of Guanghan was again dispatched as Censor to enter the south-central region. Because Li Shu's grandfather Yi* 毅 *had previously been the Governor of Ning Province for the Jin, Shu had old ties with many of the men*

---

32. Most editions of HYGZ follow Li Qi in emending Bao to Yue 約. Here I follow Ren 506n13 (commenting on the passage marked in the text, p. 501, with note 14). ZZTJ 96/3024 records that at this time all of the remaining sons of Li Xiong were killed.

33. JS 7/181 places this event in the third month of 339, and places Li Hong's capture in the fourth month. It also refers to Li Hong as "Shi Jilong's general." Perhaps both errors arise from the JS editors' relying on a source from Shi's state. See JS 7/189–90n19, 73/1923.

of the south. It was for this reason that he was sent. Li Shu's elder cousin Li Yan[b] 李演 submitted a memorial from Yuesui urging Li Shou to return to loyalty to Jin, abandoning the title of Emperor and proclaiming himself King. Shou was angered and had him killed.

The General of Chariots and Cavalry Wang Tao 王韜 *was made Military Advisor.* [HYGZ 9/125.11–127.5]

Shou dispatched his Cavalier Attendant-in-Ordinary Wang Gu and the Palace Attendant-in-Ordinary Wang Guang 王廣 to convey his respects to Shi Jilong 石季龍.[34] Jilong had previously sent Shou a missive suggesting that they ally to invade and plunder (Jin) and promising that they would divide the empire. Shou was greatly pleased and proceeded to construct ships on a grand scale. Troops were put on alert and ordered to mend their armor while both officials and infantry readied provisions. The Prefect of the Imperial Secretariat Ma Dang was named Inspector-General of the Six Armies Bearing Credentials and Axe of Authority (*liujun dudu jia jieyue* 六軍都督假節鉞).

Third year of Hanxing (340). Sixth month. Li Shou issued a rescript saying, "The remnant ashes of the Jiankang regime[35] have long escaped Heaven's punishment. Now I intend to raise a myriad to personally carry out Heaven's judgment."

Ninth month. [SLGCQ, in TPYL 123/81-b]

A camp was erected on the eastern march and a great inspection held with an army of more than seventy thousand men. The naval armada came up the Yangzi. As they passed Chengdu, their drums and the clamor of their shouts filled the river. Li Shou mounted the city wall to observe them. His many officials[36] all said, "Our country is small and out troops few, while Wu-Gui is remote and unapproachable. Planning to take it is not easy." Xie Siming also insistently remonstrated with the utmost sincerity. Shou thereupon ordered his various officials to discourse upon the advantages and disadvantages of this course of action. Gong Zhuang remonstrated, "How can

34. Also known as Shi Hu 虎 (295–349), ruler of the Latter Zhao state. Hu came to the throne in 334 when, following the death of his uncle Shi Le 勒, Hu killed Le's son Shi Hong 弘. Shi Hu was renowned for his cruelty, his exactions on the populace, and his vast harem. Shi Hu's transformation into a rain deity is discussed in Cohen 1978.

35. Here, as above, Shou uses Wu-Gui, referring to the area around the Jin capital, to avoid imparting legitimacy to the Jin state.

36. So also SLGCQ (TPYL 123/8a–b), but ZZTJ 96/3038 attributes this speech directly to Xie Siming.

Your Majesty's allying with the northern barbarians compare to allying with Jin? The barbarians are a nation of wolves and dholes. After Jin has perished, you will not be able to escape facing north and serving them. If you contend with them for the empire, then we occupy a different position of relative strength. Here the states of Yu 虞 and Guo 虢 provide an established precedent, a clear warning from the past.[37] I hope that Your Majesty will consider this well." The many officials all considered Gong Zhuang's words correct; they prostrated themselves and tearfully remonstrated. Li Shou thereupon desisted. His troops all cheered, wishing him a myriad years of life.

The Great General Stabilizing the East Li Yi[a] was dispatched on an expedition against Zangke. The Grand Warden Xie Shu took refuge in the walled city and held him off for several days; the city was not taken. Presently Li Yi[a]'s provisions were exhausted and he led his troops back.

Li Shou appointed his Heir Apparent concurrently Great General and Overseer of the Affairs of the Imperial Secretariat.[38]

Li Shou was heir to Li Xiong's liberality and frugality. When he had newly usurped the throne, he followed the course of Li Xiong's administration and had not yet expressed his own ambitions and desires. Now Li Hong and Wang Gu returned from Ye 鄴 (Shi's capital) full of praises for Shi Jilong's awesome power and the beauty of his palaces as well as the prosperity of Ye. Li Shou also heard that Shi Jilong made cruel use of the penal code and Wang Xun[39] used executions and punishments to restrain his underlings; both were able to control their states. Li Shou admired and envied them. Whenever someone committed a minor offense, Shou would invariably kill him to establish his majesty. Because the suburbs and outlying districts of the capital were not full and the city was deserted with an insufficient supply of craftsmen and tools, Li Shou moved everyone above the third adult per household to Chengdu in order to fill the city. He erected an Imperial Armory and an Imperial Storehouse, mobilizing the skilled workmen of the provinces and commanderies to fill them. He erected buildings on a vast scale and channeled

37. Yu and Guo were neighboring states during the Spring and Autumn period. Yu allowed troops of the much larger state of Jin to pass through its territory in order to attack Guo. After Guo was defeated, Jin's troops went on to subjugate Yu. See *Zuozhuan* 96/Xi 5/9.

38. SLGCQ (TPYL 123/8b) records that this appointment was made in 341. ZZTJ 96/3046 specifies the twelfth month of that year.

39. Wang replaced Li Yi as the Jin Governor of Ning Province. See above, p. 171.

streams into the city, striving for extravagance. He also enlarged the Imperial Academy (*taixue* 太學) and erected a Banquet Hall.[40] Exhausted by the corvée labor, the sighs of the common people filled the roads. Nine out of ten families thought of rebellion. Shou's Archer-in-Waiting of the Left Cai Xing 蔡興 vigorously remonstrated, but Shou considered it slander and had him executed. The Archer-in-Waiting of the Right Li Yi[b] 李嶷 had often fallen afoul of the imperial will through straightforward comments; Shou, bearing resentment toward him on more than one count, on some other pretense threw him in jail and killed him.

Sixth year (of Hanxing, 343). The six commanderies of Xinggu 興古, *Yongchang* 永昌, *Yunnan* 雲南, *Shushi, Yuesui, and Heyang* 河陽 *were separated from Ning province to become Han* 漢 *province.* [SLGCQ, in TPYL 123/8b]

Summer. Fourth month. The (Jin) Governor of Yi Province Zhou Fu 周撫 *and the Grand Warden of Xiyang* 西陽 *Cao Ju* 曹據 *attacked Li Shou, defeating his General Li Heng* 李恆 *at Jiangyang.* [JS 7/185]

When Li Shou's illness became critical, he often saw Li Qi and Cai Xing haunting him.

Ninth year (343).[41] Li Shou died. At the time he was forty-four *sui*[42] and had been on the throne six years.[43] He was falsely given the posthumous title Illustrious Cultured Emperor (*Zhaowendi* 昭文帝) and the temple name Middle Exemplar (*Zhongzong* 中宗). His burial tomb was called Anchangling 安昌陵.

When Shou first was made king, he was fond of learning and loved scholars. He was himself close to the path of goodness. Every time he would read of a good commander, a worthy minister, or one who possessed meritorious achievements, he would always recite it over and over to himself. For this reason, he was able to attack and conquer in all four directions, expanding the state a thousand *li*. Whereas Li Xiong displayed his benevolent heart above, Li Shou also displayed his benevolent heart below and was called a worthy minister. When he assumed the imperial throne, he replaced the ancestral temple,

40. WS 96/2111 parallels this paragraph quite closely but omits this last sentence.

41. JS originally read "eighth year," at variance with HYGZ 9/127.6, which gives 343, and with SLGCQ (in TPYL 123/8b) and JS 7/186, both of which specify the eighth month of that year. See JS 121/3052n15.

42. SLGCQ, quoted in TPYL 123/8b, gives Shou's age at death as forty *sui*.

43. JS originally read "five years." Emended in accordance with our emendation of the date of his death. Cf. JS 121/3052n16.

establishing his father, Xiang[a], in the Temple of the Primordial Ancestor of the Han (*Han Shizu miao* 漢始祖廟) and moved Li Te and Li Xiong to the Temple of Great Perfection (*Da Cheng miao* 大成廟). He also sent down a missive saying that he was of a different clan from Li Qi and Li Yue. All the institutions of government were altered. From the great ministers on down, he predominately used his own subordinates and aides; the old officials from the time of Li Xiong and the men of the Six Commanderies all were cashiered.

When Li Shou first fell ill, Xie Siming and others argued for recognizing the royal house (of Jin), but Shou did not agree. Li Yan[b] submitted a missive from Yuesui urging Shou to return to allegiance, renouncing the title of emperor and declaring himself King. Shou was angered and killed him in order to frighten Gong Zhuang, Xie Siming, and the others. Gong Zhuang wrote seven poems, attributing them to Ying Qu 應璩 (190–252), in order to rebuke Li Shou.[44] Shou replied, "By examining poems one can discern intentions. If these poems are the work of a contemporary author, they are the words of a worthy savant. If they are the work of an ancient author, they are merely the common words of a dead ghost."

Shou always wanted to emulate the actions of Emperor Wu of Han (r. 140–87 B.C.E.) and Emperor Ming of the Wei (r. 227–239). He was embarrassed to hear of affairs of the time of his father and cousins. Those submitting memorials were not permitted to speak of the government of the previous generation because Shou thought himself superior to them.

44. ZZTJ 96/3035, under the year 339, records this incident but gives the author's name as Du Xi 杜襲 and the number of poems as ten. Under 340, ZZTJ (96/3038–3039) records that, having failed to persuade Shou to submit to Jin, Gong Zhuang feigned deafness and never again came to Chengdu.

Li Shi[a]

李勢

Li Shi[a] 李勢, sobriquet Ziren 子仁, was Li Shou's eldest son. Originally Shou's wife, Madame Yan, had no children. When Li Xiang[a] killed Li Feng, he took Feng's daughter for Shou. She gave birth to Shi[a]. Li Qi prized Shi[a]'s bearing and appearance and appointed him General of the Reserve Army (*yijun jiangjun* 翊軍將軍) and Heir Apparent to the King of Han (i.e., Shou). Shi[a] was seven feet nine inches in height, and his waist measured fourteen spans.[1] He was adept at adapting to the exigencies of the moment,[2] and he impressed the people of his time. When Li Shou died, Shi[a] inherited the counterfeit throne, proclaiming a general amnesty, and changing the reign title to Taihe 太和 (Great Harmony).[3] He honored his mother, Madame Yan, as Empress Dowager and his wife, Madame Li 李,[4] as Empress.[5]

The Prefect of the Grand Astrologer's Office Han Hao 韓皓 memorialized that the Dazzling Deluder (Mars) was "guarding" the con-

1. Approximately six feet three inches. A span is sometimes three inches and sometimes five. Here five seems more likely, giving a girth of 66.5 inches.

2. *Fuyang* 俯仰, lit., "turning up and down." The usage derives from a passage in *Zhuangzi*, which Watson translates: "Have you never seen a well sweep? Pull it, and down it comes; let go, and up it swings. It allows itself to be pulled around by men; it doesn't try to pull them. So it can go up and down and never get blamed by anybody." See *Zhuangzi* 38/14/38–39; Watson 1968:160.

3. WS 96/2112.5 records at this point that he sent an emissary to present tribute, presumably to the Toba Wei.

4. The Bona edition (121/8a) and Tokugawa edition (121/13a) give her natal surname as Ji 季, but we have just been told she is the daughter of Li Feng.

5. The preceding paragraph is closely paralleled in SLGCQ (TPYL 123/8b). The portion of the HYGZ dealing with Li Shi[a]'s reign was lost by the Song, and the received text is an addition based upon ZZTJ. Ren (519n14) argues that this addition was made by Lü Dafang and not Li Ji, as has been commonly supposed. In any case, it is not from the hand of Chang Qu and makes no significant divergences from the JS text.

stellation Heart[6] because the rituals of the ancestral temple had been discontinued. Li Shi[a] ordered the many officials to debate the matter. His Minister of State Dong Jiao and Palace Attendant Wang Gu were of the opinion that the Emperors Jing (Li Te) and Wu (Li Xiong) had brought success to the enterprise and that Emperor Xian (Li Xiang[a]) and King Wen (Li Liu) had inherited their foundation, that the closest relatives are never distant, and that they should not be alienated or estranged. Shi[a] ordered that Li Te and Li Xiong should again receive sacrifice and that both should be styled King of Han.

Li Shi[a]'s younger brother, the Great General King Guang of Han, in view of the fact that Shi[a] had no sons, sought to be named Imperial Brother-Heir (*taidi* 太弟), but Shou would not permit it. Ma Dang and Xie Siming, considering that Shi[a]'s siblings were not many and that if he discarded one of them he would be even more isolated and imperiled, insistently urged him to permit it. Li Shi[a] suspected Ma Dang and company of plotting with Guang. He dispatched his Grand Warden Li Yi[a] to attack Li Guang at Fu and ordered Dong Jiao to apprehend and behead Ma Dang and Xie Siming, exterminating their families to the third generation.[7] Li Guang was demoted to Marquis of Linqiong and committed suicide. Xie Siming was a strategist and remonstrated forcefully. Ma Dang had won the hearts of the people. From this time on there were no more men of principles or remonstrators.

From Jinshou, Li Yi[a] raised troops and rebelled.[8] Many of the men of Shu followed him, and his force reached several tens of thousands. Li Shi[a] climbed the city walls and fought to repel them. Li Yi[a], riding alone, rushed the gate, and one of the gatekeepers shot and killed him. His force then collapsed and scattered. Having "executed" Li Yi[a], Shi[a] proclaimed a general amnesty and changed the reign title to Jianing 嘉寧 (Excellect Tranquillity).

Originally there had been no Lao 獠 in the Shu region.[9] Now

6. Heart (*xin* 心) is the fifth of twenty-eight lunar mansions against which the Chinese plotted the movements of the planets. It is located in Scorpio and Antares. To "guard" (*shou* 守) is, according to Needham, a technical term meaning to remain in one constellation for longer than twenty days. See Needham 3/399, 235, 240.

7. ZZTJ 97/3067 places this event during the eighth month of 345. WS 96/2112.5–6 is unequivocal concerning Li Guang's intentions, stating that Guang was planning a surprise attack on Shi[a].

8. ZZTJ 97/3072 places this rebellion in the winter of 346.

9. The Lao 獠 are to be identified with the modern Jielao (or Gelao, 犵獠), relatives of the modern Thai peoples. The Lao lived in pile dwellings, did not

they began to emerge from the mountains. As far north as Qianwei and Zitong, they were scattered throughout the mountain valleys in more than a hundred thousand villages. They could not be controlled and were a major source of trouble for the commoners.

Since Li Shi[a] was haughty and miserly, he would often kill a man in order to seize his wife.[10] Wild and lascivious, he paid no heed to affairs of state. The barbarian Lao (or Yi and Lao) rebelled, yet his defenses were scattered and incomplete; daily the borders of the state shrank. On top of this, there was famine. By nature fearful and jealous, Li Shi[a] killed and maimed the great officers, making unrestrained use of punishments. Men were all filled with fear and trepidation. He repudiated and dismissed the ministers and aides of his father and ancestors, drawing near to him and employing the inferior men who surrounded him. These lackeys relied on his favor to bully and reward.[11] Li Shi[a] also remained constantly in the inner quarters of the palace and seldom saw the high officials of state. When the astrologer repeatedly set forth the warnings of calamitous portents, Shi[a] gave Dong Jiao the added title Grand Preceptor, exalting him in name but actually hoping to have him share the baleful portents.

The Grand Marshal Huan Wen 桓溫 led a marine force on a campaign against Li Shi[a].[12] Wen bivouacked at Qingyi 青衣 (north of Yaan). Li Shi[a] mobilized a large army to guard against attack and also stationed Li Fu[a] 李福 and Zan Jian 昝堅 with several thousand men from Shanyang to Heshui in order to hold off Huan Wen. It was said that Huan Wen would ascend by means of footpaths, and the commanders all wanted to set an ambush south of the Yangzi in order to await the royal troops. Zan Jian disagreed and led the armies to cross from north of the Yangzi toward Qianwei at Mandarin Duck Bend 鴛鴦碕. But Huan Wen emerged south of the Yangzi from Shanyang. Only when he had arrived at Qianwei did Zan Jian discover that he was on a different route from Huan Wen. He then turned back and crossed to the north of the Yangzi at Shatou Ford

---

possess the crossbow, and are said to have had the custom of drinking through the nose. See Beauclair 1970; Ruey 1948.

10. WS 96/2112.7 adds, "He also took the daughter of Li Yi[a] as his Empress."

11. WS 96/2112.9 here adds, "He erected and decorated buildings, paying no heed to the remonstrances of his officials."

12. The JS Annals (8/193.7) record the launch of this expedition on December 10, 346. At the time, the court was controlled by the Empress of the deceased Emperor Kang 康. Huan Wen made this expedition on his own initiative, only submitting a memorial notifying the court of his actions before embarking. See JS 98/1529.

沙頭津 (twenty *li* north of Pengshan). By the time Zan Jian arrived, Huan Wen had already reached Chengdu's Shilimou 十里陌.[13] Zan's force scattered of itself. Reaching the city walls, Huan Wen set fires and burned the gates to the larger city. Li Shiª's troops were terrified and none remained resolute of will.

The Supervisor of the Palace Secretariat (*zhongshujian* 中書監) Wang Gu, Cavalier Attendant-in-Ordinary Chang Qu, and others urged Li Shiª to surrender. Shiª asked the Palace Attendant Feng Fu 馮孚 about it. Fu replied, "Of old, when Wu Han 吳漢 campaigned against Shu, he completely exterminated the Gongsun clan.[14] Now Jin has issued a missive saying they will not pardon the Lis. I fear that even though you surrender, there will be no way of assuring your safety." Shiª thereupon exited by night through the East Gate and fled with Zan Jian to Jinshou. He then sent a letter of surrender to Huan Wen that read, "Seventeenth day of the third month of the second year of the counterfeit Jianing reign period (April 13, 347).[15] Li Shiª of Lueyang prostrates himself, guilty of a capital crime. With all humility I address His Excellency, the Great General. My forebears were refugees who, relying on natural defenses and taking advantage of a dispute, came into illegal possession of Min and Shu (i.e., the Sichuan region). In my benighted weakness I came to control the last few threads of this enterprise. Stealing a few seasons of peace, I have not yet been able to change their plan. I have impertinently troubled your vermilion carriage[16] to brave perilous defiles. My unreasoning and doltish soldiers have transgressed against the Heavenly Majesty. Mortified and ashamed, my essential spirits (*jinghun* 精魂) have dissolved and scattered. I would gladly accept the executioner's blade in order to consecrate the drums of your army.[17] As for the

13. The exact location of Shilimo is unknown. Ren (513n7) would place it ten *li* south of Chengdu's Yangzi Bridge 江橋, near modern Shiyangchang 石羊場.

14. This refers to the reintegration of Sichuan into the Han empire after the defeat of Gongsun Shi in 36 C.E. See HHS 13/543.

15. JS 8/193.11 puts Li Shiª's surrender on April 25, 347. The same source placed Huan Wen's attack on Chengdu on the *yimao* 乙卯 day of the third month, but there was no *yimao* day in that month; it should perhaps be the *yimao* day of the second month, March 23. Another possibility would be to assume *yimao* is a mistake for the graphically similar *jimao* 己卯, which would give April 7.

16. A vermilion carriage was restricted to high officials and emissaries of the emperor. See *Wenxuan* (Liuchen ed.) 46/10a, 21/8b.

17. In ancient China it was the practice before a battle to consecrate with the blood of a sacrificial victim, human or otherwise, the battle drums used to convey commands and encourage the troops. Human sacrifice for this purpose

Great Jin dynasty, its heavenly net is loose-woven and vast.[18] Its mercy extends to the Four Seas, and its grace exceeds the shining sun. In harried confusion I cast myself into the wilderness. That same day I arrived in Baishuicheng 白水城 (northwest of modern Zhaohua) and respectfully sent my personally appointed Cavalier Attendant-in-ordinary Wang You 王幼 bearing a missive announcing my surrender and also ordering the provincial and commandery officials to discard their halberds and lay down their staffs. I am like a fish in a dried-up pond awaiting its imminent demise." Soon he appeared at the gate of Huan Wen's encampment with his hands tied behind his back, accompanied by a carriage carrying his coffin. Huan Wen released his bonds, burned his coffin, and transported Li Shi[a] together with his uncle Li Fu[a], his cousin Li Quan, and more than ten other relatives to Jiankang. Shi[a] was enfeoffed Marquis Returning to Duty (*guiyihou* 歸義侯). In the fifth year of Shengping (361) he died in Jiankang. He occupied the throne five years before his defeat.[19]

Li Te first raised arms in the first year of the Taian reign period (302), and the state went through six generations and forty-six years before perishing in the third year of the Yonghe reign period of Emperor Mu (347).

THE HISTORIAN'S COMMENTS

In antiquity, when the virtue of the Zhou dynasty was just coming into prominence, King Tai of Zhou 周太王 suffered the hardships connected with crossing Liang Mountain.[20] When the Han throne

---

is not, however, recorded for this period. See *Zuozhuan* 142/Xi 33/3, Legge 1861–1872:V, 225.

18. This expression is based on a line in *Laozi*, chapter 73, which Waley (1934:233) translates: "Heaven's net is wide; / coarse are the meshes, yet nothing slips through." This becomes a common metaphor for the all-encompassing inescapability of the state's legal system but here seems to refer to the care and compassion it extends to all its subjects.

19. Huan's biography (JS 98/1569.9) records his elevation of the Cheng Archer-in-Waiting of the Imperial Secretariat Wang Shi 王誓, the Supervisor of the Palace Secretariat Wang Yu 王瑜, the General Stabilizing the East Deng Ding, and the Cavalier Attendant-in-ordinary Chang Qu as Military Advisors, calling them the "best of Shu." Before the army had returned to the Jin capital, Wang Shi, Deng, and Wei Wen had rebelled. JS 8/193–195 records the rebellion of Deng Ding and Wei Wen the following month, their enthronement of Fan Chang-sheng's son, Fan Ben 范賁, as Emperor in the seventh month, and their ultimate defeat in the fourth month of 349.

20. King Tai, grandfather of King Wen of Zhou, suffered incursions from the Jong 戎 and Di 狄 surrounding his home of Bin 豳 (west of modern Xunyi,

seemed eternal, Empress Xuan 宣后 raised troops that crossed the Huang River.[21] Thus we know that the rift that caused the Rong and Di peoples to disrupt China has been deep since ancient times. How much more is this true of the mixed ethnic groups of Ba and Pu 濮.[22] Their varieties are truly numerous. They rely on plunder and robbery to provide for the necessities of life and through long practice, savage fierceness has become their habit. Li Te inherited vicious cunning from earlier generations and in his youth was bold in valorous errantry. When he gave a great sigh at the Sword Gate, his ambition was to swallow up all of Sichuan.[23] When Jin's administrative net lost its knots,[24] he and his followers took advantage of Luo Shang's indecision. Galloping horses and donning quivers, with one voice they gathered like clouds.[25] They slaughtered and massacred Shu and Hanzhong, ate grass in Ba and Liang.[26] Not half a bean was left in the fertile fields, and the ashes of broken bones covered Huayang (i.e., Sichuan). Truly it was the ruler losing the Way that brought about this degradation.

Zhongjun (Li Xiong) was innately outstanding and cut a martial figure. He was praised for his extraordinary majesty. Through many years of carrying a lance he was able to bring the hegemonic enterprise to success. He tread upon Liu Bei's former base of power and subsumed under his rule the former territory of Gongsun Shu. He taxed lightly and rectified decadent customs. By simplifying the laws,

---

Shaanxi). Gifts of goods and treasures did not dissuade them from their desire to possess the land over which King Tai ruled. Rather than subject his followers to continual warfare, King Tai resolved to leave, but the people were so enamored of his virtuous rule that they followed him to his new home at the Zhou Plains 周原. See *Shiji* 4/113–114.

21. The Huang River, in modern Qinghai, marked the boundary of Han rule in Central Asia. I have found no reference to Empress Xuan's role in any Central Asian adventure. This could perhaps be a mistake for Queen Mother Xuan, mother of King Zhao of Qin (r. 306–251 B.C.E.). She had an illicit relation with a Qiang king, giving birth to two sons, then killed him in her palace and dispatched a military force that significantly expanded Qin influence to the west, although perhaps not as far as the Huang River. See HHS 87/2874.

22. On the Pu, see above, p. 43, note 112.

23. Here Sichuan is indicated by its astral counterpart, the constellations Jing 井 (Well) and Luo 絡 (Net). They are said to have been formed by the essence of the Min mountains. See *Wenxuan* 4/26a.

24. This usage is based upon the metaphor of the state as a net controlled by guide-ropes (*gangji* 綱紀) in the hands of the emperor.

25. This is a quotation from JS 120/3025n14, translated above, p. 133.

26. Cf. JS 121/3035.15. After reducing Chengdu, Li Xiong and his forces withdrew to Qi and subsisted on wild taro.

he delighted his new country. Thus he had the appearance of conforming to the standards of a good ruler, but in fact he was inferior to Sun Quan. As for making one's son the Heir Apparent, this is a teaching shared by the sages of the past. That he should inherit one's body and the foundation (of the state) is the fertile precedent cultivated by our predecessors. But Xiong was ignorant of the far-reaching plans needed to administer a state; he practiced the minor virtues of a common fellow. He transmitted control of the state to his adopted son and entrusted strong troops to his true posterity. No one bothered to gather his abandoned bones, for the rifts (among his descendants) leading them to take up arms were already deep. Before the stars had made one Jupiter cycle (i.e., twelve years), disorders that would overturn the nest had arrived. Although some may say this was the path of Heaven, was it not also due to the schemes of men?

Li Ban incurred disaster through liberality and love, whereas Qi hastened his disaster though cruel violence. These were different paths but equally mistaken, different methods but the same destruction. Wukao (Li Shou) relied upon the inherited power of his family and exhausted his troops in stealing the throne. His crimes were those of Zhou Dai 周帶[27] a hundredfold over; his poison was worse than that of Wei of Chu 楚圍.[28] He was fortunate indeed to reach a natural death. Ziren (Li Shi[a]) carried on where he left off, succeeding to his benighted cruelty. Leading the remnant ashes of the state, he dared to oppose a great power (i.e., Jin). When he issued armor to make a dawn expedition, his reasons were the same as those of a cornered animal; when he cut the crossbar of the city gate and fled into the night, he was not dutiful like an approaching bird.[29] His head should have been hung from the gate of the capital in order to make clear the meaning of capital punishments, but instead he was honored as Liu Shan had been.[30] Was this not indeed favorable treatment!

27. Dai was the younger half brother of King Xiang of Zhou 周襄王 (r. 651–619 B.C.E.). Dai tried twice to usurp the throne and took as queen a Di 翟 woman cast aside by King Xiang. See *Shiji* 4/152–154.

28. Mi Wei 羋圍, later canonized as King Ling of Chu 楚靈王, came to the throne by assassinating his nephew and his sons. See *Shiji* 40/1703–1708.

29. This refers to the Bi 比 hexagram of the *Yijing*. The commentary to the fifth line of the hexagram says that a bird that approaches is to be spared, while one that turns its back and flees should be killed. The import would seem to be that Li Shi[a] was deserving of death. See *Zhouyi zhengyi* 2/13a.

30. Liu Shan, last ruler of the Three Kingdoms state of Shu, was enfeoffed and accorded favorable treatment after surrendering to the Wei. See SGZ 33/901–902.

EULOGY

When the Jin loosened the reins of control, the baleful influences of the hundred and six accumulated.[31] Heaven displayed an upside-down turtle and dragons fought in the field.[32] Li Te took advantage of a quarrel to steal our Ba and Yong. The dynasty lasted for five generations, nearly four Jupiter cycles (i.e., forty-eight years). Usurping, killing, and moving the kingdoms, the tracks of their benighted insanity followed upon each other. When virtue is not cultivated, even strategic locations are not reliable.

31. This uses a numerological term, *bailiu* 百六, referring to the one hundred six inauspicious years that occur within each cycle of four thousand six hundred seventeen years. See *Wenxuan* 47/31b; Bokenkamp 1994:65–66.

32. Both are inauspicious portents. See HS 26/1293; *Zhouyi zhengyi* 1/26b.

APPENDIX
Official Titles and Ranks Appearing in the Translation

The following is a listing of the official titles and titles of nobility appearing in the translation and the Chinese originals that they translate. Since it is sometimes difficult to differentiate between formal titles and functional descriptions, I have included some terms, in lower case, that are not treated as titles in the translation. I have consulted the translations suggested by Hucker (1985), Rogers (1968), Mather (1959), and Bielenstein (1980), but the final selections are my own. I have tried to err on the side of literal rather than functional translation.

秀異
Accomplished Prodigy

戶曹掾
Administrator of the Revenue
Section

僕射
Archer-in-Waiting

軍祭酒
Army Libationer

軍師
Army Preceptor

侍御史
Attendant Censor

僚屬
bureaucrats

中領軍
Capital Captain

中護軍
Capital Protector

散騎常事
Cavalier Attendant-in-ordinary

騎督
Cavalry Inspector

中軍督騎
Cavalry Inspector of the Central
Army

御史
Censor

丞相
Chancellor

右丞相
Chancellor of the Right

都戰帥
Chief Battle Leader

司隸校尉
Colonel Director of Retainers

材官校尉
Colonel of Skilled Officers

東羌校尉
Colonel of the Eastern Qiang

翊軍校尉
Colonel of the Reserve Army

南夷校尉
Colonel of the Southern
Barbarians

西夷校尉
Colonel of the Western
Barbarians

將帥
commander

牙門將
Commander of the Serrated-
Flag Gate

使持節
Commissioner Bearing
Credentials

都尉
Defender

將兵都尉
Defender Commanding Troops

騎都尉
Defender of Cavalry

車都尉
Defender of Chariots

大長秋
Director of the Palace Domestic
Service

龍驤將軍
Dragon-Soaring General

公
Duke

東羌獵將
Eastern Qiang Hunting
Commander

五官
Five Officials

將軍
General

揚烈將軍
General Arousing Ardor

撫軍將軍
General Assuaging the Army

冠軍將軍
General Cresting the Armies

領軍將軍
General Directing the Army

建威將軍
General Establishing
Intimidation

折衝將軍
General Foiling the Charge

威寇將軍
General Intimidating Bandits

奮威將軍
General of Aroused Intimidation

車騎將軍
General of Chariots and Cavalry

驃騎將軍
General of Doughty Cavalry

武威將軍
General of Martial Intimidation

驍騎將軍
General of Spirited Cavalry

衛將軍
General of the Guards

翊軍將軍
General of the Reserve Army

右將軍
General of the Right

前將軍
General of the Van

征西將軍
General of the Western
Expedition

安北將軍
General Pacifying the North

平南將軍
General Quelling the South

平西將軍
General Quelling the West

揚烈將軍
General Rousing Ardor

鎮軍將軍
General Stabilizing the Army

鎮東將軍
General Stabilizing the East

鎮北將軍
General Stabilizing the North

鎮南將軍
General Stabilizing the South

鎮西將軍
General Stabilizing the West

宣威將軍
General Who Spreads
Intimidation

刺史
Governor

太尉
Grand Commandant

大司馬
Grand Marshal

太師
Grand Preceptor

太保
Grand Protector

太宰
Grand Steward

太傅
Grand Tutor

太守
Grand Warden

諫議大夫
Grandee Remonstrant

大將軍
Great General

征東大將軍
Great General of the Eastern
Expedition

征北大將軍
Great General of the Western
Expedition

鎮北大將軍
Great General Stabilizing the
North

鎮南大將軍
Great General Stabilizing the
South

大都督
Great Inspector-General

天地太師
Great Preceptor of Heaven and
Earth

尚書
Imperial Secretary

六郡人部曲督
Inspector of Militias for the People of the Six Commanderies

東羌督
Inspector of the Eastern Qiang

都督內外諸軍事
Inspector-General for Internal and External Military Affairs

督郵
Investigator

王
King

侯
Marquis

司馬
Marshal

謀主
Master of Counsels

功曹
Merit Officer

參軍
Military Advisor

西夷護軍
Military Protector of the Western Barbarians

爪牙
minions

相國
Minister of State

司空
Minister of Works

司徒
Minister over the Masses

別駕
Mounted Escort

錄尚書
Overseer of the Affairs of the Imperial Secretariat

監軍
Overseer of the Army

侍中
Palace Attendant

中常侍
Palace Attendant-in-ordinary

中郎
Palace Squire

牧
Pastor

令
Prefect

太史令
Prefect of the Grand Astrologer's Office

太官令
Prefect of the Grand Provisioner

尚書令
Prefect of the Imperial Secretariat

中書令
Prefect of the Palace Secretariat

督護
Protector-General

東督護
Protector-General of the East

軍司
Provost of the Army

王太后
Queen Mother

主簿
Recorder

輔政
Regent

從事
Retainer

治中從事
Retainer Administering the
Palace

內史
Seneschal

長史
Senior Aide

六郡都督假節鉞
Six Armies Bearing Credentials
and Axe of Authority

中書監
Supervisor of the Palace
Secretariat

丞
Vice-Administrator (of a
commandery)

守
Warden

東羌良將
Worthy Commander of the
Eastern Qiang

Bibliography

PRIMARY SOURCES

Baihu tong 白虎通. *Byakkotsū sakuin* 白虎通索引. Ed. by Itō Tomoatsu 伊東倫厚 et al. Tokyo: Tōhō shoten, 1979.

Chunqiu Zuozhuan zhengyi 春秋左轉正義. *Shisanjing zhushu* edn. Taipei: Yiwen chubanshe, 1976. Photo-reprint of 1816 carving.

Dushi fangyu jiyao 讀史方輿紀要. By Gu Zuyu 顧祖禹. Basic Sinological Series 國學基本叢書 edn. Taipei: Commercial Press, 1968.

Fengsu tongyi tongjian 風俗通義通檢. By Ying Shao 應劭 (fl. ca. 190). *Index du Fong sou t'ong yi*. Centre franco-chinois d'études Sinologiques. Publication 3. Taipei: Ch'eng-wen Publishing Co., 1968. Reprint of Beijing, 1943.

Guanzi 管子. Ed. by Dai Wang 戴望. Basic Sinological Series edn. Shanghai: Commercial Press.

Hanshu 漢書. By Ban Gu 班固 (32–92). Beijing: Zhonghua shuju, 1962.

Hou Hanshu 後漢書. By Fan Ye 范曄 (398–445). Beijing: Zhonghua shuju, 1971.

Huayangguo zhi 華陽國志. By Chang Qu 常璩 (fl. 350). Basic Sinological Series edn. Shanghai: Commercial Press, 1938.

Huayangguo zhi jiaobu tuzhu 華陽國志校補圖注. By Chang Qu. Ed. by Ren Naiqiang 任乃强. Shanghai: Guji chubanshe, 1987.

Huayangguo zhi jiaozhu 華陽國志校注. By Chang Qu. Ed. by Liu Lin 劉琳. Chengdu: Ba Shu shushe, 1984.

Jingdian jilin 經典集林. By Hong Yixuan 洪頤烜 (1763–?). In *Baibu congshu jicheng*. Taipei: Yiwen chubanshe, 1968.

Jinshu 晉書. By Fang Xuanling 房玄齡 (578–648). Beijing: Zhonghua shuju, 1974.

Jinshu jiaozhu 晉書斠注. Liu Chenggan 劉承幹 and Wu Shijian 吳仕鑑, eds. Taipei: Yiwen shuju. Reprint of Peking, 1928.

Jiu Tangshu 舊唐書. Ed. by Liu Xu 劉昫 (887–946). Beijing: Zhonghua shuju, 1975.

Liji zhengyi 禮記正義. *Shisanjing zhushu* edn. Taipei: Yiwen chubanshe, 1976. Photo-reprint of 1816 carving.

Lixu 隸續. By Hong Gua 洪适 (1117–1184). In *Lishi Lixu* 隸釋隸續. Beijing: Zhonghua shuju, 1983.

Lunyu. See *Lunyu yinde* 論語引得. Harvard-Yenching Institute Sinological Series, no. 16. Beijing: Yenching University Press, 1940. Reprint, Taipei: Chengwen, 1966.

Maoshi zhengyi 毛氏正義. *Shisanjing zhushu* edn. Taipei: Yiwen chubanshe, 1976. Photo-reprint of 1816 carving.

Mencius. See *Mengzi yinde* 孟子引得.

Mengzi yinde 孟子引得. Harvard-Yenching Institute Sinological Series, supplement no. 17. Beijing: Yenching University Press, 1941. Reprint, Taipei: Chengwen, 1966.

Mozi 墨子. See *Mozi yinde* 墨子引得. Harvard-Yenching Institute Sinological Series, supplement no. 21. Beijing: Yenching University Press, 1948. Reprint, Taipei: Chengwen, 1966.

Mozi jiangu 墨子閒詁. By Sun Yirang (1848–1908). Kanbun taikei, vol. 13. Tokyo, 1913.

Sanguozhi 三國志. By Chen Shou 陳壽 (233–297). Beijing: Zhonghua shuju, 1963.

Shangshu zhengyi 尚書正義. By Lu Deming 陸德明 (?–ca. 628). *Shisanjing zhushu* edn. Taipei: Yiwen chubanshe, 1976. Photo-reprint of 1816 carving.

Shiji 史記. By Sima Qian 司馬遷. Beijing: Zhonghua shuju, 1962.

Shiki kōchū kōshō 史記校注考證. Ed. by Takigawa Kametarō 瀧川龜太郎. Tokyo: Tōhō Bunka Gakuin Tōkyō Kenkyūjo, 1932–1934.

Shiliu guo chunqiu jibu 十六國春秋輯補. By Cui Hong 崔鴻 (?–ca. 525). Ed. by Tang Qiu 湯球. Basic Sinological Series edn. Beijing: Commercial Press, 1958.

Shitong tongshi 史通通釋. By Liu Zhiji 劉知幾 (661–721). Commentary by Pu Qilong 浦起龍. Basic Sinological Series edn. Shanghai: Commercial Press, 1935.

Shuowen jiezi zhu 說文解字注. By Xu Shen 許慎 (fl. ca. 55–149), commentary by Duan Yucai 段玉裁 (1735–1815). Taipei: Lantai shuju, 1974. Reprint of 1808 Jingyunlou edn.

Songshu 宋書. By Shen Yue 沈約 (441–513). Beijing: Zhonghua shuju, 1974.

Suishu 隋書. By Wei Zheng (580–643). Beijing: Zhonghua shuju, 1974.

Taiping guangji 太平廣記. Edited by Li Fang 李昉 (925–996) et al. Peking: Zhonghua shuju, 1961.

Taiping huanyu ji 太平寰宇記. By Yue Shi 樂史 (930-1007). Taipei: Wenhai chubanshe, 1963.

Taiping yulan 太平御覽. Edited by Li Fang 李昉 (925–996) et al. Beijing: Renmin wenxue chubanshe, 1959.

Taipingjing hejiao 太平經合校. Ed. by Wang Ming 王明. Beijing: Zhonghua shuju, 1960.

Tang huiyao 唐會要. Ed. by Wang Pu 王溥 (922–982). Basic Sinological Series edn. Shanghai: Commercial Press, 1935.

Tongdian 通典. By Du You 杜佑 (735–812). *Shitong* 十通 edn. Palace edition of 1747. Reprint, Taipei: Xinxing shuju, 1958–1959.

Wangshi hejiao Shuijing zhu 王氏合校水經注. By Li Daoyuan 酈道元 (d. 527). Ed. by Wang Xianqian 王先謙. Sibu beiyao edn.

Wenxuan 文選. Commentary by Li Shan 李善 (?–689). Edited by Hu Kejia 胡克家 (1757–1816) 1809. Reprint, Taipei: Yiwen chubanshe, 1967.

Xin Tangshu 新唐書. Edited by Ouyang Xiu 歐陽修 (1007–1072) et al. Beijing: Zhonghua shuju, 1975.

Xunzi 荀子. See *Xunzi yinde* 荀子引得. Harvard-Yenching Institute Sinological Series, supplement no. 22. Beijing: Yenching University Press, 1949. Reprint, Taipei: Chengwen, 1966.

Yantielun jianzhu 鹽鐵論簡注. Ed. by Ma Feibai 馬非百. Beijing: Zhonghua shuju, 1984.

Yi Zhoushu jixun jiaoshi 逸周書集訓校釋. Ed. by Zhu Youceng 朱右曾. Taipei: Shijie shuju, 1957. Reprint of *Huang Qing jingjie* edn.

Yuhan shanfang jiyishu bubian 玉函山房輯佚書補編. By Wang Renjun 王仁俊 (1866–1913). In *Yuhan shanfang jiyishu xubian sanzhong* 玉函山房輯佚書續編三種. Shanghai: Shanghai guji chubanshe, 1989.

Zhanguoce 戰國策. Basic Sinological Series edn. Shanghai: Commercial Press, Reprint, Taipei: Commercial Press, 1967.

Zhouli zhushu 周禮注疏. *Shisanjing zhushu* edn. Taipei: Yiwen chubanshe, 1976. Photo-reprint of 1816 carving.

Zhouyi zhengyi 周易正義. *Shisanjing zhushu* ed. Taipei: Yiwen chubanshe, 1976. Photo-reprint of 1816 carving.

Zhuangzi. See *Zhuangzi yinde* 莊子引得. Harvard-Yenching Institute Sinological Series, no. 20. Beijing: Yenching University Press, 1947. Reprint, Taipei: Chengwen, 1966.

Zuozhuan 左傳. Harvard-Yenching Index Series edn.

SECONDARY STUDIES

Akatsuka Kiyoshi 赤塚忠. 1977. *Chūgoku kodai no shūkyō to bunka: In ōchō no saishi* 中國古代の宗教と文化：殷王朝の祭祀. Tokyo: Kadokawa Shoten.

Allan, Sarah. 1991. *The Shape of the Turtle: Myth, Art, and Cosmos in Early China.* Albany: State University of New York Press.

Beauclair, Inez de. 1970. *Tribal Cultures of Southwest China.* Taipei: Orient Cultural Service.

Beck, B. J. Mansvelt. 1980. "The Date of the *Taiping Jing.*" *T'oung Pao* 66:149–182.

Benn, Charles D. 1991. *The Cavern-Mystery Transmission: A Taoist Ordination Rite of A.D. 711.* Honolulu: University of Hawai'i Press.

Bielenstein, Hans. 1959. "The Restoration of the Han, Part II." *Bulletin of the Museum of Far Eastern Antiquities* 31.

———. 1980. *The Bureaucracy of Han Times.* Cambridge: Cambridge University Press.

Bilsky, Lester James. 1975. *The State Religion of Ancient China.* Asian Folklore and Social Life Monographs, 71. 2 vols. Taipei: Orient Publishing.

Birrell, Anne. 1993. *Chinese Mythology.* Baltimore: Johns Hopkins University Press.

Blakeley, Barry B. 1988. "In Search of Danyang. I: Historical Geography and Archaeological Sites." *Early China* 13:116–152.

Bokenkamp, Stephen. 1994. "Time after Time: Taoist Apocalyptic History and the Founding of the T'ang Dynasty." *Asia Major,* 3rd series, 7.1:59–88.

———. 1997. *Early Daoist Scriptures.* Berkeley: University of California Press.

Boltz, Judith M. 1987. *A Survey of Taoist Literature Tenth to Seventeenth Centuries.* Berkeley: Institute of East Asian Studies.

Boltz, William G. 1982. "The Religious and Philosophical Significance of the 'Hsiang erh' Lao tzu 老子想爾注 in the Light of the Ma-wang-tui Silk Manuscripts." *Bulletin of the School of Oriental and African Studies* 45.1:95–117.

Cahill, Suzanne E. 1993. *Transcendence and Divine Passion: The Queen Mother of the West in Medieval China.* Stanford: Stanford University Press.

Chalfant, Frank H. (Fang Falian), and Roswell S. Britton (Bo Ruihua). 1935. *The Couling-Chalfant Collection of Inscribed Oracle Bone.* Shanghai: Commercial Press.

Chang, K. C. 1983. *Art, Myth, and Ritual: The Path to Political Authority in Ancient China*. Cambridge, Mass.: Harvard University Press.

————. 1986. *The Archaeology of Ancient China*. 4th edition. New Haven: Yale University Press.

Chavannes, Edouard. 1895–1905. *Les Mémoires historiques de Se-Ma Ts'ien*. 5 vols. Paris: E. Leroux. Reprint, Paris: Maisonneuve, 1967.

Chen Guofu 陳國符. 1963. *Daozang yuanliu kao* 道藏源流考. 2 vols. Beijing: Zhonghua shuju.

Chen Mengjia 陳夢家. 1936. "Shangdai de shenhua yu wushu" 商代的神話與巫術. *Yanjing xuebao* 20:485–576.

————. 1937. "Shangdai dili xiaoji" 商代地理小記. *Yugong banyuekan* 7.6-7:101–108.

————. 1956. *Yinxu buci zongshu* 殷墟卜辭綜述. Beijing: Zhongguo kexueyuan kaogu yanjiusuo.

Chen Yongling 陳永齡, ed. 1987. *Minzu cidian* 民族词典. Shanghai: Shanghai cishu chubanshe.

Cheng Faren 程發軔. 1967. *Chunqiu Zuoshizhuan diming tukao* 春秋左氏傳地名圖考. Taipei: Guangwen shuju.

Cheung, Siu-woo. 1995. "Millenarianism, Christian Movements, and Ethnic Change among the Miao in Southwest China." In *Cultural Encounters on China's Ethnic Frontiers*, edited by Stevan Harrell, 217–247. Seattle: University of Washington Press.

Ch'ü, T'ung-tsu. 1961. *Law and Society in Traditional China*. Paris: Mouton.

————. 1972. *Han Social Structure*. Seattle: University of Washington Press.

Chunqiu jingzhuan yinde 春秋經傳引得. *Combined Concordances to Ch'un-ch'iu, Kung-yang, Ku-liang and Tso-chuan*. 4 vols. Harvard-Yenching Sinological Series, no. 11. Beijing: Yenching University Press, 1937. Reprint, Taipei: Chengwen, 1966.

Cohen, Alvin P. 1978. "Coercing the Rain Deities in Ancient China." *History of Religions* 17.3/4: 244–265.

————. 1979. "Avenging Ghosts and Moral Judgement in Ancient Chinese Historiography: Three Examples from *Shih-chi*." In *Legend, Lore, and Religion in China: Essays in Honor of Wolfram Eberhard on His Seventieth Birthday*, edited by Sarah Allan and Alvin P. Cohen, 97–108. San Francisco: Chinese Materials Center.

————. 1982. *Tales of Vengeful Souls: A Sixth Century Collection of Avenging Ghost Stories*. Taipei: Variétés Sinologiques.

Deng Shaoqin 鄧少琴. 1983. *Ba Shu shiji xintan* 巴蜀史蹟新探. Chengdu: Sichuan renmin chubanshe.

DeWoskin, Kenneth J. 1981. "A Source Guide to the Lives and Techniques of Han and Six Dynasties Fang Shih." *Bulletin of the Society for the Study of Chinese Religions* 9:79–105.

Dong Qixiang 董其祥. 1983. *Ba shi xinkao* 巴史新考. Chongqing: Chongqing chubanshe.

———. 1987. "Ba Yu wu yuanliu kao" 巴渝舞源流考. In *Ba Shu kaogu lunwen ji* 巴蜀考古论文集, edited by Xu Zhongshu 徐中舒, 167–177. Beijing: Wenwu chubanshe.

Dong Zuobin 董作賓. 1942. "Yindai de Qiang yu Shu" 殷代的羌與蜀. *Shuowen yuekan* 3.7:103–115.

———. 1948–1953. *Xiaotun dierben Yinxu wenzi yibian* 小屯第二本殷墟乙編. 3 vols. Nanjing, 1948; Nanjing, 1949; Taipei, 1953.

Dubs, Homer H. 1938–1955. *The History of the Former Han Dynasty.* 3 vols. Baltimore: Waverly Press.

———. 1942. "An Ancient Chinese Mystery Cult." *Harvard Theological Review* 35.4:221–240.

———. 1958. "The Archaic Royal Jou Religion." *T'oung Pao* 47:217–259.

Dull, Jack L. 1966. "A Historical Introduction to the Apocryphal (Ch'an-wei) Texts of the Han Dynasty." Ph.d. diss., University of Washington.

Eberhard, Wolfram. 1968. *Local Cultures in South and East China.* Translated by Alide Eberhard. Leiden: E. J. Brill.

———. 1982. *China's Minorities: Yesterday and Today.* The Wadsworth Civilization in Asia Series. Belmont, Calif.: Wadsworth Publishing.

Egan, Ronald C. 1977. "Narratives in *Tso-chuan.*" *Harvard Journal of Asiatic Studies* 37.2:323–352.

Eno, Robert. 1990a. *The Confucian Creation of Heaven: Philosophy and the Defense of Ritual Mastery.* Albany: State University of New York Press.

———. 1990b. "Was There a High God *Ti* in Shang Religion?" *Early China* 15:1–26.

Fang Guoyu 方国瑜. 1984. *Yizi shigao* 彝族史稿. Chengdu: Sichuan minzu chubanshe.

Fu Lecheng 傅樂成. 1977. *Han Tang shi lunji* 漢唐史論集. Taipei: Lianjing chubanshe.

Funaki Katsuma 船木勝馬 et al., eds. 1974–. "*Kayōkokushi* yakuchū kō" 華陽國志譯注稿. *Tōyō daigaku Ajia Afurika bunka kenkyūjo kenkyū nenpō* 東洋大學アジア・アフリカ文化研究所研究年報 Part I, 1974:25–86; Part II, 1975:19–71; Part III, 1976:63–147; Part IV, 1977:53–135; Part V, 1978:93–128; Part VI, 1982:11–71; Part VII, 1986:75–129; Part VII, 1988: 61–127; Part IX, 1989:75–122; Part X, 1991:73–121; Part XI, 1992:45–110; Part XII, 1994:67–134.

Graham, David Crockett. 1958. *The Customs and Religion of the Ch'iang*. Washington, D.C.: Smithsonian Institution.

Granet, Marcel. 1922. *The Religion of the Chinese People*. Translated by Maurice Freedman. New York: Harper & Row, 1977.

Gu Jiegang 顧頡剛, ed. 1926–1941. *Gushi bian* 古史辯. Beijing and Shanghai; reprint, Shanghai: Guji chubanshe, 1982.

Guo Ruoyu 郭若愚, Zeng Yigong 曾毅公, and Li Xueqin 李學勤. 1955. *Yinxu wenzi zhuihe* 殷墟文字綴合. Beijing.

Hammond, Charles E. 1995. "The Demonization of the Other: Women and Minorities as Weretigers." *Journal of Chinese Religions* 23:59–80.

Harrell, Stevan. 1990. "Ethnicity, Local Interests, and the State: Yi Communities in Southwest China." *Comparative Studies in Society and History* 32.3:515–548.

———, ed. 1995. *Cultural Encounters on China's Ethnic Frontiers*. Seattle: University of Washington Press.

He Yaohua 何耀华. 1988. *Zhongguo xinan lishi minzuxue lunji* 中国西南历史民族学论集. Kunming: Yunnan renmin chubanshe.

Holtzman, Donald. 1957. "Les débuts du Système Médiéval des Choix et de Classement: Les neuf catégories du l'Impartial et juste." In *Mélanges* (Institut des Hautes Études Chinoise):387–414.

Honey, David B. 1990. *The Rise of the Medieval Hsiung-nu: The Biography of Liu Yuan*. Bloomington, Ind.: Research Institute for Inner Asian Studies.

Hori Toshikazu 堀敏一. 1975. *Kindensei no kenkyū: Chūgoku kodai kokka no tochi seisaku to tochi shoyūsei* 均田制の研究——中國古代國家の土地政策と土地所有制. Tokyo: Iwanami Shoten.

Huang Fanguang 黃繁光. 1975. "Cheng-Han de xingwang" 成漢的興亡. *Shixue huikan* 史學彙刊 6 (April 1975):119–191.

Huang Lie 黃烈. 1965. "You guan Dizu laiyuan yü xingcheng de yixie wenti" 有關氏族來源與形成的一些問題. *Lishi yanjiu* 歷史研究 2:97–114.

Huang Xiaodong 黄晓东 and Zeng Fanmu 曾凡模. 1993. "Ba wenhua yuansheng xingtai chutan" 巴文化原生形态初探. In *Sanxingdui yu Ba Shu wenhua* 三星堆与巴蜀文化, edited by Li Shaoming 李绍明, Lin Xiang 林向, and Zhao Dianzeng 赵殿增, 54–60. Chengdu: Ba Shu shushe.

Hucker, Charles O. 1985. *A Dictionary of Official Titles in Imperial China*. Stanford: Stanford University Press.

Hulsewé, Anthony Francois Paulus. 1965. "Texts in Tombs." *Asiatische Studien* 18/19:78–89.

Hummel, Arthur W. 1943. *Eminent Chinese of the Ch'ing Period*. Washington, D.C.: Government Printing Office.

Ikeda Suetoshi 池田末利. 1976. *Shōsho* 尚書. Zenshaku kanbun taikei edn. Tokyo: Shūeisha.

Jao Tsung-yi (Rao Zongyi). 1959. *Yindai zhenbu renwu tongkao* 殷代貞卜人物通考. Hong Kong: Hong Kong University Press.

Jin Baoxiang 金寶祥. "Hanmo zhi Nanbeichao nanfang manyi de qianxi" 漢末至南北朝南方蠻夷的遷徙. *Yugong* 5.12 (1936): 17–20.

Johnson, David. 1981. "Epic and History in Early China." *Journal of Asian Studies* 40.2: 255–271.

Kaltenmark, Max. 1953. *Le Lie-sien tchouan (Biographies légendaires des Immortels taoistes de l'antiquité)*. Université de Paris, Publications du Centre d'Études Sinologiques de Pékin. Pékin: Université de Paris.

———. 1961. "Religion and Politics in the China of the Ch'in and the Han." *Diogenes* 34 (summer):17–43.

———. 1979. "The Ideology of the T'ai-p'ing Ching." In *Facets of Taoism: Essays in Chinese Religion*, edited by Holmes Welch and Anna Seidel, 19–52. New Haven: Yale University Press.

Kamata Tadashi 鎌田正. 1963. *Saden no seiritsu to sono tenkai* 左傳の成立とその展開. Tokyo: Taishūkan.

Kandel, Barbara. 1979. *Taiping jing, the Origin and Transmission of the 'Scripture on General Welfare': The History of an Unofficial Text*. Hamburg: Gesellschaft für Natur- und Volkerkunde Ostasiens.

Kanō Naosada 狩野直禎. 1963. "Kayōkokushi no seiritsu o megutte" 華陽国志の成立を迴って. *Seishin joshi daigaku ronsō* 聖心女子大学論叢 21:43–81.

———. 1966. "Goko jidai no gōzoku: Ha-Shoku no gōzoku to Sei-Kankoku" 五胡時代の豪族: 巴蜀の豪族と成漢国. *Rekishi kyōiku* 14.5:19–25.

Karlgren, Bernhard. 1926. *On the Nature and the Authenticity of the Tso-chuan.* Göteborg: Elanders Boktryckeri Akteibolag.

———. 1950. *The Book of Documents.* Göteborg: Elanders Boktryckeri Aktiebolag.

Keightley, David N. 1978. "The Religious Commitment: Shang Theology and the Genesis of Chinese Political Culture." *History of Religions* 17:211–235.

———. 1979. *Sources of Shang History.* Berkeley: University of California Press.

Keyes, Charles F. 1976. "Toward a New Formulation of the Concept of Ethnic Group." *Ethnicity* 3:203–213.

Keyes, Charles F., ed. 1981. *Ethnic Change.* Seattle: University of Washington Press.

Kleeman, Terry F. 1993. "The Expansion of the Wen-ch'ang Cult." In *Religion and Society in T'ang and Sung China*, edited by Patricia Ebrey and Peter N. Gregory, 45–73. Honolulu: University of Hawai'i Press.

———. 1994a. *A God's Own Tale: The Book of Transformations of Wenchang, Divine Lord of Zitong.* Albany: State University of New York Press.

———. 1994b. "Mountain Deities in China: The Domestication of the Mountain God and the Subjugation of the Margins." *Journal of the American Oriental Society* 114.2 (April-June 1994): 226–238.

Knechtges, David R. 1982. *Wenxuan or Selections of Refined Literature, Volume 1: Rhapsodies on Metropolises and Capitals.* Princeton: Princeton University Press.

Kusuyama Haruki 楠山春樹. 1983. "Taiheikyō rui" 太平經類. In *Tonkō to Chūgoku Dōkyō*, edited by Editorial Committee, 119–136. Tokyo: Daitō shuppansha.

Lau, D. C. 1979. *Confucius: The Analects.* Middlesex: Penguin Books.

Legge, James. 1861–1872. *The Chinese Classics.* 5 vols. London: Trubner.

———. 1885. *Li Chi: Book of Rites.* 2 vols. Sacred Books of the East, vol. 27 and 28. Oxford: Oxford University Press. Reprint, New York: University Books, 1967.

Lemoine, Jacques. 1982. *Yao Ceremonial Paintings.* Bangkok, Thailand: White Lotus Co.

Levi, Jean. 1986. "Les fonctionnaires et le divin—Luttes de pouvoir entre divinités et administrateurs dans les contes des Six

Dynasties et des Tang." *Cahiers d'Extrême-Asie* 2:81–110.

———. 1987. "Les fonctions religieuses de la bureaucratie celeste." *L'Homme* 101 (January-March):35–57.

———. 1989. *Les fonctionnaires divins*. Paris: Seuil.

Lévi-Stauss, Claude. 1964. *Totemism*. Translated by Rodney Needham. London: Merlin Press.

Levy, Howard. 1956. "Yellow Turban Religion and Rebellion at the End of the Han." *Journal of the American Oriental Society* 76:214–224.

Lewis, Mark Edward. 1990. *Sacred Violence in Early China*. Albany: State University of New York Press.

Li Fuhua 李复华 and Wang Jiayou 王家祐. 1987. "Guanyu 'Ba Shu tuyu' de jidian kanfa" 关于巴蜀古土语的语几点看法. In *Ba Shu kaogu lunwen ji* 巴蜀考古论文集, edited by Xu Zhongshu 徐中舒, 101–112. Beijing: Wenwu chubanshe.

Li Shaoming 李绍明, Lin Xiang 林向, and Xu Nanzhou 徐南洲, eds. 1991. *Ba Shu lishi, minzu, kaogu, wenhua* 巴蜀历史·民族·考古·文化. Chengdu: Ba Shu shushe.

Li Shaoming 李紹明, Lin Xiang 林向, and Zhao Dianzeng 赵殿增, eds. 1993. *Sanxingdui yu Ba Shu wenhua* 三星堆与巴蜀文化. Chengdu: Ba Shu shushe.

Li Shiping 李世平. 1987. *Sichuan renkou shi* 四川人口史. Chengdu: Sichuan daxue chubanshe.

Li Xueqin 李學勤. 1959. *Yindai dili jianlun* 殷代地理簡論. Beijing: Kexue chubanshe.

———. 1985. *Eastern Zhou and Qin Civilizations*. Translated by K. C. Chang. New Haven: Yale University Press.

———. 1991. "Chu Bronzes and Chu Culture." *New Perspectives on Chu Culture during the Eastern Zhou Period*, edited by Thomas Lawton, 1–22. Princeton: Princeton University Press.

Liang Zhaotao 梁钊韬, Chen Qixin 陈啓新, and Yang Heshu 杨鹤书. 1985. *Zhongguo minzuxue gaikuang* 中国民族学概况. Kunming: Yunnan renmin chubanshe.

Lin Huixiang 林惠祥. 1936. *Zhongguo minzu shi* 中國民族史. Reprint, Taipei: Commercial Press, 1978.

Liu Jiusheng 刘九生. 1986. "Ba Zong jianguo de zongjiao beijing" 巴賨建国的宗教背景. *Shaanxi shida xuebao (zhexue shehui kexue)* 陕西师大学报 (哲学社会科学) 1986.1:94–101.

Loewe, Michael. 1982. *Chinese Ideas of Life and Death: Faith, Myth, and Reason in the Han Period*. London: George Allen & Unwin.

———. 1979. *Ways to Paradise: The Chinese Quest for Immortality*. London: Allen & Unwin.

———, ed. 1993. *Early Chinese Texts: A Bibliographical Guide*. Early China Special Monograph Series, No. 2. Berkeley: Society for the Study of Early China and the Institute of East Asian Studies, University of California.

Luo Kaiyu 罗开玉. 1991. "Banshun 'qixing' yu Zongren" 板楯「七姓」与賨人. In *Ba Shu lishi, minzu, kaogu, wenhua* 巴蜀历史·民族·考古·文化, edited by Li Shaoming 李绍明, Lin Xiang 林向, and Xu Nanzhou 徐南洲, 132–143. Chengdu: Ba Shu shushe.

Maruyama, Hiroshi 丸山宏. 1986. "Shōitsu dōkyō no jōshō girei ni tsuite—'chōshōshō' o chūshin to shite" 正一道教の上章儀禮について——冢訟狀を中心として. *Tōhō shūkyō* 68 (Nov. 1986):44–64.

Maspero, Henri. 1927. *China in Antiquity*. Translated by Frank A. Kierman. Amherst: University of Massachusetts Press, 1978.

Mather, Richard B. 1959. *Biography of Lu Kuang*. Chinese dynastic histories translations, no. 7. Berkeley: University of California Press.

———. 1976. *Shih-shuo Hsin-yü: A New Account of Tales of the World*. Minneapolis: University of Minnesota Press.

Meng Mo 蒙默, Liu Lin 刘琳, Tang Guangpei 唐光沛, Hu Zhaoxi 胡昭曦, and Ke Jianzhong 柯建中. 1989. *Sichuan gudai shigao* 四川古代史稿. Chengdu: Sichuan renmin chubanshe.

Meng Wentong 蒙文通. 1981. *Ba Shu gushi lunshu* 巴蜀古史论述. Chengdu: Sichuan renmin chubanshe.

Mollier, Christine. 1990. *Une apocalypse taoïste du Ve siècle. Le Livre des Incantations divines des Grottes abyssales*. Mémoires de l'Institut des Hautes Études Chinoises. Paris: College de France, Institut des Hautes Études Chinoises.

Morohashi Tetsuji 諸橋徹次. 1957–1960. *Dai Kan-Wa jiten* 大漢和辭典. 13 vols. Tokyo: Taishūkan shoten.

Needham, Joseph. 1959. *Science and Civilisation in China. Volume 3: Mathematics and the Sciences of the Heavens and the Earth*. Cambridge: Cambridge University Press.

Ngo, Van Xuyet. 1976. *Divination, Magie, et Politique dans la Chine ancienne*. Paris: Presses Universitaires de France.

Norman, Jerry, and Tsu-lin Mei. 1976. "The Austroasiatics in Ancient South China: Some Lexical Evidence." *Monumenta Serica* 32:274–301.

Ōfuchi Ninji 大淵忍爾. 1991. *Shoki no Dōkyō* 初期の道教. Oriental Studies Library, No. 38. Tokyo: Sōbunsha.

Prusek, Jaroslav. 1971. *Chinese Statelets and the Northern Barbarians, 1400–300 B.C.* Dordrecht, Holland: Riedel.

Pulleyblank, E. G. 1983. "The Chinese and Their Neighbors in Prehistoric and Early Historic Times." In *The Origins of Chinese Civilization,* edited by David N. Keightley, 411–466. Berkeley: University of California Press.

Qi Qingfu 祁庆富. 1990. *Xi'nanyi* 西南夷. Changchun: Jilin jiaoyu chubanshe.

Qian Yuzhi 钱玉趾. 1993. "Bazu yu Shuzu wenhua kaobian" 巴族与蜀族文字考辨. In *Sanxingdui yu Ba Shu wenhua* 三星堆与巴蜀文化, edited by Li Shaoming 李绍明, Lin Xiang 林向, and Zhao Dianzeng 赵殿增, 205–209. Chengdu: Ba Shu shushe.

Qu Wanli 屈萬里. 1969. *Shangshu jinzhu jinyi* 尙書今注今譯. Taipei: Commercial Press.

Ran Guangrong 冉光荣, Li Shaoming 李绍名, and Zhou Xiyin 周锡银. 1985. *Qiangzu shi* 羌族史. Chengdu: Sichuan minzu chubanshe.

Ren Naiqiang 任乃强. 1984. *Qiangzu yualiu tansuo* 羌族源流探索. Chengdu: Sichuan renmin chubanshe.

———. 1986. *Sichuan shanggushi xintan* 四川上古史新探. Chengdu: Sichuan renmin chubanshe.

Rickett, W. Allyn. 1985. *Guanzi: Political, Economic, and Philosophical Essays from Ancient China.* Princeton: Princeton University Press.

Riegel, Jeffrey K. 1989–1990. "Kou-mang and Ju-shou." *Cahiers d'Extrême-Asie* 5:55–83.

Rogers, Michael C. 1968. *The Chronicle of Fu Chien: A Case of Exemplar History.* Berkeley: University of California Press.

Roth, Harold. 1991. "Psychology and Self Cultivation in Early Taoistic Thought." *Harvard Journal of Asiatic Studies* 51.2:599–650.

———. 1992. *The Textual History of the Huai-nan Tzu.* Ann Arbor: Association of Asian Studies.

Ruey, Yih-fu (Rui Yifu 芮逸夫). 1948. "Lao wei Gelao shizheng" 僚爲仡佬試證. *Bulletin of the Institute of History and Philology, Academia Sinica* 20.1:343–357.

Sage, Steven F. 1992. *Ancient Sichuan and the Unification of China.* SUNY Series in Chinese Local Studies. Albany: State University of New York Press.

Sawa Akitoshi 澤章敏. 1994. "Gotōbeidō seiken no soshiki kōzō" 五斗米道政權の組織構造. In *Dōkyō bunka e no tenbō* 道敎文化への展望, edited by Dōkyō bunka kenkyūkai 道敎文化研究會, 131–152. Tokyo: Hirakawa shuppan.

Schafer, Edward H. 1977. *Pacing the Void: T'ang Approaches to the Stars*. Berkeley: University of California Press.

Schipper, Kristofer M. 1985. "Taoist Ordination Ranks in the Tun-huang Manuscripts." In *Religion und Philosophie in Ostasien (Festschrift für Hans Steininger)*, edited by Gert Naudorf, Karl-Heinz Pohl, and Hans-Herrman Schmidt, 127-148. Königshausen: Neumann.

———. 1994. "Purity and Strangers: Shifting Boundaries in Medieval Taoism." *T'oung Pao* 80:61–81.

Seidel, Anna K. 1969. *La divinisation de Lao Tseu dans le taoïsme des Han*. Publications de l'École Française d'Extrême-Orient, vol. 71. Paris: Ecole Française d'Extrême-Orient.

———. 1969–1970. "The Image of the Perfect Ruler in Early Taoist Messianism: Lao-tzu and Li Hung." *History of Religions* 9.2-3:216–247.

———. 1984. "Le sutra merveilleux du Ling-pao Suprême." In *Contributions aux études de Touen-houang*, edited by Michel Soymié, vol. 3, 305–352. Publications de l'École Française d'Extrême-Orient 135, Paris.

———. 1987. "Traces of Han Religion in Funeral Texts Found in Tombs." In *Dōkyō to shūkyō bunka*, edited by Akizuki Kan'ei, 714–678. Tokyo: Hirakawa shuppansha.

Shaughnessy, Edward L. 1980–1981. "'New' Evidence on the Chou Conquest." *Early China* 6:57–79.

———. 1991. *Sources of Western Zhou History*. Berkeley: University of California Press.

Shima Kunio 島邦男. 1958. *Inkyo bokuji kenkyū* 殷墟卜辭研究. Hirosaki: Chūgokugaku kenkyūkai.

———. 1971. *Inkyo bokuji sōrui* 殷墟卜辭綜類. 2nd revised edition. Tokyo: Kyūko shoin.

Shiratori Yoshirō 白鳥芳郎. 1975. *Yōjin monjo* 傜人文書. Tokyo: Kōdansha.

———. 1981. "The Yao Documents and Their Religious Ceremonies." In *Proceedings of the International Conference on Sinology: Section on Folklore and Culture* 中央研究院國際漢學會議論文集民俗與文化組, 311–318. Academia Sinica, Nankang, August 1980 (Taipei).

Shuihudi Qinmu zhujian zhengli xiaozu 睡虎地秦墓竹简整理小组. 1990. *Shuihudi qinmu zhujian* 睡虎地秦墓竹简. Beijing: Wenwu chubanshe.

Sichuansheng bowuguan 四川省博物馆. 1960. *Sichuan chuanguanzang fajue baogao* 四川船棺葬发掘报告. Beijing: Wenwu chubanshe.

Sichuansheng Guanxian wenjiaoju 四川省灌县文教局. 1974. "Dujiangyan chutu Dong Han Li Bing shixiang" 都江堰出土东汉李冰石像. *Wenwu* 文物 7:27–28.

Sichuansheng minzu yanjiusuo 四川省民族研究所, ed. 1982. *Sichuan shaoshu minzu* 四川少数民族. Chengdu: Sichuan minzu chubanshe.

Skar, Lowell. 1992. "Preliminary Remarks on Yao Religion and Society." Unpublished typescript.

Stein, Rolf A. 1963. "Remarques sur les mouvements du taoïsme politico-religieux au IIᵉ siècle après J.C." *T'oung Pao* 50:1–78.

———. 1979. "Religious Taoism and Popular Religion from the Second to Seventh Centuries." In *Facets of Taoism: Essays in Chinese Religion*, edited by Holmes Welch and Anna Seidel, 53–82. New Haven: Yale University Press.

Strickmann, Michel. 1977. "The Mao Shan Revelations: Taoism and the Aristocracy." *T'oung Pao* 63.1:1–64.

———. 1979. "On the Alchemy of T'ao Hung-ching." In *Facets of Taoism: Essays in Chinese Religion*, edited by Holmes Welch and Anna Seidel, 123–192. New Haven: Yale University Press.

———. 1982a. *Le Taoisme du Mao Chan: Chronique d'une révélation*, Mémoires de l'Institut des Hautes Études Chinoises, v. 17. Paris.

———. 1982b. "The Tao among the Yao." In *Rekishi ni okeru minshū to bunka* 歴史に於ける民衆と文化, edited by Sakai Tadao Sensei koki shukuga kinen no kai, 23–30. Tokyo: Kokusho kankōkai.

Stuart, G. A. 1911. *Chinese Materia Medica: Vegetable Kingdom*. Shanghai: American Presbyterian Missionary Press.

Sun Hua 孙华. 1987. "Ba Shu fuhao chulun" 巴蜀符号初论. In *Ba Shu kaogu lunwen ji* 巴蜀考古论文集, edited by Xu Zhongshu 徐中舒, 89–100. Beijing: Wenwu chubanshe.

Takezoe Shin'ichirō 竹添進一郎. *Zuozhuan huijian (Saden kaisen)* 左傳會箋. Kanbun taikei ed. Tokyo, 1911.

Tan Qixiang 譚其驤. 1982. *Zhongguo lishi dituji*. 8 vols. Shanghai: Ditu chubanshe.

Tang Changru 唐長儒. 1954. "Fan Changshen yu Bashi ju Shu de guanxi" 范長生與巴氏據蜀的關係. *Lishi yanjiu* 歷史研究 1954.4:115–122.

———. 1955. *Wei Jin Nanbeichao shi luncong* 魏晉南北朝史論叢. Beijing: Xinhua shudian.

———. 1983a. "Shiji yu Daojing zhong suojian de Li Hong" 史籍與道經中所見的李弘. In *Wei Jin Nanbeichao shilun shiyi* 魏晉南北朝史論拾遺, 208–217. Beijing: Zhonghua shuju.

———. 1983b. "Wei Jin qijian beifang Tianshidao de chuanbo" 魏晉期間北方天師道的傳播. In *Wei Jin Nanbeichao shilun shiyi* 魏晉南北朝史論拾遺, 218–232. Beijing: Zhonghua shuju.

———. 1990. "Clients and Bound Retainers in the Six Dynasties Period." In *State and Society in Medieval China*, edited by Albert E. Dien, 111–138. Stanford: Stanford University Press.

Taniguchi Fusao 谷口房男. 1973. "*Kayōkokushi* jinmei sakuin" 華陽國志人名索引. *Tōyō daigaku Ajia Afurika bunka kenkyūjo kenkyū nenpō* 東洋大學アジア・アフリカ文化研究所研究年報 1973:12–130.

———. 1976. "Shindai no Teizoku Yōshi ni tsuite" 晉代の氏族楊氏について. *Tōyō daigaku bungakubu kenkyū kiyō* 東洋大学文學部研究紀要 30:31–57.

Tong Enzheng 童恩正. 1979. *Gudai de Ba Shu* 古代的巴蜀. Chengdu: Sichuan renmin chubanshe.

Twitchett, Denis. 1992. *The Writing of Official History under the T'ang*. Cambridge: Cambridge University Press.

Twitchett, Denis, and Michael Loewe, eds. *Cambridge History of China. Volume I: The Ch'in and Han Empires, 221 B.C.–A.D. 220*. Cambridge: Cambridge University Press, 1986.

Ushioda Fukizō 潮田富貴藏. 1954. "Kandai Seinan Shina no rekishi chiri" 漢代西南支那の歷史地理. *Ōsaka daigaku kyōyōbu kenkyū shūroku* 大阪大學敎養部研究集錄 2 (March):21–45.

Von Glahn, Richard. 1987. *The Country of Streams and Grottoes: Expansion, Settlement and the Civilizing of the Sichuan Frontier in Song Times*. Harvard East Asian Monographs 123. Cambridge, Mass: Council on East Asian Studies, Harvard University.

Waley, Arthur. 1934. *The Way and Its Power*. London: George Allen & Unwin. Reprint, New York: Grove Press, 1958.

Wang Guowei 王國維. 1917. *Jinben Zhushu jinian shuzheng* 今本竹書紀年疏證. Reprint, Taipei: Shijie shuju, 1977.

Wang, John C. 1977. "Early Chinese Narrative: The *Tso-chuan* as

Example." In *Chinese Narrative: Critical and Theoretical Essays,* edited by Andrew H. Plaks, 3–20. Princeton: Princeton University Press.

Wang Ming-ke 王明珂. 1992. "The Ch'iang of Ancient China through the Han Dynasty: Ecological Frontiers and Ethnic Boundaries." Ph.D. diss., Harvard University.

———. 1994a. "Guoqu de jiegou: Guanyu zuqun benzhi yu rentong bianqian de tantao" 過去的結構－－關於族群本質與認同變遷的探討. *Xin Shixue* 5.3:119–140.

———. 1994b. "Shema shi minzu: yi Qiangzu wei li tantao yige minzuzhi yu minzushi yanjiuhang de guanjian wenti" 什麼是民族：以羌族爲例探討一個民族誌與民族史研究上的關鍵問題 ("What Is an Ethnos? A Key Issue in Ethnographic and Historical Studies of Peoples in the Case of the Ch'iang"). *Bulletin of the Institute of History and Philology, Academia Sinica* 中央研究院歷史語言研究所集刊 65.4:989–1027.

———. n.d. "Huaxiahua de licheng: Wu Taibo chuanshuo yanjiu" 華夏化的歷程：吳太伯傳說研究. Typescript.

Wang, Yü-ch'üan. 1949. "An Outline of the Central Government of the Former Han Dynasty." *Harvard Journal of Asian Studies* 12:134–187.

Watson, Burton. 1968. *The Complete Works of Chuang-tzu.* New York: Columbia University Press.

Wu Chenglo 吳承洛. 1937. *Zhongguo duliangheng shi* 中國度量衡史. Shanghai: Commercial Press.

Xu Zhongshu 徐中舒. 1987. *Ba Shu kaogu lunwen ji* 巴蜀考古论文集. Beijing: Wenwu chubanshe.

Xu Xitai 徐锡台. 1979. "Zhouyuan chutude jiaguwen suojian renming guanming diming jianshi" 周原出土的甲骨文所见人名官名地名简释. *Guwenzi yanjiu* 1:184–202.

Yang Bojun 杨伯峻, ed. 1981. *Chunqiu Zuozhuan zhu* 春秋左传注. Beijing: Zhonghua shuju.

——— and Xu Ti 徐提, eds. 1985. *Chunqiu Zuozhuan cidian* 春秋左传词典. Beijing: Zhonghua shuju.

Yang Lien-sheng (Yang Liansheng) 楊聯陞. 1961. *Studies in Chinese Institutional History.* Cambridge, Mass.: Harvard-Yenching Institute.

Yang Ming 杨铭. 1991. *Dizu shi* 氐族史. Changchun: Jilin jiaoyu chubanshe.

Yang Weili 楊偉立. 1982. *Cheng Han shilüe* 成漢史略. Chongqing: Chongqing chubanshe.

Yang Zhongyi 楊中一. 1956. "Buqu yan'ge lüekao" 部曲沿革略考.
　　Shihuo 1.3:97–107.
Yasui Kōzan 安居香山. 1979. *Isho no seiritsu to sono tenkai* 緯書
　　の成立とその展開. Tokyo: Kokusho kankōkai.
———, ed. 1984. *Shin'i shisō no sōgōteki kenkyū* 讖緯思想の綜
　　合的研究. Tokyo: Kokusho kankōkai.
Yasui Kōzan and Nakamura Shōhachi 中村璋八, eds. 1971– . *Chō-
　　shū Isho shūsei* 重修緯書集成. Tokyo: Meitoku shuppansha.
Yoshioka Yoshitoyo 吉岡義豐. 1976. "Rikuchō Dōkyō no shumin
　　shisō" 六朝道教の種民思想. In *Dōkyō to Bukkyō* 道教と仏
　　教, vol. 3, 221–284. Tokyo: Kokusho kankōkai.
You Zhong 尤中. 1979. *Zhongguo xinan de gudai minzu* 中国西南
　　的古代民族. Kunming: Yunnan renmin chubanshe.
Zang Lihe 臧勵龢. 1936. *Zhongguo gujin diming da cidian* 中國
　　古今地名大辭典. Shanghai: Commercial Press.
Zhang Guanying 張冠英. 1957. "Liang Jin Nanbeichao shiqi min-
　　zu da biandong zhong de Linjun man" 兩晉南北朝時期民族
　　大變動中的廩君蠻. *Lishi yanjiu* 歷史研究 1957.2:67–85.
Zhang Xiong 張雄. 1993. "Cong Xia-Shang shiqi Exi wenhua yicun
　　kan zaoqi Bazu: Jian tan 'Ba' 'Shu' fei xiangtong zushu" 从夏商
　　时期鄂西文化遗存看早期巴族－兼谈巴蜀非相同族属. In
　　Sanxingdui yu Ba Shu wenhua 三星堆与巴蜀文化, edited by Li
　　Shaoming 李绍明, Lin Xiang 林向, and Zhao Dianzeng 赵殿增,
　　33–40. Chengdu: Ba Shu shushe.
Zhang Zexian 张泽咸 and Zhu Dawei 朱大渭. 1980. *Wei Jin Nan-
　　beichao nongmin zhanzheng shiliao huibian* 魏晋南北朝农民战
　　争史料彙编. 2 vols. Beijing: Zhonghua shuju.
Zhang Zongyuan 章宗源. 1936. *Suishu jingji zhi kaozheng* 隋書
　　經籍志考證. In *Ershiwishi bubian* 二十五史補編, 4943–5037.
　　Shanghai: Kaiming shudian.
Zhong Bosheng 種柏生. 1982. *Buci zhong suojian Yin wang tian-
　　you diming kao* 卜辭中所見殷王田游地名考. Taipei: (privately
　　printed).
Zhongguo ge minzu zongjiao yu shenhua dacidian Editorial Board
　　中国各民族宗教与神话大词典编审委员会, ed. 1990. *Zhong-
　　guo ge minzu zongjiao yu shenhua dacidian* 中国各民族宗教与
　　神话大词典. Beijing: Xueyuan chubanshe.
Zhou Fagao 周法高. 1974. *Hanzi gujin yinhui* 漢字古今音彙.
　　Hong Kong: The Chinese University Press.
Zhou Yiliang 周一良. 1963. *Wei Jin Nanbeichao shi lunji* 魏晋南
　　北朝史论集. Beijing: Zhonghua shuju.

Zhu Shijia 朱士嘉. 1934. "Huayangguo zhi banben kaolüe" 華陽
國志版本考略. *Yanjing daxue tushuguan bao* 燕京大學圖書館
報 71:1–4.

Zürcher, Erik. 1959. *The Buddhist Conquest of China*. Leiden:
Brill.

———. 1980. "Buddhist Influence on Early Taoism." *T'oung Pao*
66:84–147.

Index

ABOUT THE AUTHOR

Terry F. Kleeman is assistant professor of East Asian Religions at the College of William and Mary. After graduating from the University of Miami, he earned an M.A. in Asian Studies at the University of British Columbia and a Ph.D. in Oriental Languages at the University of California at Berkeley. He studied at National Taiwan University, Taishō University in Tokyo, and the École Practique des Hautes Études, Sorbonne, Paris. He was a visiting researcher at the Institute of Oriental Culture, University of Tokyo, during 1989. He is the author of *A God's Own Tale: The Book of the Transformations of Wenchang, the Divine Lord of Zitang* (Albany: SUNY Press, 1994) and numerous articles in *Journal of the American Oriental Society, Asia Major, Tōhō Shūkyō,* and elsewhere.